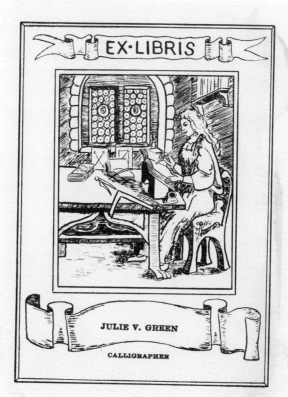

EX·LIBRIS

JULIE V. GREEN

CALLIGRAPHER

No Other Foundation

No Other Foundation
The Church Through Twenty Centuries

Jeremy C. Jackson

Cornerstone Books
Westchester, Illinois

For my mother and
in memory of my father

No Other Foundation: The Church Through Twenty Centuries
Copyright © 1980 by Jeremy Jackson.
All rights reserved.
Printed in the United States of America.

Library of Congress Catalog Card Number 79-92017
ISBN 0-89107-169-5

Contents

Introduction

THIS IS NOT a textbook on Christian church history. There are many such available, in multivolume sets or between the covers of one book. Kenneth Scott Latourette, one of the greatest church historians of the past generation, managed to bequeath a wonderfully readable and enviably well researched version of church history not only in many volumes, but also in one. The latter, his concise *Christianity Through the Ages* (1965), is perhaps the most stimulting short treatment available in English. For establishing the basic story of the Christian church there are, then, many good and accessible works and I do not presume to compete with them.

There is, however, I am convinced, a need for something a bit different: a history of the church which ventures to interpret the meaning of the past for our own day while yet keeping in touch with the objective facts. What something means to us depends, of course, on how we look at things. How I am looking at things is clarified by an explanation of the genesis of this book.

The twenty-two chapters which follow are, save for chapter 4, substantially the transcription of a series of lectures given at South Presbyterian Church, Syracuse, New York, on successive Sunday evenings from September 1974 to June 1975. I was mindful, as the lecturer, that there is a difference between regular academic teaching, such as I was then engaged in as a professional historian at Syracuse University, and addressing the members of one's own church on the Lord's Day concerning God's dealing with the church in the past.

Not that the standards of accuracy or scholarly integrity are different. They are the same. Rather, the purpose is different. That is to say, I was not only conveying information but also, in faith, instructing God's people. Such instruction requires both an attention to the principles of life set forth in Scripture and a charitable discrimination of approximate fidelity to these principles in history.

In preparing each lecture, therefore, I sought to evaluate the subject in the light of biblical truth and to apply it to our own circumstances as a twentieth-century church. While thinking as a Protestant, as the last sentence implies, I was thinking even more as a plain Christian, for Christianity is defined by the Bible, not by the Reformers or the Westminster Standards.

All of this implies selection, according to the principles just outlined, and I make no apology for omitting events, people and movements which find a place in the textbooks. I mention the Eastern Orthodox tradition but once or twice, for example. It has little direct relation to mainline Western church history and the sorts of general lessons which may be drawn from its teachings and experience may be drawn just as well from Christendom as a whole. Even the selection I have made is, inevitably, a selection of a selection. Certainly, rich lessons may be drawn from the story of a George Müller or a Thomas à Beckett, but the book has to close somewhere.

The idea of converting the original lectures into a book was not mine. As a social historian interested in European history between about 1400 and 1800, I had no particular expertise in church history. The thought of writing such a book, when first suggested to me, horrified my sense of what is professional. At the same time, I was urged by my original audience and encouraged by other friends, notably Mr. Richard Baltzell, to sacrifice professional pride and look at the matter from another viewpoint. If, in other words, a church audience was stimulated spiritually and intellectually by the lectures, should not one take seriously the possible benefits of making the material more widely available? What is spoken to laymen may be written to laymen.

Admittedly, as I noted earlier, the same canons of integrity obtain for whomever one is writing. One does all things well, not for the scholar, nor yet for the man in the street, but for the Lord. So, I must still observe that it is as a social historian and not as a church historian that I write. But I can add that I have written as a social historian with broad interests both in time and subject matter; that I have taken care to check my generalizations; and that, since the church is always embedded in society, it is not such a bad idea for a social historian to scrutinize the church in that society.

I may perhaps note here that in the book I use the word *church* in a loose way. The church is, of course, the body of the redeemed in Christ Jesus the Lord. The apparent harvest of the church is, however, replete with tares as well as wheat. Rather than use a capital *C* for church when I mean the actual, known-only-to-God Body of Christ, and a lowercase *c* for what purports to be a part of that Body, I have, therefore, preferred to allow the context in each case to clarify the usage.

The lectures became a book, not only through the promptings of the original listeners but also by their financial support. "I have received full payment, and more; . . ." (Phil. 4:18). With the blessing and tangible encouragement of Pastor Donald E. Wallace and the Session of South Presbyterian Church, a three-man committee (Dr. Gordon Danielson, Mr. Charles Ritchie, and Professor Johannes Smid) directed and channelled support for what became known as "The Church History Project." For six months (June to December, 1976), I was given partial financial backing to work part-time, at breakneck speed, to produce the first draft of the manuscript.

Consciously, all of us saw ourselves as joint participants in the project, praying, giving, writing, advising, thus illustrating the truth of Paul's description of the body of Christ in action. In a real way, then, this book is a testimony in the history of its writing as well as in its content, to biblical principles of Christian church life.

There is, of course, a gap between the preparation of a manuscript and the publication of a book. For advice and suggestion at this stage I want to thank Dr. Harold O. J. Brown and Mr. Franky Schaeffer. For constructive prompting and very specific criticisms of the early chapters I am much indebted to my editor, Mr. Jan Dennis.

Having said all this, I do, as author, bear total responsibility for the failings of the book. Likewise, although the wisdom and example of Dr. Francis A. Schaeffer have crucially influenced my own apprehension of what church history is about, I can only blame any misapprehensions upon myself.

No Other Foundation

Finally, many friends have encouraged, prayed, and helped in the formation of this work. To each I am quietly grateful. In an exceptional way, however, my mother-in-law, Elsa Van Buskirk, has stood by me in all sorts of ways, and most especially in typing out the final draft. Her generosity is matched only by that of my wife, from whom I have learned most and received most.

1

Old Testament Problems and Precedents

W HAT IS RIGHT reveals what is wrong. And to speak of the Church means there is something which is not the Church. Yet if by the Church we refer to people in harmony with God, there was a short period of time when all history was the history of the Church. I am, of course, talking of the time before the Fall.

It is only after the Fall that a division appears among men such that those whose desire is to please God constitute the 'Church' amidst the alien society of those whose desire is to please themselves. This is why belief in a historic Fall is so momentous. Without this belief, in a world so obviously disjointed, the history of the Church comes to mean the history of mankind's efforts to override accidental human blemishes. All religion is, then, self-made religion. It is man sewing fig leaves together to cover his nakedness—"the first liturgical garments of the first apostate religion" as a friend once remarked. It is men building the city of Babel whose very name is an epitaph to all humanistic religion. For while *babel* means "gate of God" it is also related by an etymological twist to the word for "confusion." In any case, self-made religion is poles apart from the religion which starts with Adam and Eve rejecting their fig leaves, to be clothed by the skins prepared by God.

So, even in a subject like church history, you cannot get started without insisting upon cardinal beliefs: a Personal God; a creation out of nothing which was perfect only because of its origins; a creation fallen because of willful disobedience; a creation which God alone can and purposes to redeem. Without these beliefs, the traditional idea of the Church is stuff and nonsense. What is worship, if 'god' is a vague concept who certainly never did anything concrete enough to make you feel worshipful? And if the Church's commission is to evangelize, where do you find the enthusiasm to preach salvation to people who are "saved" anyway, who never "fell"? Likewise, the hope of the Second Coming of Jesus Christ and a restoration of all creation is meaningless without the reality of the Fall. This is not to mention belief in a Savior dying and being raised, to rescue us from the curse of the Fall. Indeed, a lost humanity is replaced by the idea of innocent mankind. Adam and Eve in the Garden of Eden becomes, then, a parable of a future state to which man, by earnest effort, is progressing.

In this light, insistence upon the fundamentals of the faith is not pedantry but life and death. As Paul said, if these things be not true, if Christ be not raised, then we are not raised either—"Let us eat and drink, for tomorrow we die." To affirm that the Church does exist, and that therefore there is something which is not the Church, thereby providing the context for the Church's mission, brings us to a second vital consideration, launching us into the important historical epoch beyond the Fall.

The period of Noah is rarely pondered *as* a period because either it is seen as dominated by a few spectacular events, such as Abel's murder and the Flood, or it is brushed aside as a preliminary to the main plot: the covenant with Abraham. But it is worth noting that between the Fall and Abraham the scope of the story has not narrowed to a single race and its neighbors. Rather, we are still dealing with the whole of humanity. It is as if the *Old* Testament phase of God's dealings with mankind followed a time when God's direct call was universal and preceded a *New* Testament era when, through Christ, the call is once again directly to all men.

This can remind us that the Gospel is for the entire world. And, indeed, the covenant with Abraham was not intended to be to the detriment of the rest but the reverse: to so preserve belief in the Creator and adhere to His ways, and so to be the cradle for mankind's Savior, that *all* men might be saved. The curse of the Jew was exclusiveness, a parochialness contrary to God's wish. As God said to Israel in Ezekiel 36:32: "It is not for your sake that I will act."

This directly applies to the Christian Church. Our parochialism is mirrored in absolute denominationalism, in our tendency to identify what is important and worthwhile by standards of America, the West or whatever society we inhabit. It is ironic but instructive that the Greek word *paroikia* (for example, in 1 Pet. 1:17), from which we get our word parochial, means "sojourning." Sojourning in the Bible, of course, always bears reference to the situation and mentality of the believer. Like Abraham, like the heroes of faith in Hebrews 11, the Christian has a universal frame of reference beyond what is visibly apparent. He is not a citizen of earth; he is a sojourner on earth. To be dragged down into the earth's values is to be parochial in the modern sense. It is, in fact, because Christians have compromised so much with the world that parochial has lost its original meaning. Losing the sense of being exiles, we become parochial.

To read the story of the epoch of Noah is to be strongly reminded that we must always be conscious of our true identity. We must not allow the weight of ungodliness around us to make us think we are abnormal. The Christian is in touch with normalcy in the most universal sense. It was Noah who knew what he was doing because he knew God and God spoke with him. Everybody else was living in a world of fantasy. Relative to men, Noah was odd. Relative to God, the world was out of step. This does not mean that mercy is withheld from mankind. God is the creator of all men and all things. He is no respecter of persons, denominations, or local ways of life and thought. God's rain falls upon the just and the unjust alike. Having said all this, it remains true that what visibly distinguishes the just from the unjust is that the former *thanks* God for the rain. The Westminster Shorter Catechism says that "The chief end of man is to glorify God and to enjoy him forever." To thank him for all he has done is one fulfillment of this end.

A final principle that the period of Noah can illustrate is the built-in tendency to rebel against God. To be born into the "right" sort of spiritual family is clearly no guarantee of individual spiritual allegiance. One may dwell upon the line of promise through Seth, by contrast to the line of rebellion through Cain, only to notice that with the exception of Noah and seven family members all the Sethites perished along with everybody else. The record of Noah's issue is no more reassuring. The story of the Tower of Babel is the story of their effort to establish their own identity apart from God—to make a name for themselves, as the Bible puts it. The name Adam, given by God to man, connotes createdness. The emphasis is on God's creativity. The naming associated with Babel emphasizes *man's* creativity.

God's response was two-fold. He first of all intervened to confuse their communication, their language. He thereby prevented a sort of geometrically proportioned increase in human knowledge. It is worth noting here that the reason why the "tower builders" of the twentieth century have enjoyed such an explosion of knowledge is because they are reaping the results of the establishment of a universal language two or three centuries ago. I am referring not to English but to mathematics and derivative scientific symbol systems. These are universally understood and though one could cite other factors in modern scientific and technological advance a shared symbol system is basic to it. We often ask, "What will man do next?" In his providence, God was delaying the answer to that question when he made confusion out of the humanistic culture of Noah's descendants.

There was a second dimension to God's response, however. God judges but he also saves. His plan of salvation involves Abraham and the Jews.

In making a covenant with Abraham and his descendants, God was not washing his hands of the rest of the world. In fact, the reverse. Abraham and his people are to be the visible reflection of the just and loving God. They are the trustees of a special revelation of God's nature and of the meaning of life—a revelation which, in written form, we call the Scriptures. To preserve belief in himself and to be the cradle of mankind's savior, God gave the Jews a Law and a ritual to guide their faith which also clarified the significance of Christ's sacrifice when it took place. Though it was only a minority, a remnant, of the Jews who were ever truly faithful, that there should still have been seven thousand who feared God in the dark days of Ahab and Jezebel is a better batting average than Noah and his seven family members. This is striking testimony to the benefit of the Law given to Abraham's children.

The Jews were, collectively, an apostolic people—that is, sent by and witnesses to, Jehovah. Even when apostate, they cannot help being apostolic, mutely testifying in all their sufferings and, more recently, in their remarkable return to Palestine, to the God who chose them out, whose Word is always fulfilled. "How odd of God to choose the Jews," the saying goes. Not that God is supposed to be odd, but the Jews. But eventually, if the Jew is odd, God is too. As with Noah, however, so with the Jew: oddness depends on your perspective. Relative to man, the Jew was odd. Relative to God and the universe God has made, the Jew basked in normality, he was correctly centered. In this sense, to attack the Jew was, and still is, to attack the apple of God's eye (Zechariah 2:8).

For the Jew, of all people, to become parochial and exclusive was the worst contradiction of all. As the visible exhibition of God's existence and character, there was no place for self-congratulation. To quote that verse from Ezekiel again: "It is not for *your* sake that I will act."

Although any approach to the history of the Christian Church must start with the experience of mankind in general and of the Jew in particular before Christ's advent, it is certainly not my business to do much more than emphasize a few basic principles. The broad epochs of Jewish history, specifically, are well enough known: from Abraham in about 1900 B.C.; through the 400-year exile in Egypt till Moses and the Exodus around 1400 B.C.; to the beginning of the kings, about 1000 B.C., and the tragic deportations in the seventh and sixth centuries before Christ. Rather than belabor the obvious, then, I want to emphasize three important aspects of Jewish life and history which are directly applicable to the Christian Church: the covenants and the Law; theocracy; and the "remnant."

Characteristic of the covenants given through Abraham and Moses was a certain order and dynamic. Although likened to treaties, it might be more appropriate to liken treaties to them. That God relates to men is, after all, prior to men's being able to relate to one another. Fundamental to all the covenants is the grace or givingness of God. There is, indeed, reciprocity, but not between equal powers. The sole initiator of the covenants is God. You can see this very clearly in the Ten Commandments which begins with God the initiator saying: "I am the Lord your God, who brought you out of the land of Egypt, out of the house of bondage." God is here giving himself to the Jews, in the sense of declaring himself their God, and then instancing a proof of this

16

No Other Foundation

fact in his recent deliverance of them. This is God's part of the covenant which is then followed by the Jews' part: "You shall have no other gods before me." The rest of the Ten Commandments constitute, as it were, the absolute instancing of how "having no other gods before me" works out in practice. The whole covenant is reminiscent of the Lord's Prayer which is given to God's people under the new covenant. "Our Father," Jesus invites us to say: God is graciously our Father as much as or in a greater way than he was the Lord God of Moses. This Father, to whom in the first phrases of the Lord's Prayer we express our worship, gives us our daily bread and forgives us. But woe betide if, thus forgiven in Christ, we fail to forgive our fellows. "Be merciful as your heavenly father is merciful," Jesus further expressed it. This is, when understood in all its dimensions, our side of the covenant.

Our side of the covenant evokes the complex law and ceremonial practice whereby the Jews were to regulate their lives according to the principles of the covenant. Crucially, the law and the ceremonial were not ends in themselves but pointed "beyond the veil" to God himself. They did not constitute the covenant; they evidenced it. This distinction is so crucial that it is not surprising that the Jews' spiritual delinquency may be defined by reference to it. The Jew went wrong *either* by not keeping the Law at all (formal apostasy, characteristic of the epoch before the exile to Babylon) *or* by keeping it hypocritically, making it an end in itself (informal apostasy, characteristic of the epoch after the exile). These twin forms of unbelief are the critical marks of an apostate Christian Church: downright heresy or dead orthodoxy. Which is worse? Well, Jesus seemed to criticize the hypocritical Pharisees even more than the heretical Sadducees. But both were condemned because each rejected the Word.

There is disagreement over the definition of theocracy: does it mean a priest-governed or a God-governed society? And the two are by no means synonymous. Before things declined in Israel, theocracy meant "God-governed," not "priest-ridden": "I will be your God and you shall be my people."

I mention this because there has always been an issue in the Christian Church over whether and in what circumstances one may claim to be living in a theocracy and, if so, whether one is justified in re-applying Old Testament social and religious laws and penalties. In the sixteenth-century Reformation, for example, where entire, sovereign cities by formal decision opted for a particular religious stance, was one justified in applying the laws and penalties of Ancient Israel with respect to blasphemy, cursing, and so on? Or does the new covenant, in which God's Spirit is given to all who believe, invalidate the public provisions for enforcement of the old covenant?

The principles involved here are, incidentally, much broader than might at first appear. All societies have to face them and any discussion of censorship takes place in their context. When we come to deal with the Reformation we shall grasp this nettle. Suffice it to say here that in the old covenant as well as the new, hypocritical enforcement of rules replaces loving remonstrance and correction as soon as real belief fades.

The covenant was made with all of Abraham's seed and, as Paul points out in his Epistle to the Romans, this covenant has not been abrogated in so far as it pertains to the Jew. Nevertheless, as Paul also points out, it was a minority, a "remnant," that kept the covenant in truth and which therefore recognized in Jesus the fulfillment of the Law. Just as the work of Christ is *suf*ficient for all but *ef*ficient for only those who believe, "who are the called according to his purpose," so the old covenant was sufficient for all Jews but efficient only for those "circumcised in heart as well as flesh." This latter group is the remnant and I want to say two things about them.

Firstly, the remnant Jew or Christian, like Abraham, breathes a climate in which he is prepared to leave all for God's sake. Even if he is not called to leave Haran, like Abraham, he is actively prepared to. And God knows our preparedness: "As a man thinketh, so is he." As the last Old Testament prophet, John the Baptist, put it: "He must increase but I must decrease." This has always been a live issue for the Christian Church and at the end of the twentieth century it is getting more so, not less.

Secondly, the remnant is prepared to die spiritually. Indeed, it is dying daily. As such, it is prepared, like Jesus, to risk itself not merely for friends but for enemies, too. This is no more poignantly revealed than in those astonishing prayers of repentance uttered by Ezra and Daniel for their people, in which they humbly identify themselves with the guilt of their fellows. "O my God, I am ashamed and blush to lift my face to thee, my God, for our

iniquities have risen higher than our heads, . . ." (Ezra 9:6). "O
Lord, . . . we have sinned and done wrong and acted wickedly
and rebelled, . . . " (Dan. 9:4-5). This is clear also in Moses'
frequent intercession for the Jews in the wilderness and in Job's
intercession both for his children and for his "comforters." A
striking New Testament instance of the same thing is Paul's compassion for the unbelieving Jew. Having closed the eighth chapter
of Romans with the ringing declaration that absolutely nothing
can separate us from the love of God in Christ Jesus, he opens the
ninth chapter by saying that if possible he would even be ready to
suffer such separation if thereby his fellow Jew would believe.

If preparedness to leave all seems in retrospect like a "heroic"
aspect of the remnant, this other willingness to identify with pain
and sin is decidedly *un*glamorous. For Jesus, the supreme exem-
plar, the infinite substitutionary burden-bearer, it meant "going
outside the camp."

We see, then, in Noah, Babel and Abraham, fundamental
themes of all history thereafter. We see the backdrop of a loving,
just, personal Creator. We see a mankind, from the Fall, always
in rebellion and ingenious in its rebellion. And we see men, chosen by and choosing God, testifying in word and deed to his
existence. Now, as then, we are given a name—the name of
Jesus—in which alone we can boast. The builders of Babel set out
to establish their own name, their own identity; the name of
Abraham, as the Bible explicitly tells us, was given by God.

If we boast in ourselves, our denominations, our spiritual gifts,
our petty preferences, we are parochial—no longer a witness to
the God who is Creator of *all*. We are boasting of something less
than the name of Christ. When we hesitate to preach to the
Buddhist, we are not being liberal or broadminded. We are being
exclusive and parochial. We are honoring the distinctions of men,
rather than the universal Word of God. We are ashamed of the
Cross. Our message to *all* men must be: "God made you and
sustains you and by the Gospel he calls you. What is your response?"

Far from being ashamed of the Gospel of Christ, "it is the
power of God to salvation to everyone who believes, to the Jew
first and also to the Greek" (Romans 1:16). Just so, Noah "preached
righteousness" to the ancient world before the Flood.

For Further Study

The purpose of the study suggestions at the end of each chapter is not to help you become an overnight expert on the subjects discussed. I do not claim that myself! Nor is it to uncover the sources I have relied upon, about which I make a brief comment in the "Bibliographical Note" at the end of the book. Rather what I have in mind is to pass on the names of books, and sometimes other sources, which I have found interesting, provoking or just plain enjoyable. I hope you do, too.

Cantor, Norman F. "Judaism, the Ancient Near East, and the Origins of Christianity," a conversation with William F. Albright. In *Perspectives on the European Past: Conversations With Historians*. Vol. 1. New York: Macmillan Co., 1971.

Kitchen, K. A. *Ancient Orient and Old Testament*. Downers Grove, IL: Intervarsity Press, 1966. Refreshingly pugnacious. The footnotes give an idea of what mastery in a field entails.

The New Bible Dictionary. J. D. Douglas, ed. Grand Rapids, MI: Wm. B. Eerdmans Publishing Co., 1962. Why this? Because it is the best single-volume reference tool for the Bible. Flora, fauna, biographies, the meaning of puzzling words, historical background, etc.

Schaeffer, Francis A. *Joshua and the Flow of Biblical History*. Downers Grove, IL: InterVarsity Press, 1975. Schaeffer was a preacher before he was a writer and these sermons contain a vital message.

2

New Testament Structures

THROUGH JESUS CHRIST the history of the West—to speak only of the West—has been radically transformed. This makes the more astonishing historians' disregard of him. Beyond the usual statements that he was a great and good man, a marvelous teacher and a martyr to principle is a strange silence, a quiet refusal to come to terms with facts that turn these easy opinions upside down. On the always desperate and certainly untenable assumption that Christ is what men made him, textbooks generally lavish more attention on Paul, Augustine, Aquinas and Luther, than on the Cornerstone himself. Quite simply, Jesus is virtually nondiscussable unless one takes his own claims seriously. Yet the convictions of his followers are clear enough and so, to preserve the comfortable notion that Jesus was a great man misunderstood, we are told that he was falsified by his press. It is, indeed, always easier to attack the king by attacking his servants. Paradoxically, thereby, one fulfills the words of Christ when he warned his followers that men would treat them as they were treating him.

Christ *is* an enigma unless you accept the New Testament record. Hence, the frenzied "explanations" to reveal a different Christ—whether "mushroom cult" extravaganzas or some of the overingenious identifications of Jesus with the "Teacher of Righteousness" (or at least the ethos) of the Essene sect, revealed in the Dead Sea Scrolls. A well-qualified theologian alludes to the "perverse attitude" which

while quite unwarrantably hospitable to the latest irresponsible speculation by the journalistic charlatans, insists on treating such serious documents as those which comprise the New Testament as though they had long ago been discredited. I have met otherwise intelligent men who ask,

No Other Foundation

apparently in all seriousness, whether there may not be truth in what I would call patently ridiculous legends about (let us say) an early portrait of Jesus or the shroud in which he is supposed to have been buried, and who grow excited over the Gospel of Thomas or some other late apocryphal document, but who brush aside the much earlier and more sober canonical Gospels as unreliable legends not worthy of serious consideration. (C. F. D. Moule, *The Phenomenon of the New Testament: An Inquiry Into the Implications of Certain Features of the New Testament* [Naperville, IL: A. R. Allenson, 1967], pp. 2-3.)

Moule is documenting that profound repression of the truth which Paul describes in Romans chapter 1, where he mentions those who refuse to honor God and become "futile in their thinking and their senseless minds darkened. Claiming to be wise, they become fools" and exchange "the truth about God for a lie," worshipping and serving "the creature rather than the Creator." This worshipping of the creature, this claim to be wise, in the guise of fifty-seven scholarly brands, has marred much biblical study. It has, instead of opening the door to the Truth, made it more difficult for ordinary people to see Christianity as it really is.

In the last chapter we spoke of the basic Old Testament setting for the Church. Here we are concerned about the immediate context in the first century culture of Rome and Greece.

When humanists, of the Renaissance and since, looked back to Rome, they were mostly looking back to the great days of the Roman Republic which were mostly over by the time of Christ. Over a century before Christ's birth, the decline of republican ideals was evidenced in bloody contests for political control. The series opened in 146 B.C. with the clubbing to death of Tiberias Gracchus. The last game began with the stabbing of Julius Caesar in 44 B.C. In the ensuing melee, Caesar's adopted nephew, Octavian, won out. His victory at Actium in 31 B.C. (often remembered as the naval battle at the end of Richard Burton and Elizabeth Taylor's *Anthony and Cleopatra*) heralded a great period of peace. With the spread of Roman power, this peace was extended to the Western world as a whole.

Such was the popular relief after decades of civil conflict, that Octavian received the title *Augustus* ("worshipful"), was hailed "Savior of the World," assumed the priestly position and title of *Pontifex Maximus* ("supreme priest"), and pragmatically accepted a sort of patriotic Emperor worship which would later spell death for Christians who refused to participate. Though in essence a dictator, Augustus Caesar, as he is usually called, preserved the outward republican forms. The title Emperor, for example, is a military title meaning "general," hence fostering the illusion that he was not really a king. The degree to which he was, indeed, more than a king is the degree to which "emperor" has ever since meant someone with more than kingly power. And the degree to which Augustus' subversion of the older constitution was not seen for what it was is reflected in a private Roman tombstone inscription of 6 B.C.: "It was since the pacification of the universe and the restoration of the Republic that, at length, happy and quiet times came our way."

"Happy and quiet times"—the longing for peace. It is ironic that around the time of this inscription the *real* Prince of Peace was born. Scripture hints that the same irony is going to be repeated. That the circumstances of Christ's Second Coming will parallel those of his first. There will be the peace-giving reign of an arch-dictator, a super-Augustus, ruling not a Roman but a world empire, and equally attracting the grateful applaud of a naive population which imagines its freedom is restored after years of disorder and conflict. Once more, people will be able to trade, to drink and to make merry. And, as in the days of Noah the Flood came as a surprise, so will it be at Christ's return.

The grandiose rule of the Roman Emperors was, of course, based on a well-articulated scheme of imperial control. The hard-won and coolly maintained exercise of power was the reality behind all the titles. When this was forgotten, the titles assumed a hollow ring. In that small, troublesome but strategically important strip called Palestine, Roman rule was partly carried out by regular governors (civil service appointees) from Rome and partly by the able but incestuously brutal Edomite family of the Herods. Herod the Great, the father of the family, was alive when Jesus was born. His sons divided the territory of his administration after his death. Of these, it was Herod Antipas, who inherited his father's sly cunning and taste for the bizarre, whom Jesus termed "that fox." Unfortunate as the Jews of the day might consider themselves to be, they were yet fortunate to enjoy legal license to practice the one thing which they regarded as personally distinctive: their religion. Because the Jews backed Julius Caesar on his way to success, he had reciprocated by granting the privilege of a tolerated religion, with the freedom to practice it and maintain independent judicial bodies even outside Palestine.

If Rome's republican greatness was a thing of the past in Jesus' day, even more was the glory of Athens and Greece the stuff of memory. Historians of this epoch in discussing the continuing influence of Greek culture do not even accord that influence its native adjective; they call it Hellenic. They thereby indicate a diluting, a trivializing, such as all systems of thought and ways of life undergo when copied by those to whom they are not instinctive.

Nevertheless, whether Greek or Hellenic, the influence of Greece was crucial in the Mediterranean world. It provided a clear and distinctive vocabulary of thought. It did, in fact, provide a vocabulary. To such a degree had the conquered culture overcome the Roman conqueror, that the education of Roman children was carried on in Greek. Greek was the universal language of the day, as natural a vehicle for Paul's Epistle to the Romans as of his various letters to churches in Asia Minor. Considering the dispersion of Jews in the Mediterranean world, probably more were familiar with the Scriptures in the Greek (the Septuagint version) than in Hebrew. No missionary language schools were required for evangelization, then.

In Palestine Hebrew was not only eclipsed by Greek as a language of thought and discussion; it was even superseded locally by Aramaic, much as, say, Welsh bows to English, or the languages of American ethnic groups are secondary in public life. One can in any case, returning to the Greek, see how natural it was for John not only to write the Gospel in Greek but also to borrow part of the vocabulary of Greek thought to express a Christian idea. The word *Logos* is a case in point: he was not taking a Greek idea and stitching it into a Christian pattern. He was taking a biblical truth and giving a new and electric vitality to a Greek term. In similar ways, modern missionary Bible translators take native words and fill them with fresh meaning.

To be most specific about the importance of Greek in the history of the Christian Church: it was not just the convenience of a common language or the adaptability of a few terms. More basically, it was the congruence of a language ideally suited for expressing thought vigorously and precisely, to a Gospel proclamation which had everything to gain by being set forth in a straightforward, honest fashion.

New Testament Structures

Any historical study of a great and successful cultural and religious movement must try to explain what made it attractive and distinctive. To take the matter of distinctiveness first, there was little to mark off the so-called Nazarene Jews from other Jews. Jews, as such, were, it is true, sufficiently remarkable in the Roman world. Not having idols in their Temple, they were regarded as atheists by some. The historian Tacitus, in a famous comment on the Roman general Pompey's having found the Holy of Holies devoid of images, wrote: "Their sanctuary was empty; their mysteries meaningless." Yet, paradoxically, not a few gentiles were attracted to the dignity, seriousness and intellectual challenge of Jewish religion.

Christianity, however, offered even worse conundrums than official non-Christian Judaism. There were, as many have pointed out, few immediately obvious differences between Christian and non-Christian Jews. But when one considered these differences, *what* differences! It was enough to the average gentile that the Jew should believe in a God who acted concretely in history and through a specific race. But the Christian further claimed that a young man, crucified in living memory by a Roman governor, was the Son of this God and Savior of the world. To add insult to injury, they further insisted that he had been raised from the dead and had ascended to heaven! Small wonder that after Paul's message in Athens "some mocked."

What could not be gainsaid, though, was the power to love and forgive that the Christian claimed was given him by God. It was the evidence in life of the message preached that made a supposedly heretical Jewish sect into the most dynamic spiritual force in the Mediterranean by the end of the second century. This was the secret of its attraction: a living faith based on living facts. The facts certainly came first, as in Old Testament Judaism, and so we must examine them to determine the content of the faith. Such an examination is the more pertinent in our own day when the cliche so often trotted forth is that Christianity is whatever you happen to make it.

The Resurrection of Jesus Christ was central because it demonstrated that Jesus was who he said he was. He is the Christ, sent by God, otherwise God would not have raised him. Accordingly, any Christianity which begins and ends with Christ is false. Jesus, and the Apostles after him, made it abundantly plain that the

No Other Foundation

Father was and is pre-eminent. We are united with Christ, as Paul explains, so that we can be accepted of the Father. It is in this context, then, that Paul declares, "If Christ has not been raised, your faith is futile, and you are still in your sins" (1 Cor. 15:17).

If the Christian claimed that Christ was living in him, this was not by way of self-hypnosis or self-discipline, but by the living reality of the Holy Spirit. The real, the objective, Holy Spirit; not an "it" but a person; the third Person of the Triune God; the third of the Triune personal expressions of God; the One whose divinity is not derived from his divine work but whose divinity makes his comforting and empowering divine. "The life I now live in the flesh I live by the power of the Son of God": *that* power of Christ was the Spirit who drove him into the wilderness and performed mighty works through him. Only because of the Spirit who was to come could Christ predict the mighty works of his followers. Otherwise, his prediction must sound like an election year promise. The Spirit did come and works through us as, like Jesus, we *will* to die daily. Thus willing, like the Early Church, the Spirit enables us to die and enables us to rise. We cannot die without living; as one valve closes, the other opens.

What is true personally is true corporately. Remember that with Abraham God swore by himself because there was no greater to swear by? Remember that when the Jews challenged Jesus' authenticity, he had the "blasphemous" audacity to suggest that he and the Father together supplied the two witnesses demanded by Jewish law? The point here is that only God can testify to God. The Early Church knew this in practice. They, and we, cannot testify to God. Only God can do this, and He does it through his Spirit within us. Only that witness cuts ice. Jesus told his disciples to wait for the promised Spirit after he was ascended. Then, and only then, would they have power. Then, and only then, could they be "my witnesses in Jerusalem, and in all Judaea and Samaria and to the end of the earth" (Acts 1:8).

On this subject, a last thing to bear in mind: as someone has remarked, the Church did not possess the Spirit; the Spirit possessed the Church. Further, when the Spirit is at work, we do not see him, we see Christ. If people claim to be attracted to the Spirit, be sure that they are either dangerously sloppy in their thinking or else more in love with spiritual power than with Christ.

There is an incident recorded in Acts (19:1-7) where Paul, at Ephesus, bumps into a group of disciples who had received John's baptism but had "never even heard that there is a Holy Spirit." I sometimes wonder whether, for different reasons, people today are unaware of the Spirit. The principle of the leading of the Church by the Spirit is very clear in Acts; every turn and twist in the Church's doings is directed by him. As in Creation and Redemption, so in the mission of the Church, God's initiative is total. How far is this apparent today? How far can our mission be explained, because it is couched, in terms and methods derived from Madison Avenue?

At the heart of witness is the Spirit who witnesses. At the heart of his witness is a particular communication, the Word of God. This word is powerful, a two-edged sword. It is wielded, when wielded properly, by the Spirit: "the sword of the Spirit which is the word of God" (Eph. 6:17).

The essence of the Gospel preaching was and must always be the Word of God in person and inscripturated. Rather than limit such preaching, seven men were chosen to take over practical tasks of essential service in Acts chapter six in order that the apostles should not have to "give up preaching the word of God to serve tables." Over and over again in the Acts such preaching is emphasized.

Use of the Bible is not a form of magic, however. "Let the word of Christ dwell in you richly," says Paul when touching upon the sort of verbal exchanges that the Colossian Christians should be enjoying (Col. 3:16). If we have not ourselves received the Word of God, if it does not dwell in us, then to mouth Scripture will not reproduce the effects of Scriptural preaching delivered by those who have. The Word of God is still the Word of God, of course, and has its effect, notwithstanding. But its effect is, understandably, more complete when that mind of God which it speaks is also present in the life of the believer who has "the mind of Christ" (1 Cor. 2:16).

The mind of the world is always intent upon falsifying and diluting God's Word. The Pharisees made it "of none effect" by their tradition, Jesus charged (Matt. 15:6). The effective demonstration of Christ's Messiahship from the Scriptures was so potent that there is a suspicion, to say the least, that some of the alternative renderings introduced by non-Christian Jewry into a revised version of the Greek Old Testament in the 120's A.D. were calculated to make this demonstration more difficult. One might note that an atmosphere of distrust towards God's written Word enters here and there into modern translations. And this need not surprise us. For example, despite much good and clear translation in the New English Bible, what can be the possible impact of its rendition of Genesis 11:1—"Once upon a time . . ."? This phrase has only one current, idiomatic meaning: "Get ready for a fairy tale."

For the first Christians, however, the plain, true Gospel was proclaimed, even if it was foolishness to non-Jews and a stumbling block to Jews.

The effect of the facts we have discussed is prophesied in Jesus' moving parable of the Prodigal Son in Luke 15. It is illustrated by the traditional story of the old disciple John being asked three times over what Jesus had said apart from the other things recorded. "Love one another," he replied. "Love one another. Love one another." Remember Jesus' question to Peter: "Lovest thou me?" and its follow-up: "Feed my sheep." There is no love without following. "Love is of God" because "God is love." This love is precise and objective. It involves all those obediences we find in Psalm 119 and the Sermon on the Mount. Note the marriage in John's Second Epistle of love and commandment. You cannot be a heretic, he says, and know anything about love.

To the pagan world, which we shall turn to directly in the next chapter, what was so arresting and compelling was this quality of love which made of one body its many individual embodiments.

The continuing reality of this love is vividly demonstrated in this anecdote from the experience of Richard Wurmbrand:

With about thirty other Christians I remember being in a prison cell in Rumania. One day the door was opened and a new prisoner was pushed in. It took us a little time to recognize him in the half-darkness of the cell. When we did recognize him we were amazed to see not a fellow Christian but a well-known Captain of the Secret Police who had arrested and tortured many of us. We asked him how he had come to be a fellow prisoner.

He told us that one day a soldier on duty had reported that a twelve-year-old boy, carrying a pot of flowers, was asking to see him. The Captain was curious and allowed the boy to enter. When the boy entered he was very shy. "Comrade Captain," he said, "You are the one who arrested my father and mother, and today is my mother's birthday. It has always been my habit to buy her a pot of flowers on her birthday—but now, because of you, I have no mother to make happy.

"My mother is a Christian and she taught me that we must love our enemies and reward evil with good. As I no longer have a mother, I thought these flowers might make the mother of your children happy. Could you please give them to your wife?"

The Communist torturer is also a man. There is a chord in his heart that still vibrates at the word of truth and burning love. The Captain took the boy's flowers and embraced him with tears in his eyes. A process of remorse and conversion began. In his heart he could no longer bear to arrest innocent men. He could no longer inflict torture. In the end he had arrived with us in prison because he had become a defender of Christians. *(Underground Saints* [Old Tappan, N.J.: Spire Books, Revell Co., 1968] pp. 197-8.)

For Further Study

France, R. T. *Jesus and the Old Testament: His Application of Old Testament Passages to Himself and His Mission.* Downers Grove, IL: Inter-Varsity Press, 1971. We need to know the whole Bible and Jesus' use of Scripture should encourage us.

Johnson, Paul. *A History of Christianity.* New York: Atheneum, 1976. Read Part 1, "The Rise and Rescue of the Jesus Sect" (pp. 3-63). I mention this for negative reasons: here is a well-written reworking of an old travesty of the truth—"Paulianity."

Moule, C.F.D. *The Phenomenon of the New Testament: An Inquiry Into the Implications of Certain Features of the New Testament.* Naperville, IL: A. R. Allenson, 1967. An exegetical aid to appreciating deeply the reality of being one body in Christ. And other things.

Phillips, J. B. *The Ring of Truth.* New York: Macmillan Co., 1967. What he learned from translating the New Testament.

3

Expansion and Heresy:
The Principles of Practice

T HE GOSPEL WAS first to the Jew and then to the Greek. The
man who said this was not a Judaizer but Paul, the great
apostle to the Gentiles. Luke, in the book of Acts, notes
that the Gospel spread from Jerusalem out into the wider world.

Without the Jew, there would be no Gospel; and the Jew
proved to be, at the same time, both the most receptive and the
most hostile soil. The considerable variation within Judaism as it
had spread abroad usually guaranteed, above all outside Judaea, a
sympathetic hearing to the apostles. This might quickly turn into
bitter hostility but not without, at the very least, the garnering of a
few souls. The evidently powerful use of the Old Testament scriptures to back up the Christian claim, presumably based upon an
exegesis established by Christ himself after the Resurrection, was
central to synagogue preaching. But it was not easy, as Michael
Green has pointed out, for a Jew to see a non-political, crucified
Jesus as the sum and wisdom of Israel's proud heritage. Furthermore, as the content of the Gospel became more and more
familiar to Jews and as the number of Jews won over to Christ
loomed as a threat to non-Christian Judaism, a strongly defensive
reaction set in. Significantly, in view of the pattern of God's past
dealings with the Jews, the destruction of the Temple in A.D. 70
did not make the Jew agree with the argument of the book of
Hebrews—it hardened him. The book of Judges is explicit about
the incidence of forty-year periods of trial for Israel in which they
could demonstrate their allegiance to Jehovah. If Jesus was
crucified around A.D. 30, the forty years' preaching of the Gospel
was over by A.D. 70. As in the ancient past, so now, God's judg-

ment inevitably fell and that hardening of the Jew, to which Paul refers in Romans, set in.

In this mood, the non-Christian Jew was more and more anxious to distinguish himself from the Christian Jew. That the Christians should come under the umbrella of religious toleration accorded to Jews, on the "ignorant" Gentile assumption that Christianity was just another variation in Judaism, was especially galling. Perhaps we can imagine the Jewish reaction if we gauge our own response to the idea that Christian Scientists, Jehovah's Witnesses, Mormons, and the like, are Christian groups. At all events, the Christian was more and more thrust out on a limb. Tragically, a complementary prejudice was born with fateful consequences for the future. The Jew, on his side, made himself immune to evangelization. The legacy has been that, to this day, a Jew frequently considers it sufficient answer to the universal claims of the Gospel to reply, "Oh, I'm a Jew." The Christian, on his side, obligingly accepted this evasion. The Jew was consigned to a sort of "no man's land" (eventually a ghetto) where grace could not penetrate. Noticeable evangelization among Jews seems to have ended in the first decades of the second century.

When the Jew said no, the Gentile had a chance to say yes. Apart from direct preaching, Christianity made headway in proportion as Christians lived Christ. The poor and uneducated saw that they were acceptable on equal terms by the followers of one who is no respecter of persons. The rich and educated, tired and disillusioned with religious alternatives and the decadence of Imperial culture, responded to a religion which not only satisfied the mind but also spoke with the authority which the Roman centurion had recognized in Christ decades before. Compared to its rivals, Christianity was sober and yet exhilarating. There was no initiation rite such as that which involved handling the genitals of Demeter or being doused with the blood of a Cybelene bull. Christian joy and oneness came from a different source. And though Christians supported one another sacrificially, there was no pressure of financial obligation. By contrast, the mystery cults usually charged a whopping entry fee.

By A.D. 100, Christianity had straddled the contradictions of the Roman world: it had entered the Imperial household, yet owned adherents among slaves. And both in theory and practice, the opposite poles of wealth and poverty were not allowed to produce a pecking order in the Church. Not that there were not tensions to which, for example, James addressed himself sternly in the second chapter of his Epistle. But the degree to which the principles of Christ triumphed may be measured in Edward Gibbon's humanist complaint that Christianity sapped the Empire of its vigor. But Gibbon was also less than sympathetic to the nature of that specifically Christian vigor which, thirteen hundred years after the demise of the Roman Empire, was still giving life in his own day.

This was a vigor which depended not on the great of this world but on the greatness of God in the humblest believer. For all that God used and uses outstanding individuals to lead the advance, the "army" still marches at the speed of its foot soldiers. Historians agree that it was grass-roots evangelization at work and at home which wrought change in the Roman Empire. The epoch of an impressive, visible structure was in the future. The first immense thrust of the Gospel till the mid-second century took place, as far as we can tell, without benefit of church buildings and choirs, not to mention the printed word. What a benefit and privilege these things are! But who would want them if the Gospel were not honored? The answer in the late twentieth century is: Far too many.

Although the lapse of time between the Creation and the Fall of man is not specified, the Genesis account makes fairly clear that it was distressingly short. The theme of the rest of this chapter is the pressures so quickly brought to bear upon the expanding New Testament church by inner declension and heresy. For every Old Testament Achan there was a New Testament Ananias and Sapphira.

The word heresy comes from a Greek word meaning "choice." This word used in the New Testament has a further connotation of "party." In other words, heresy is the selfish exercise of choice, and heretics tend to form parties or pressure groups to popularize their choices. And heresy begets heresy, because to back down means to admit your foolishness, to admit you have made a mistake—something none of us likes to do. Yet you can hardly stand still: having left one mooring post you inevitably set sail for another.

Like true belief, of which heresy is a distortion, it is always lived as well as thought. "From the heart of man," said Jesus, "stem all wrong thoughts and deeds." There is no belief which is not lived and no *un*belief which is not lived. "By their fruits shall you know them." All heresy is rooted in disaffection. We can never therefore take lightly a plain distortion of Christian, biblical truth, whether in ourselves or others. We can be certain that it springs from an antecedent and unchecked waning in our love for God. The doctrinal distortion is a rationalization of our behavioral self-will.

The certain antidote is repentance and a prayerful obedience to God's Word. The certain mark of developing heresy is someone's determined refusal to heed the Bible's testimony when it is pointed out to him. When we see that all heresies are partial or more total distortions of the truth, that they reflect spiritual willfulness, and that none of us is so spiritually strong as to be immune from error, then we have to be very grateful for a written revelation of God's truth to protect and guide us. Otherwise, we should be in a state of continual wavering and, as the book of Judges says, we would emulate the Jews who forsook the true worship of God and did what was right in their own eyes. It is precisely this that we see nowadays. For where people have given up on the Bible as an absolute standard, morality apes the preferences of the hour. "Where there is no guidance, a people falls" (Proverbs 11:14).

Before itemizing the key heresies of the New Testament world, let us agree that all of us are guilty of a form of heresy when we do not believe God when he tells us to trust him fully. Heresy is a denial of truth: and we are heretics daily as we deny the truth that it is not we ourselves that live but Christ who lives in us. Heresy is not something that appears overnight in our garden: it is something that we plant and cultivate. There is no heresy which did not have its small personal beginning in individual unbelief. And remember, if for every Apostle Paul there were thousands of less well-known, less well-endowed people of faith, then for every famous heretic there were thousands of little known, less intellectually articulate spiritual vagrants. If the Church today is weak, is it not because *we* are weak? "Let him that thinketh he standeth, take heed lest he fall."

One of the tricks that history plays on us—a trick sometimes passed by the guardians of knowledge—is to so label a heresy as

to hide it. Even among well-instructed Christians, who could pass
an identification test on Docetism, Gnosticism, Nestorianism,
Donatism, Manichaeanism, Arianism, Nicolaitanism? For a history test you might need to know these. But the only crucial test
we all have to face is the examination of our own consciences.

So, foregoing for a moment the names, I shall describe what
underlies the heresies. Let us start with a useful axiom: all major
heresies major in denying Christ. Once you have absorbed this
fact, you are not only prepared to study the various forms of
denial, you are also prepared to deal wisely with any potential
heretic who knocks on your door tomorrow morning—find out
what he thinks of Christ. And do not be satisfied with a vague
answer. If he cannot subscribe to the Bible's full testimony about
Christ, then nothing else he has to say is worth a scrap. It is *he*
who needs to listen to *you*. Don't waste the opportunity.

I hardly need to explain why heresies focus on Christ. The idea
of a salvation by God's grace, involving God's becoming man,
effected by a gibbet and an empty tomb, successively offends
every human constituency. The Incarnation is an insult to intelligence; Calvary and the empty tomb play havoc with mere religiosity; grace nullifies the self-made man. All heresy is a recoiling from the shock of these facts.

The self-made man cannot, as such, accept the finished state of
Christ's work. The New Testament teaches what the Old Testament also makes plain, that we can know God only by his free
gift, by his grace. Only at his invitation, only by his means, may
we approach him. There is nothing to add. A life of obedience to
God is the Holy Spirit's signature in our life, confirming that we
do, indeed, belong to the family. It does not *make* us members of
the family. This hallmark of biblical religion is a standing rebuke
to the self-made man approach. Yet, all other religions are full of
what we must do, on a regular basis, to be assured of salvation.
And the history of Christianity is strewn with such heresy. The
so-called Judaizers in the Early Church set the pace. Paul has to
emphasize over and over the free nature of God's grace. The
Epistle to the Hebrews eloquently and forcefully preaches the
finished, unrepeatable nature of Christ's sacrifice for us. The instinct to ingratiate ourselves with superiors, and thus with God, is
basic. This is the fountain of all heresies. Perhaps for this very
reason it is usually overlooked in discussions of heresy. It does

not seem particularly theological. Indeed, no great thought is required to do what is second nature to fallen man.

The trouble with mere religiosity is that it is safely located in space and time outside the rhythm of life. The darkened cathedral, the scent-laden atmosphere of the temple, the esoteric reaches of abstract theology, the impregnable fortress of private religious sensibility—all these are ways of separating truth from life. And they all result in dehydrating that truth whose hallmark is streams of living water. Christ is a living contradiction to this mentality: he made his grave with the wicked and as risen he ate breakfast. There *is* no "religious" truth. Either truth *is* truth or it isn't. And if it is, all of life is involved on the same level. Be circumcised in the heart as well as the flesh, said Isaiah. "Whatever you do, do all to the glory of God," advised Paul (1 Cor. 10:31). The heresy that reflects the human instinct for separating the "sacred" from the "profane" always pretends that you can live life to the full, religiously and humanly, just so long as you do not confuse the two realms. Hypocrisy is not a bad word to describe it.

To deny either Christ's humanity or his divinity is not far removed from the mentality we have just described. The important difference is that each denial emphasizes one thing to the actual or virtual exclusion of the other. A despairing, even perhaps masochistic, streak in humanity leads some to feel that all things visible are evil and that the only salvation is to be found in the invisible. Applied to Christianity, the real humanity of Christ is denied. He becomes a shadowy, mystical figure, another symbol to add to many others in the pantheon of man-made religion. The tradition of Plato fuels this mentality; the religious traditions of India, now encroaching on the West, reinforce it. The cry is not so much to keep spirit and life apart as to flee life entirely. The opposite is true of those who boldly declare only for what they can see. To them, Christ is the great ethical teacher but no more. Salvation means grappling with what we know and see and coming to terms with it. The escape is not into a world of mystical experience but into the world of practical, concrete busyness. Christ is not divine. Rather, he is a sort of cultural technician. But culture has changed in two thousand years and so we revere Christ's teachings in principle rather than in practice. Other technicians must take over. The tradition of Aristotle has fortified this emphasis on what seems immediately useful and a trust in the unaided powers of the human mind. The visible achievements of the West have seemed to underwrite this faith and promote the conviction that if some answers are lacking today they will be found tomorrow.

What these twin misconceptions have in common is a refusal to accept the Incarnation. Human intelligence concludes either that everything is spiritual or everything is material. Depending on your choice, it is either an insult to the soul or an insult to the body to say that god became man or that the best man was a god. The first four verses of John's first Epistle contradict both. We have heard, seen and touched "the eternal life which was with the Father," he writes.

It is apparent that these three major roots of heresy are intertwined. This is to be expected. Jesus deliberately contrasts the children of God the Father with the children of the Devil. "You are of your father the devil, and your will is to do your father's desires," he tells the Pharisees (John 8:44). Just as the children of the heavenly Father do his will, in various ways, according to background, opportunity, capacity; so do "the children of this world," according to the same variants, do the will of "the father of lies." Heresy, remember, is bound up with choice. There is one major choice but several fundamental expressions of it. To encounter, as one often does nowadays, a combination of seemingly contradictory heresies in a single person, is not surprising if one bears in mind that heresy is a lie, a contradiction. Contradiction is of the essence of heresy. The worldly man, Paul says, is "ready to say Yes and No at once" (2 Cor. 1:17). By contrast, James writes (5:12), "Let your yes be yes and your no be no" James is here echoing Christ's own words, the one in whom, Paul adds, all God's promises "find their Yes" (2 Cor. 1:20).

What heretical plants sprang from the root-system we have traced? There were basically two types, reflecting the related issues of man's approach to God and God's approach to man.

In the days of the Apostles, the attempt to approach God on a basis other than that of Christ's work alone was already apparent. While the form of such an attempt may often be a deviation from, rather than a full denial of, Christian doctrine, it is significant that Paul was emphatic in his condemnation of contemporary "Judaizing." He saw in the insistence upon circumcision (especially Gentile circumcision), and other "works," something more than cultural pride. He saw it as, in principle, "another Gospel."

In the generations following, the issue was sometimes very clear-cut, as we may see in the case of Pelagianism, roundly condemned by Jerome and Augustine in the early fifth century. Pelagius, a British monk unleashed on the Mediterranean world, placed an axe to the tree of grace, asserting the original innocence of all newborn children and the ability of man to fulfill God's law on his own account.

But the issue might be less clear-cut. Not everyone is sure that the church fathers were right to condemn the Montanists so severely. Starting in the late second century, Montanism stood for an ecstatic spiritual experience and a heavy, even sensationalist, emphasis on the soon-coming of Christ. Perhaps the leaders of the church were over-reacting in hounding the Montanists. It is not, after all, far removed from emphases in the church today which are not favored by all but not necessarily deemed heretical. On the other hand, implicit in Montanism, as in other movements since, is a claim to a continuing revelation of new truths by the Spirit. If the church's leaders were responding to this, their wisdom should not be too hastily impugned.

Montanism and Pelagianism were relatively unimportant, however, compared to Gnosticism. Gnosticism (from a word meaning "knowledge") is a broad term covering any religious tendency which stresses as necessary for salvation secret inner knowledge and escape from the "evil" of the physical world, including our own bodies. A generic, early form of Gnosticism seems to be attacked by Paul in his Colossian letter, and the spiritual elitism apparent in Colossae naturally accompanied a view which posited higher and higher stages of spiritual illumination. Of course, if salvation involves being delivered from our actual physical nature, it is unthinkable that God in Christ would assume such a form. Thus, Gnosticism quickly shades off into a denial of Christ's humanity. At its most innocent, Gnosticism might be a dangerous emphasis needing correction. At its worst, it was a thoroughgoing mysticism, in which the employment of the name of Christ and other distinctive Christian terms was merely gratuitous. We see similar masquerades today, with the supposed identification of Christ with alien concepts of "inner light" and so on.

Mature Gnosticism is generally identified with the ideas of Valentinus, who almost became bishop of Rome in the mid-second century. Manicheanism, with which Augustine flirted before his conversion, may be seen as a severe form of Gnosticism. The realm of the spirit (good) is sharply divided from that of matter (evil), yielding the idea of a dualistic conflict between the two forces. Salvation, then, is escape from the realm of matter. One can clearly sense here the general influence of Platonic thinking on the immortality of the soul alone, after the evil carcass has fallen away.

While not always identified with Gnosticism, the ideas of Valentinus' contemporary Marcion reveal characteristic traits. Distinguishing between a bad Old Testament materialistic God and a good New Testament spiritual Christ, Marcion cut down Scripture to his own size (selected, edited portions of Luke and Paul's epistles) and censored life itself (forbidding obvious physical activities such as marriage or physical relations within marriage). The material self-indulgence of the Nicolaitans condemned in Revelation 2:6 would be the opposite side of the coin to Marcion's tendency, as would be also Jefferson's editing of the Bible to suit his own brand of self-confident humanism. Whether by cutting out portions of the Bible or importing one's own special interpretation, these approaches to God all major in exalting a human idea of what is truly spiritual over the plain statement of Scripture. In our own times, Mormons, Unificationists, Jehovah's Witnesses, and those who excuse the vices of the age on the grounds that love allows them, link hands with Marcion and Valentinus.

A special footnote may be added to the discussion of man's approach to God: Donatism, which engaged the attention of Augustine and the North African churches around 400. The context of Donatism cannot here concern us. Its super-spiritual emphasis upon a pure church, with a corresponding rejection of any church or individual seeming less than pure, implicitly detracted from the ongoing awareness of that grace of God in everyday life which helps us to confess our failings and forgive those of others. It must be noted, however (as the history of Donatism shows in places), that if rejection of Donatist exclusiveness is based on a smug or shallow attitude to sin—"that grace might more abound"—then it is hard to decide who is worse: the heretic or his accuser.

Gnosticism, as we have seen, combines the themes of man's

approach to God and God's to man: if man has to transcend aspects of his created nature to know God, then the God-man can hardly be human. This denial is fundamental to the other heresies we must consider. Indeed, John in his First Epistle makes the flat statement that the refusal to accept that "Jesus Christ is come in the flesh" is "the spirit of antichrist" (1 John 4:3). Whatever the particular variation of concept and expression, none of these heresies can stomach the Scriptural testimony that Jesus was the uncreated Word who yet took upon himself full human form, being tempted as we are, yet without sin.

Docetism (from the Greek "to seem"), in the early second century, asserted that Jesus only seemed to be a man and that his crucifixion was an illusion. The reverse tack was taken by Adoptionism, that troubled the church two or three generations later. Here, Jesus was only a man but indwelt by the Spirit of God who "adopted" him for his ministry and then left him just before the crucifixion.

A century after Docetism, Sabellius detracted from the real divinity of Christ, giving coherence to current heterodoxy about the Godhead. He argued that the Father, Son and Holy Spirit are not persons so much as modes or guises by which the one God makes himself known. On the surface, this view is relatively innocent compared to Docetism. But what can it possibly mean for a "mode" of the one God to declare to another "mode": "Why hast thou forsaken me?" Salvation is at stake.

Nestorianism (named after a fifth century patriarch of Constantinople), confronting the Sabellian analysis as it might apply to the person of Christ alone, went to the other extreme, rigidly distinguishing between his human and divine natures. But if Christ's nature be so split, the tendency is to end up downplaying one in favor of the other. So, if Nestorius seemed to his opponents to reduce Christ to a holy *man*, his younger contemporaries, the Monophysites, (from the Greek, "one nature"), made him seem only divine.

But before ever Nestorius and the Monophysites were heard of, a far more serious overreaction to Sabellius had informed the classic fourth-century battle over the nature of Christ. The sharp distinction which Nestorius made later on between the natures of Christ was applied by an Alexandrian priest called Arius to the persons of the Godhead. And just as Nestorianism tended to destroy the unity of Christ's person, so Arianism detracted from the unity of God. To emphasize Christ's distinction from the Father, Arius downplayed the divinity of the Son, asserting that he was actually created by the Father. There was also, it is true, a whiff of Platonism here: perhaps Christ's assumption of physical form inhibited Arius from seeing him as fully God.

If it was left to the Council of Chalcedon in 451 to give final form to orthodox conviction as regards the nature of Christ (true God, true man, yet truly one), the fifth century bishops were able to build upon the insistence of the Council of Nicaea (325) and the Nicene Creed that Christ is truly God ("one substance with the Father"), yet fully incarnate.

That Arianism should have been the occasion for the first and fundamental battle over the nature of Christ probably says more about contemporary political circumstances than about the actual state of theological debate. The advent of Constantine, an emperor sympathetic to Christianity whether or not Christian, who had a direct interest in ecclesiastical and theological order, forced the issue to a head. Likewise, whereas historians often say that the Nicene perspective survived only by a hair's-breadth after 325, it appears possible that political circumstances artificially inflated the degree to which it was really threatened. Bishops and theologians might flirt with Arian views to spite such ecclesiastical foes as Athanasius. But when their bluff was called they were clearly not prepared to *be* Arians. Very few challenged the definitive form of the Nicene Creed accepted by the Council of Constantinople in 381.

This is not to downplay the struggles and theological contributions of Athanasius, the five-times exiled bishop of Alexandria. Nor is it minimizing the issue at stake. Rather it is to suggest that there was an underlying health in the church which was able to survive disputes carried on in a manner which shocks our modern (anemic?) sensibilities. It is to suggest, too, that if the great creeds of the undivided church are the universally accepted enunciation of orthodox Christology and Trinitarian belief, they also lack that prime authority which resides in Scripture alone. Lacking this, they invite, willy-nilly, especially during their formulation, the activity of that ungenerous party spirit which sometimes marks the orthodox as well as the heretical. "There must be divisions among you," the Apostle remarked, "that those who are genuine among you may be recognized" (1 Corinthians 11:19).

Have you been congratulating yourself on your orthodoxy over the last few pages? Such congratulation is the thin end of the wedge of the gospel of works. Do you emphasize victory over sin, without taking seriously the evidence of your ongoing frailty? Then you are a spiritualizer. Or do you bemoan the desperateness of the battle against sin, implying that outward joy is unrealistic or else not for you? If so, then at bottom your Christ is still on the Cross—he is, perhaps, a symbol of suffering humanity. Are you, finally, entirely unmoved? Then ask yourself whether you ever allow God to speak to you by his Word outside the confines of habitual religious observance. "Religion that is pure and undefiled before God and the Father is this: to visit orphans and widows in their affliction, and to keep oneself unstained from the world" (James 1:27).

For Further Study

Green, Michael. *Evangelism in the Early Church*. Grand Rapids: Wm. B. Eerdmans Publishing Co., 1970. Answers most of the questions you'd like to ask on the subject, on the basis of a sound Biblical theology and thorough knowledge of the Mediterranean world at the time.

Lucretius Carus, Titus. *Lucretius on the Nature of the Universe*. Translated and with Introduction by Ronald Latham. Baltimore: Penguin Books, 1951. Expresses basic view of the world held by most people at most times, I think. Written a century before the Apostles.

Packer, J. I. *I Want to be a Christian*. Wheaton, IL: Tyndale House, 1977. An excellent antidote to all our little heresies. The way the material is arranged is almost as important as the material itself.

Plato. *The Republic*. Translated with Introduction and Notes by Francis MacDonald Cornford. New York: Oxford University Press, 1951. What was so attractive about Platonism? Find out directly, for a change.

4

Persecution and the Church's Life: The Practice of Principles

ERESY IS PRESENT in the Church from the start. Persecution is its twin brother. Where there is a Judas there is a Pontius Pilate. Much of the New Testament is written consciously against a background of suffering. The author of Hebrews pens the great chapter on the heroes of faith to encourage his readers not to shirk suffering. Paul frequently couches mention of the Second Coming in the context of the present suffering of believers. Paul's own career is a litany of sufferings. Jesus warned his followers of rough treatment: "If they persecuted me, they will persecute you" (John 15:20).

Persecution, like heresy, does not arise by accident. It is a natural growth. All societies, at all times, have been more or less hostile to the stranger and the eccentric. Part of the persecution of the Christian had and still has, therefore, nothing to do with the Gospel as such. It is worth remembering this. Although the Christian is, inevitably, a stranger and exile like Abraham, his life will also commend him and his Lord to others. It fell to Jeremiah's lot to be universally despised. This, however, was exceptional. The book of Proverbs and a number of Jesus' sayings underline the fact that the man who fears God can make even his enemies to be at peace with him.

Having said this, the Cross of Christ *is* an offence. The opinions and conduct of the Christian do constitute a judgment upon society. Those who heed the judgment will be saved. Those who do not are apt to turn and bite. This is the special sense in which the persecution of the Christian, in the first century or now, is natural.

In the world of the Roman Empire, which, in common with all settled societies till the fragmentation of modern times, stressed complex and visible levels of membership and belonging, the Christian often came across as a holdout.* After all, how could he enter a civil service job if it involved swearing an oath to Caesar as God? We should be sensitive to this predicament; Christians in various Iron Curtain countries cannot take similar jobs without joining the Communist Party. Recalling that persecution is not a one-way street, we need to say that Communist Party members in some Western countries face similar exclusion. The difference here is that whereas the Christian is bound by the law of God not to dissimulate, the Communist is under no such absolute prohibition and so can infiltrate at will.

It was not only government service that presented problems, however. Membership of basic trade and craft organizations sometimes involved questionable practices and religious oaths. Just as guilds in medieval Europe had patron saints, their Roman antecedents did homage to Mithras, Diana, and other gods and goddesses. And what about teaching? Could one in good conscience cover the whole curriculum if it meant instilling respect for pagan deities? A similar problem begins to face Christian teachers in the modern world; only the details are changed. How will the Christian deal with "desexed" textbooks which, in denying the distinctions in God's creation, inculcate in our children basic tenets of pantheistic culture?

The Christian's use of leisure time might also set him apart. How could he derive pleasure from brutal gladiatorial sports? And quite apart from intellectual and aesthetic considerations, the freedom he had in Christ was certainly not elastic enough to take in the pornographic slush that steadily engulfed stage entertainment. I hardly need press the modern parallels here.

The way the Christian actually *did* use his leisure time could be even more incriminating than the way he did not. What exactly were these Christians doing in their strange gatherings?

*Specifically in the next paragraphs, including the direct quotes from contemporaries, as generally in my treatment of the Christian in Roman society, I am indebted to Michael Green's excellent *Evangelism in the Early Church.*

Persecution and the Church's Life

A perhaps willful misunderstanding of the celebration of the Lord's Supper gave birth to the rumor that Christians were cannibals, consuming someone's flesh and blood. Much talk of love and the appellations "brother" and "sister" aroused suspicions of incest (there was, indeed, incest at Corinth) or at least sexual doings. Oddly enough, such ideas were current in some sixteenth-century circles about life in Calvin's Geneva. The promiscuous imagination fed on the thought of ex-monks and ex-nuns whipping it up!

More seriously, the very cohesion and seriousness of the Christian assemblies made civil authorities fear political intrigue and dissension. Tacitus, reflecting popular prejudice, wrote in the late first century that Christians were "hated by the populace for their crimes" and gave his judgment that they "were both guilty of and deserving the severest penalties." Capitalizing upon the prejudice, Nero could accuse the Roman Christians of arson and, by way of symbolically appropriate retribution, burn them as living torches in the imperial gardens.

In a roundabout way but for the wrong reasons, Nero had a point. Although the level of official persecution fluctuated wildly, the Christian Gospel was always a rapier pointed at the heart of the state. For if, as Francis Schaeffer has very well expressed it, the state regards itself as absolute, the Gospel represents a greater absolute to judge it. Even the Christian's respect for authority, enjoined by Christ and Paul and Peter, was activated by that higher authority who is God. This was never better illustrated than in the late third century when, for purposes of unity and also to express confidence in them, the Christians were invited to have Christ added to the Pantheon of accepted gods. The Christian refusal was like a whiplash across the bare flesh of a society bereft of values. It prompted the last savage wave of persecution before toleration was granted in the early fourth century.

What made the church conspicuous enough to be offered official recognition was a combination of steady growth in numbers and a distinctive moral and intellectual profile. Speaking of numbers: before the advent of the "science" of political economy in the eighteenth century it is impossible to be sure of the population of even whole regions, let alone minor groups such as Christians in the Roman Empire. From a statistically insignificant proportion around the year 100, it is guessed that the church may have accounted for 10 percent of imperial population in the Mediterranean lands about the year 250. This year, incidentally, marked a concerted attack upon the church by the emperor Decius, heralding a strong drive toward social and political cohesion after fifty years of assassinations and declining morale. It is interesting that this drive was matched religiously and philosophically by a growing preference for monotheism and a unified cult amidst the very chaos of cults. While this would at first intensify the attack upon Christianity as a recalcitrant force, it also prepared the way for its eventual acceptance in the fourth century.

Perhaps, indeed, it is more important to know the point at which the church's presence was thus felt to be an obstruction, than to know how many heads there were. For Decius's insistence that all (and he especially meant Christians) should express public loyalty by sacrificing to the Roman gods, thereby receiving paper certification, began the first official assault since the first century. Not that there was not persecution in the intervening period. But whereas the state, which enjoyed fairly stable leadership till about 200, was content to deal passively with Christians, prosecuting and executing them only as charges were brought, active aggression was left up to the local populations. Especially after the decimation of many of the homogeneous Jewish enclaves after the successive Jewish revolts of 66-70, 115-117, and 135 (the last, Bar Kochba's insurrection), the brunt of local prejudice tended to be borne by the increasingly more conspicuous exclusivist group, the Christians.

Prejudice against minorities is most rampant during times of hardship. Some historians, echoing an observation of Tertullian (died ca. 240), have therefore sought to plot the curve of provincial persecution on the graph of famines, military threats and crippling inflation. The Nazis' assault on the Jews in the context of economic, social and political crisis is a modern example of the same correlation; Solzhenitsyn's *Gulag Archipelago* documents in detail how the ups and downs of prison camp fortunes tended to follow the pattern of crisis in Soviet policy. If we had adequate documentation, we could no doubt paint an interesting background to two of the most notorious attacks upon the church in the late second century. At Lyons and Vienne in the south of France, mass tortures and executions were carried out in 177, not instigated by but weakly acquiesced in by imperial government. A decade or so earlier, at Smyrna in Asia Minor, mob action abetted by local Jewish hostility in this wealthy port town exploded against Christians, providing the setting for the martyrdom by burning of bishop Polycarp, whose moving testimony has refreshed the church ever since: "Eighty-six years have I served him and he has done me no wrong. How then can I blaspheme my King who saved me?" No wonder an informal martyrology began to develop after about 150!

Lyons, Smyrna: these cities are over a thousand miles apart. All around the Mediterranean congregations had sprung up, not least on the long North African coast. This region, hard to visualize now as a once great stronghold of Christianity, was a vital granary for the Roman Empire. The Gospel had taken hold in many populous areas, especially around Carthage (modern Tunisia and Algeria) and Alexandria, in the Nile Delta. Hippo, west of Carthage, would produce one of the very greatest Christian minds in the history of the church—Augustine (died 430)— and Alexandria certainly represented the most lively early center of theological debate, hosting men of the calibre of Origen (died 253) and Athanasius (died 373), to name two among many.

Rome, by comparison, not to slight Clement (died early second century), was far less productive of influential theologians than either the great North African cities, or Antioch and Asia Minor. Yet the price of theological originality was a climate of bickering and division which laid the spiritual foundations for the rapid assimilation of the southern and eastern Mediterranean to Islam in the seventh century. The relative stability of the Roman Christians may have been due, in part, to the baptizing of those qualities of deliberateness and order which had characterized their pagan ancestors who had founded the Republic and organized an empire.

But whether we look back to Antioch, Alexandria, Carthage, or Rome—all ecclesiastical rivals at one time or another in the early centuries—it is well to note that, even if in the breach, the history of the church was proving the truth of Jesus' words that the time would come when men would worship neither in Samaria nor in Jerusalem. Worship would not depend on a physical shrine or a national capital. If Jerusalem could be regarded in some sense as the visible center of the church till A.D. 70, its destruction in that year cut this umbilical cord. The church was well and truly

No Other Foundation

launched into an epoch only at the end of which, if one takes seriously the import of biblical prophecy, a capital will be restored in the form of the New Jerusalem whose temple is the Lord God Almighty and the Lamb.

The church is not to have a visible capital till Christ's return; she *is* to have visible leadership and visible order. She is, after all, to be visible. What sort of leadership and order has engaged the attention of Christians a great deal, not least in modern times when the slow breakdown of community, in favor of centrally directed faceless groupings, has been felt in the church as well as in society at large. As a result, we see many fledgling congregations and denominations testifying to a more, or less, authentic attempt to recover the theory and practice of New Testament church order.

Unfortunately, there is often in this attempt, as well as in some criticisms of it, a failure to distinguish between what is essential and what is beneficial. The tension between Donatists and their critics, mentioned in the last chapter, is here expressed in a related context and with similar faults on both sides. If this thorny topic is best handled by isolating the essential from the beneficial, then this task is made easier if we enlarge the screen to take in social order as a whole.

The Bible is clear that theocracy is the essence of a truly viable social order. When Israel clamored for a king after the elders of Israel had failed to give a lead, God revealed to Samuel that, implicitly, it was his (God's) kingship that was being rejected. Yet Samuel was told to tell Israel that this divergence from God's order did not have to mean an ongoing rejection of God's real authority. Likewise, even Jeroboam, in revolt against the bloodline of David, was assured that he would still be blessed as long as he did not establish a rival center of worship to Jerusalem. What we can learn from this is that there is a preferable visible order which best enables men to live in the awareness of the invisible order. Nevertheless, if the visible order is first traduced and then replaced, one may, despite the handicap, still obey God and be blessed.

This analysis seems to apply very exactly to the issue of order in the church. The lordship of the ascended Christ, expressed through his Spirit, is the essence of this order. With obvious similarities to the place of the elders in Israel, the visible order of the church taught in the New Testament is one of plural elders who differ from the deacons and other members of the congregation in function, not in quality, all Christians being equally servants to each other, as Christ also served. As in Israel, this plurality in a local setting also translated into a supra-local order, such that a congregation would participate in and respect the counsel of the elders of plural congregations over a given issue. The so-called Council of Jerusalem in Acts 15, though dealing with a special case—the appeal of one congregation to another—anticipates the fuller manifestation of this principle in subsequent councils and synods down through the ages.

In the local congregation itself, even if among the ruling elders one or more might be particularly effective rulers or bear the main teaching responsibilities, there is no suggestion whatever in the New Testament that this granted authority above other elders. The relevant passage (1 Timothy 5:17) makes clear that it is extra remuneration that is deserved by those who are thus especially engaged in the tasks of the eldership. Further, the use of the plural argues against the idea of there being normally only one elder in this category, although the possibility of Timothy's receiving advice for more than one congregation precludes one from being absolute about this.

The most obvious and immediate devolution from this pattern would be the concentration of the authority and functions of the eldership in the hands of one man, on a regular basis. One reason for such a trend might be someone's proud assertiveness—perhaps Diotrophes in John's Third Epistle is an example. Or perhaps the reason might be a lack of mutual servanthood among elders such that effective leadership, convincing teaching and godly example are not given to the flock. A possible example of this may have existed at Corinth, judging from a letter written to the church by Clement (ca. A.D. 90) on behalf of the Christians at Rome. It appears, too, that the strong recommendations of Ignatius of Antioch (died ca. 115) for one elder per congregation, sprang at least in part from his experience of dissension within plural elderships. The steady drift towards unitary leadership, which began to be the norm in the church thereafter, is often ascribed to Ignatius' influence. But, as we have seen, there are more fundamental reasons for which Ignatius' teaching served merely as an apologetic. And after all, Ignatius' elder was to be

No Other Foundation

chosen by the congregation and must come *from* that congregation. This was a far cry from subsequent developments.

"Subsequent developments," would, for instance, bring into view that familiar pattern of spiritual authority exercised over many churches by virtue of a particular physical location, such as Rome or Antioch. This pattern seems well established by the year 200. But just as leadership sanctioned by God in Israel, while honoring the principle of supra-local appeal showed no necessary respect for eldest sons or even exclusive blood-lines, so the gifts of the Spirit are not automatically showered on large, ancient cities—including Jerusalem! Pre-eminent spiritual authority in the church at any one time might not, indeed, be identified with Rome or Canterbury, but with an abbot of Clairvaux, or John Wesley whose parish was the world. The first centuries of the church are, for a fact, full of examples, not only of worthy leaders occupying prominent positions but exceedingly *unworthy* ones in the *same* positions.

At this point, to assert that the key is the office *per se,* even if the occupant is not always godly, is to be guilty of taking one's cue from secondary considerations instead of primary ones. Respect for office, which Paul showed in the case of a law-breaking High Priest, says nothing whatever about the relevance of that office in the light of the High Priesthood of Christ. Thus, one might respect the leadership of a patriarch of Alexandria in the third century, without thereby subscribing to the prevailing hierarchical system as the preferable order, the most excellent tradition of the visible church.

This distinction is crucial for it allows us to do two things simultaneously. First, to be grateful for the qualities of the church in the early days—a church which spread the Gospel, endured persecution, preserved the Scriptures and gave us creeds whose faithfulness to truth is matched only by their clarity and simplicity. Second, to discern the roots of future trouble in a pattern of order which was slowly departing from the principles enunciated by the Apostles. Ignatius, let us not forget, in arguing for a one-man eldership, used every argument possible, except that of apostolic institution—for the simple reason that there was no evidence that the Apostles ever instituted such a thing. And Ignatius was close enough in time to have known about it if they had. He was, therefore, to his credit, honest enough not to fake it, unlike

Papal Chancery clerks in ages to come. We might note here, further, that like all the leaders in the first centuries—frequently headstrong, powerful personalities—Ignatius was emphatic that his authority, about which he felt no embarrassment, was not apostolic; it was fallible.

A comment is also in place about the related issue of apostolic succession, with the particular claim which the bishops of Rome would eventually make (especially Leo in the fifth century) to a primacy based on Christ's statement: "Thou art Peter, and on this rock I will build my church"—Peter's headship of the Roman church being assumed. Quite apart from the known problems of positive historical evidence to establish continuity, and the exegetical difficulties surrounding the Matthew 16:18 proof text, there is another basic problem stemming from a further text often cited to support the idea of an institutionally consistent traditional authority. This is Paul's word to Timothy (2 Timothy 2:2): "And what you have heard from me before many witnesses, entrust to faithful men who will be able to teach others also."

What is the problem? Creation precedes redemption; life precedes new life. In other words, life itself offers a valuable insight. Abortion proponents often say that we cannot be sure when life begins in the fetus. This is a silly argument because, biologically, since the first parents life has never ended. There is always a sperm and always an egg. But the continuation of this life is not dependent upon any one set of parents, unless God so decrees it. The Capetian dynasty in France might produce heirs for 300 years but still become extinct. Then a prince could be sought in a collateral line. Similarly, in the transmission of the living Gospel, it has never ended once begun. But its continued transmission is not dependent on any one particular agency. An agency might be faithful for a long time and yet eventually prove barren. In which case, God is never without collateral lines. The key, then, is life, not the agency per se. Every family, every institution, has its day—even if sometimes recurring days. Fortunately, the faithful teaching of the Gospel is not dependent on one family or one institution. Eli can give place to Samuel. The patriarchate of Alexandria, so secure in the early centuries, was destined to be swallowed up by the Moslems. Likewise Antioch and Carthage.

Let us repeat, however, that none of these considerations should cause us absolutely to wash our hands of a church order

No Other Foundation

which is more or less foreign to apostolic principle. We may, indeed, speaking of contemporary experience rather than historical observation, choose to worship in a context a little closer to biblical order because the estrangement in question seriously inhibits or obscures "the obedience of faith." But it is the latter issue which forms the pivot. Let us look for this, for faith is the first obedience to which we are called because it is God's command that we have faith in the obedience of Christ. Here is the foundation of the doctrines of grace. Only standing on this foundation can we see clearly to deal with dependent realities which conflict to a greater or lesser extent with it.

That phrase "the obedience of faith" (cf. Acts 6:7) recalls a phrase coined in the second century: "the rule of faith." This constituted a summary of apostolic doctrines as understood by the leading Christian congregations. There might, perhaps, be differences of opinion about ecclesiastical authority and there would be disagreements later on about how to understand certain aspects of this "rule" (for example, the divine and human nature of Christ). But there was general agreement on essentials, simply stated. Before the year 200, we hear of active cooperation, in the interests of safeguarding the faith from error, on the part of prominent bishops ranging from Rome to Alexandria. The emergence of this self-conscious episcopal authority is, it seems, related to the threat of false teaching. It was an effective vehicle for guarding the faithful against interlopers, similar in intent (though derivative as regards authority) to the New Testament epistles.

The positive teaching of "the rule of faith" accompanied positive practice in the church as regards worship and regular instruction. There was no shirking catechism: young and old alike must have a reason for the faith they claimed. In particular, candidates for baptism, normally administered on Easter morning in the name of the Father, the Son and the Holy Spirit, had to undergo lengthy preparation, stretching from months to years. We may admire the serious intent here, while having some misgivings about the possible implications of requiring such a refined grasp of the Gospel as a condition for receiving the sign of God's grace in salvation. It would seem to encourage a view of baptism as something substantive in itself and therefore not far removed from the idea that infant baptism is regenerative—an idea gaining ground in some quarters in the third century.

Persecution and the Church's Life

The regular worship of the church in the early centuries has been closely studied by scholars. Its changing forms have been carefully documented. Such changes are no cause for alarm, in themselves. The Passover celebrated by Jesus embraced a traditional course of four wine cups which was not specified in the Law. Furthermore, Jesus appears to have taken part in the Feast of Dedication (Hannukah), referred to in John 10:22f., which was an inter-testamental celebration recalling the days of the Maccabees. These traditions were acceptable because not alien to what the Law *did* require. This fact is helpful when considering customs in worship and Christian observance (such as Christmas) which are not commanded in Scripture.

As we might expect, the expansion of the church, along with a grudging, haphazard toleration of Christians, which saw the increased use of public buildings and even separate church buildings from the late-second century, was accompanied by a growing formality in worship. Quite apart from other considerations, formality is a price to be paid for larger numbers. If this formality be seen in terms of the regular recitation of the Lord's Prayer, and even some set prayers in the third century; in the systematic, year-round reading of Scripture; in a preaching which is the expected office of one elder; and in the weekly celebration of the Lord's Supper—who would wish to throw stones? Would that more Christian worship today were as true to biblical patterns. And I have not even mentioned the practice of church discipline whereby the Lord's table was guarded against the presumptuous and the careless. Whatever the cost in terms of fuller participation, there was here an enduring structure which, even with the later addition of alien features, still bears the hallmark (as in the Roman Catholic mass) of sound scriptural origins.

There *were* some additions during the first few centuries, nevertheless, two of which I shall note. The adoption of the term "priest" in its theological sense to describe a pastor seems to have had its beginnings in the latter half of the third century. Initially, perhaps, this was more a linguistic assimilation to the terminology of contemporary religion than a definite departure from New Testament teaching on this matter. The time would come, however, when the "priest" would indeed claim to be enacting or reenacting a sacrifice when he administered the Lord's Supper. The other addition was actually a subtraction: the demise of congregational singing. At least, the most straightforward reading of Paul's epistles leads one to assume that everybody sang. By the third century this practice seems to have become extremely rare; soloists predominated. It is a measure of the stature of Ambrose that he should have single-handedly restored this important feature of congregational worship in the late fourth century.

Ambrose is best remembered, however, as the immediate human instrument used in the conversion of the half-pagan Augustine. And from the organization of the church we must finally turn to its positive confrontation with the surrounding culture. It is customary to designate as "Apologists" those Christian thinkers, especially in the second century, who wrote directly to a pagan audience, explaining and defending the Gospel intellectually and ethically, as well as exposing the weaknesses in rival explanations of reality. Properly speaking, though, every Christian is an apologist in some sense and the label is more useful in underlining the greater emphasis given before 200 to apologizing than to theologizing. No doubt the theologizing which becomes a more distinctive, though never exclusive, mark of the Christian mind after 200, testifies to the inner challenge faced by the church as the character of its beliefs was pondered by more and more converts fresh out of paganism. Apologetics is translating truth into current terms; theology is translating current terms into truth. The apologist informs the world; the theologian informs the church.

The Christian apologists covered the spectrum of attitudes to pagan learning which we may still observe today. At one end was a certain contempt for the classical mind, a reluctance even to quote pagan authors, and a failure, intellectually, to be a Roman to the Romans. At the other end there was a willingness bordering on compromise to speak to the issues, employing the categories of pagan debate. Justin Martyr (died 165) in his *Apologies* took advantage of his excellent training in classical philosophy to win over his foes gently. He was careful to explain those elements in the Gospel which might confuse the outsider, and he took pains to single out aspects of classical thought congenial to biblical thinking. Interestingly, Clement of Rome in the letter to Corinth referred to earlier made no bones about drawing a parallel between the harmony of the Greek city-state *(polis)* and the harmony required in the Body of Christ. But Tatian, a generation after Justin, was distinctly hostile. He tended to look for what was uncongenial in classical thought, categorizing such elements as diabolical. There is a note of scorn.

Sometimes, an apologetic was a direct response to a written attack upon Christianity. The most famous case is a book by Origen, the outstanding scholar of the church before Augustine. A Platonist called Celsus had issued a belittling study of Christian beliefs in 178—in itself a convincing testimony to the notice which the church was receiving. Origen's *Contra Celsum* was a devastating reply, logic and evidence combining to build a formidable argument.

As we have seen, every Christian is an apologist. But every Christian is a theologian, too. He does good to all men but especially to the household of faith. Irenaeus (died ca. 200) stands out as someone whose apologetic merged into his theology. His five-volume *Against Heresies* not only dealt exhaustively with current forms of Gnosticism but also gave coherent expression to Christian thought as it confronted its own world. Tertullian, however, must take pride of place in helping the church come to terms with the world on a Christian basis. He was the most gifted controversialist, with an original approach to problems (occasionally, too original), and a wonderful knack for coining and adapting terms, thereby making complex aspects of belief and practice easily discussable. "Sacrament" is one of his contributions. Another is "substance." And though the New Testament *is* the New Testament, it was Tertullian who thought to call it such.

The Christian confrontation with the world is never simply intellectual. Nor is it only to be discussed in "spiritual" terms. In our own lives we are perfectly aware of this but in studying the past we sometimes forget. The Christian is called upon to take a stand with regard to the whole orb of life and the early Christians set us a good example. One stand—of tragic interest today in view of the failure of many Christians to stand where the church has always stood—was over abortion and infanticide. The testimony of the early Fathers and various councils, stemming from the biblical injunction against the taking of human life, was most explicit. The degree to which the by no means universally accepted Hippocratic Oath, a pre-Christian standard of medical ethics which forbade abortion, could become the universal rule

No Other Foundation

till our own jaded times, was the degree to which it coincided with the consistent conviction of an ever-growing body of Christian opinion in the Roman Empire.

It is appropriate to end a chapter on the place of the church in the early centuries with a comment on its attitude to human life. Precisely when civilizations are foundering, people retreat more and more into themselves. Paradoxically, life becomes cheap simply because one's own life seems to be at such a premium. We are modern witnesses to the self-same phenomenon. We must salvage from the experience of the early church the vocation to defend human life from human predators, secure in the knowledge that all life is God's and that our own lives are forever secure. This perception nerved the early Christians to place their lives on the line in the arena and also refuse to sacrifice either truth or the unborn on the altar of personal convenience.

For Further Study

Psalm Praise. London: Falcon, 1973. One of the greatest weaknesses in much modern worship is lack of directly scriptural "psalmody"—whether the actual Psalms, or Bible passages put to music. This volume is one of the very best attempts I have seen to rectify this weakness without being too "folksy." *The Book of Psalms for Singing* (1975), put out by the Reformed Presbyterian Church of North America, is an excellent and amazingly inexpensive songbook of the entire Psalter (excluding, of course, other biblical canticles).

Stedman, Ray C. *Body Life*. Glendale, CA: Regal Books, 1972. There are several good books which seek to get to the roots of basic church organization. None is so immediate in impact and conviction as this.

Stevenson, James, ed. *A New Eusebius: Documents Illustrative of the History of the Church*. New York: Macmillan Co., 1957. Eusebius, a pet ecclesiastic of Constantine, bequeathed a history of the church which is the source of much of our knowledge. Stevenson's book fills in many of the gaps with firsthand, contemporary information.

Webber, Robert E. *Common Roots: A Call to Evangelical Maturity*. Grand Rapids, MI: Zondervan, 1978. Challenges much of our thinking about worship and Christian activity. Unfortunately marred by over-reaction; some of the roots are branches.

5

Canons, Councils, and a Catholic Church

W E HAVE SEEN how the Gospel spread in the context of heresy and persecution. The effectiveness of the Gospel is itself, at any one time, a powerful answer to ideological and physical subversion. Just so, the taking of Ai under Joshua had been a strident response to the "heresy" of Achan and the "persecution" of Ai's initial victory. Yet, Ai would not have fallen if Achan had not first been dealt with. And he was dealt with through God's making Joshua sensitive to the law of God which had been broken. In a similar way, in the epoch of the New Covenant, the preaching of the Gospel cannot be long effective if God's law, revealed in Scripture, is in any way toyed with or made secondary to essentially human expedients. "We refuse to practice cunning or to tamper with God's word," Paul wrote to the Corinthians, adding a little later: "For though we live in the world we are not carrying on a worldly war, for the weapons of our warfare are not worldly but have divine power to destroy strongholds" (2 Corinthians 4:2; 10:3-4).

At the same time, then, as the Gospel was being proclaimed in word and deed, its normative written form was being determined. Great as a Moses, Joshua or Paul might be, they pass away. As we are told at the end of the book of Joshua: "Israel served the Lord all the days of Joshua, and all the days of the elders who outlived Joshua and had known all the work which the Lord did for Israel" (Josh. 24:31). But "there arose another generation after them, who did not know the Lord or the work which he had done for Israel. And the people of Israel did what was evil in the sight of the Lord" (Judges 2:10-11). A normative Scripture is a

No Other Foundation

defence against this, and the Christian Church of the first centuries sought to counter and prevent error by affirming the distinctive doctrines and the documents which distinctively reveal
them.

The difficulty and importance of this task must be clear to
anyone looking at church history down the ages, and certainly
church history in our own day. For, just as in the second, third
and fourth centuries, so now we are faced with fundamental attacks upon doctrine, and open or more cloaked questioning of the
authority, inspiration and reliability of those books which we call
the Bible which embody the doctrine.

The word "canon" has the general connotation of measure or
standard.* It has come to signify a completed, authoritative collection of writings, inspired by God, an absolute rule for faith and
life. Crucially, if the Spirit of God inspires these writings, then he
leads people to accept them as the very Word of God and obey
them as such. It is not, therefore, canonization by a council which
gives the Scriptures authority; rather, their authority, previously
recognized and obeyed, is formally affirmed. Circumstantially,
the motive for defining the canon is negative rather than positive.
It is to say what is *not* Scripture by saying what is. In other
words, if a book is not recognized, it is not spiritually authoritative, even if interesting from other points of view.

If the recognition of a canon serves a negative purpose, the
content of the canon serves a positive purpose. It is interesting
that Moses in Deuteronomy 31:26 sees the "book of the law" as
"a witness against" the Jews, anticipating their rebellion against
the Lord. Thus, the Scripture is seen from the start as normative
for life and belief. Later on, we come across Nehemiah, Ezra,
Josiah, all being used by God to lead the Jews in a reconsecration
to the law. When the people heard the reading of the law they
were struck to their hearts and vowed to obey it.

It is important to see the dual function of a canon of Scripture in
order to have a reasonable perspective on the detailed questions
of which books were included and why. A canon embodies a
standard, and what is not up to or is clearly opposed to that

---

*I am indebted for a number of factual statements on the canon to F. F. Bruce's
still useful, general treatment: *The New Testament Documents: Are They Reliable,* 5th rev. ed. (Grand Rapids, MI: Wm. B. Eerdmans Pub. Co., 1960).

standard is excluded from or condemned by it. Although there are any number of reasonable, historical things one can say about the canon, one *can* never and *must* never lose sight of the fact that the books of the canon are given by God and that only a belief in God can secure the knowledge that they are not just human writings. When we are told in Scripture that Moses received words from God which he wrote down and that these words in front of us are those words; when we are told that Jesus was the very Word of God personified, that he said this and that and here are those sayings, we ultimately have only two courses open—to accept the words as such or to reject them.

Of course, the internal evidence that the words have an authority about them, a sense of objectivity, lacking in all other scriptures, as even nonbelieving scholars have observed, this is telling in itself. And the external evidence that the words are congruent to the world as we know it and men, and also and supremely that when we seek the God whose words they purport to be, on the terms laid down, that we find him—this is clinching proof. But by no means do all men seek God, and the certainty of the divine origin of Scripture is given only to those who do. This situation guarantees that debate about Scripture will go on. Furthermore, just as the conduct of the believer is imperfect, his thoughts are, too, including in some cases his thoughts about Scripture.

What must never be forgotten, however, is that there can be no antithesis between the Godhead and the Scriptures. For only in the Scriptures do we have any special knowledge of our creation and redemption. Anyone who claims to take God seriously but the Bible lightly is engaged in a deception. God cannot be separated from his Word. Nor can his children who are saved through that Word. Accordingly, we must give full weight in discussing the canon to the convictions of the Godly men in time past who worshipped the same God and who deemed such and such books to be Scripture. The awareness by the believer that his own experience of God's workings exactly matches that of the past generations who accepted the Scriptures, points to a common Scriptural source. In a world of change, this truism is established by the Truth.

Only after recognizing all these facts can one reasonably consider the history of the making of the canon. In fact, it is not to our purpose to become technical on this subject. As far as the Old

No Other Foundation

Testament goes, Jesus' references to "the Scriptures" and the parallel allusions of the New Testament writers fortify the impression derived from many other sources that there was what we should call an "Old Testament" in existence in the first century (indeed before).

That the Greek version of the Old Testament, dating from the second or third century B.C., should include the so-called Apocryphal books in addition to the well-known thirty-nine is less important than the fact that the so-called Hebrew Canon of thirty-nine is central and well-established. The Jew did not reject the Apocryphal books out of hand; rather, he saw them as unfit for normative, year-round, authoritative public teaching in the synagogue. For private edification they had a definite value. When the sixteenth-century Reformers reverted to the Hebrew Canon of thirty-nine books, they were simply accepting not only what appears to have been mainline Jewish opinion at the time of Christ but also the testimony of the New Testament. Jesus, for example, refers to Old Testament books very frequently but never to an Apocryphal book. If there are any references at all in the New Testament to Apocryphal books—and opinion is divided over the handful of probable allusions—the phrase "as the scripture says" never occurs in these places.

That the same Church councils which eventually formalized the canon of the New Testament in the late fourth century, formalized an Old Testament canon which included several Apocryphal books, is most likely due to the fact that the Christian Church was used to the *Greek* Old Testament (Septuagint), not the Hebrew. It is, in fact, interesting that a man like Jerome who was intimately familiar with the Hebrew should have vigorously sought the exclusion of the apocryphal books.

Coming now to the acceptance of the New Testament as we know it, all that needs to be said about the principles behind its formation has been said above. While Paul's epistles circulated as a unit from as early as A.D. 80 and while we begin to find evidence of the other New Testament books including, from at least the late-second century, the four Gospels, we also find Christian writers citing other works. This last fact is not surprising: without intending to ascribe special authority to them, we nowadays will quite naturally, in letters and books, refer to things written by able and trustworthy Christian leaders. Certainly, men have always done so.

Canons, Councils, and a Catholic Church

What provoked a specific enumerating of those writings which could be regarded as true Scripture was heretical attack. In particular, Marcion in the mid-second century preached an Old Testament harsh God and a New Testament God of love, and drew up a mutilated canon, excluding any Old Testament writings and emphasizing a misinterpreted collection of Paul's epistles and one Gospel. Marcion's "canon" stimulated the first formal efforts (as far as we know) to make a clear selection of normative as opposed to nonnormative Christian writings. The leading criterion of value seems to have been apostolic or near-apostolic provenance.

The sometimes confusing and tortuous establishing of the twenty-seven-book New Testament canon does not satisfy our desire for a clear-cut selection. It is nevertheless striking that the very books which *were* regarded as Scripture from early on and were later accepted definitively in 367 in the East and at the Council of Carthage in 397 in the West—these books turn out after centuries of minute scholarly investigation to be the best and earliest and most authentic records of Christ's life and work. It is also worth noting that the writings of the Apostolic Fathers who accepted the canonical books are generally far superior to the "apocryphal" material (such as the Shepherd of Hermas and the Epistle of Barnabas) which they rejected.

To address another issue that often worries people: whether we can trust the accuracy of those who copied the Scriptures and whether oral transmission, in so far as it played a part, can be relied upon. Birger Gerhardsson's book, *Memory and Manuscript,* emphasizes the tradition of minutely accurate oral and written transmission among Jews. We also have a remarkable example of such accuracy in a comparison between the Book of Isaiah among the Dead Sea Scrolls (dating from before Christ) and the otherwise earliest surviving copy of this prophecy, several hundred years later. The evidence shows an almost exact correlation. Furthermore, one can take the matter of possible copyists' errors too far. To make any substantial distortion in the Bible's teaching would require a series of errors which all managed to dovetail together—a possibility whose statistical likelihood would make even the largest computer tremble.

Looking at the whole subject of texts, what has to strike any objective observer is the overwhelming superiority of the textual basis of the Bible, particularly the New Testament, to the textual basis of the major Greek and Latin classics. When one considers

No Other Foundation

that, for example, the oldest manuscript of Caesar's Gallic War (written about 50 B.C.) is from the ninth century A.D., then the interval of time between the first century writing of the New Testament and the oldest extant manuscripts (dating from the second to the fourth century) is cause for wonder not scepticism.

What this long discussion boils down to, is that in the context of heresy, with the need for a fixed standard, those books were termed canonical which from an early time had been accepted as true records of Christ's work before and after Pentecost. Issuing from the hands of actual Apostles and eyewitnesses, the very spiritual power of these books exemplified Christ's recorded promise that the Holy Spirit would bring all things to the disciples' remembrance. Through these books, full of life and authority, the Early Church was indeed brought face to face with the living, authoritative Word of God, Jesus Christ. They demanded a decision and they still do. Whatever disagreements people may have about the date of this or the authorship of that, what looms out of the pages of the New Testament is the consistent portrait of a man who claimed to be God, to have risen from the dead, and of the men who, as self-confessed "eyewitnesses of his majesty," turned the world upside down.

And now we must say a few words about the councils in which the canon of Scripture was formalized.

The councils which formalized the canon of Scripture were not the first. The meeting of Apostles and elders in Jerusalem, around A.D. 48 is often spoken of as the first church council. This is a slightly grandiose appellation but if it serves to emphasize what a council is, or should be, then it is useful. The Apostles and elders met to discuss gentile admission to the church (see Acts 15). In other words, we have the acknowledged spiritual leaders gathering to discuss a vexed issue. As Acts 15 shows, they heard the evidence from both sides, came to a decision and transmitted their findings to the church in Antioch which was central to the gentile mission. Their finding was in line with scriptural teaching, furthermore. One can see the benefit here, incidentally, of contacts between churches or congregations. Although, as we shall be seeing, the problem with large, centrally administered churches is the tendency towards politicking and overmighty centralization, the problem with independent congregations is the tendency to get ingrown and petty, for little sawdust Caesars to emerge. The principle of some sort of collegiality, some sense of a larger belonging within the visible Body of Christ, is emphatically scriptural.

What, in any case, successive councils did was to respond to the ongoing needs of the church by authoritative pronouncement on questions of doctrine and practice. The norm for all judgments was the Scripture, and one can hardly admire enough the spiritual wisdom which informed the great creedal statements of the early councils. Somehow, as we have seen, the leaders of the church managed to make profound statements about the Bible's teaching (e.g., on the Trinity) which, without going beyond Scripture's testimony, were yet clear enough to embarrass heretics. One of the most famous creeds is the Nicene Creed, so-called after the Council of Nicaea of 325.

This particular council was actually called into being by Constantine, a secular ruler, a Roman emperor. This fact leads us to our last point for it underlines a change coming over the fortunes of the Christian church in the period after 300. The councils of this period become more and more identified with a movement towards organization and ossification in the church, paralleling the emergence of the church "universal" or "catholic."

In an important sense, the Church has always been catholic or, as this word means, universal. It transcends all human barriers. It is not restricted to time, place or social condition. It unites sinners, equally guilty, equally redeemed by the grace of God. The adjective "catholic" began to develop a less open meaning, a less truly universal meaning, when the criteria of catholicity became more a matter of de jure pronouncement by a hierarchy than of de facto recognition by the faithful. This is not to deny the importance of objective standards for Christian profession. Rather, it is to insist that these standards are plain enough in the Gospel so that whatever options one group of believers may embrace contrary to the convictions of other believers, their shared submission to Christ should forestall any pontificating as to who is or is not a part of the church universal.

What encouraged a devolution in the meaning of "catholic" in the fourth century was a tendency for the church to be identified with society as a whole. People, we are told, are gregarious. In other words, they go around in flocks. But they are not gregarious as far as *other* flocks are concerned. The danger of the church's becoming identified with a human grouping is that it will adopt the incidental customs of the grouping and, as it were, "baptize" them. This, in turn, will serve to exclude people elsewhere from the church because the Gospel will appear to be part and parcel of a way of life which is foreign to them.

In other words, once the church has a political, social locus, an earthly citizenship, it is tempted to miss the wood for the trees. It is tempted to become a service organization, gratifying human egos, human mores, human traditions. The Gospel is adapted to society, instead of society being adapted to the Gospel. Obviously, this is not just a fourth century problem. To tackle it squarely, in our own day, we must be as rigorous about the life and practice of the church as about our own personal walk. Indeed, the church member's seriousness about his own godliness is the essential foundation for the godliness of the church as a whole. If the church is enmeshed with respectability, material values, purely human efficiency, does this not advertise the fact that the individual members are similarly enmeshed?

It is a short step for the church subtly to qualify its doctrine to rationalize its behavior. Thus, we tend to "spiritualize" the Sermon on the Mount, to draw its sting. Its injunctions become the exception rather than the rule. Anyone who takes Jesus' words seriously is thought to be either a fanatic, whose conduct is vaguely threatening, or a super-saint, whose example is not for the likes of us.

In the fourth century, the challenge to the church took the form of social and political acceptance after centuries of persecution and unpopularity. As we saw in an earlier chapter, it was after the Emperor Aurelian (270-275) was spurned by the Christians when he offered to include Christ in the Pantheon along with Mithra that the state decided most determinedly to root out these subversive ingrates. As we also saw, this last great burst of persecution which would peak in the merciless pogroms of Diocletian, Maxentius and Galerius in the first years of the fourth century, would stop almost as suddenly as it began.

Under Constantine, Christianity in the West embarked upon a long period of toleration and respectability, stretching, with few exceptions, to our own day. It may be observed of the last wave of persecution, however, that unlike the situation under Nero it was the best emperors, those most energetic in trying to pull together the weakening bonds of exhausted Roman society, who would least tolerate the Christian refusal to submit to their will.

Constantine was born in Britain of a soldier father and a Christian mother. After Diocletian retired in 305 (to grow cabbages, it was said), the empire was divided by political and military quarrels. Constantine's own father had a tilt at power but died, bequeathing the ambition to his son. The British legions declared for Constantine and, after a series of battles, he emerged victorious. By 324 he had succeeded in drawing the eastern and western parts of the empire together.

Whatever the actual truth, the story circulated that at the outset of Constantine's drive for power he had seen in the sky the chi-rho insignia (the first two letters of Christ's name, spelled in Greek) along with the message: "By this sign you shall conquer." This story was current in the wake of Constantine's subsequent toleration of Christianity. It is unknown to this day whether, even on his deathbed, Constantine professed Christ. Certainly, while alive, he continued the public religion of Rome, struck coins and medals in honor of the sun and other gods, as well as of himself as divine emperor.

Whether Constantine's action is to be regarded as the fruit of genuine conversion, the wise policy of a leader desirous of channelling the energy of the strongest religious force in the empire, or both, Christianity enjoyed not only toleration from the year 311 but also favored treatment. Except for one brief reversal, the position of Christianity steadily improved till, in 381, Theodosius the Great made it the official state religion, all other beliefs being outlawed.

From the vantage point of many centuries it is easier to view the fact and circumstance of toleration as a handicap to the church than as an asset. But this is a jaundiced view if it is all one has to say. To obtain a fairer perspective one need only put oneself in the place of a Christian who had lost a loved one in the persecutions of Diocletian. To such a believer, and there were many, the advent of toleration was a wonderful mercy of God. Do we not likewise thank God for any signs of a let-up in persecution in Communist countries today?

Having said this, it remains true that the embrace of society

No Other Foundation

proved to be spiritually costly. The intricate problem of church/ state relations which has troubled the Western world ever since was well and truly introduced. Various dimensions of this problem will be touched upon in succeeding chapters.

Specifically, when the church was not only made the state religion but its rivals were denied toleration, Christianity was dealt a body blow. For at the very time when decades of toleration had diluted the spiritual discipline of the church, the accession to the church of pseudo-believers afraid of ostracization required a firmer discipline than ever before.

Almost inevitably, the quality of membership declined rapidly. And this very circumstance made necessary firm intervention by Christian leaders in local church affairs. This, in its turn, could not but encourage the bishops of the church in a trend towards elitist control—the sort of control that their secular neighbors in the "Christian" state exemplified.

Finally, one can see the historical logic of a bishop in Rome or Constantinople arrogating to himself the same sort of central authority which his secular counterpart in the capital exercised. After all, then as now, the most capable Christian pastors might tend to gravitate towards the large urban centers. It was a natural transition from the highly responsible and authoritative leadership of the Roman church (or the church of any great imperial city) to the leadership of a wider and wider circle of provincial churches which welcomed contact with the capital in the frightening days of Roman political decline.

It is, indeed, hard to miss the parallel between the popular response to Augustus Caesar's takeover and the steady advance in politico-ecclesiastical influence of the greatest bishops in the late Roman world. In times of crisis or great change, people— including Christian people—settle for compromise values in return for order. It is a mark of special quality, unusual sensitivity to spiritual reality, not to do so. Had we a mandate from Christ to judge the church of the fourth and fifth centuries, we might do so here. Instead, Christ warns us to remove the beam from our own eyes. To be candid, the church of our day hardly stands comparison with the church under discussion.

The link between a canon of Scripture and the church is a close one. For only the touchstone of Scripture can prevent the church being sucked into the vortex of ecclesiastical and secular politics. Our worthiest ancestors were the "subversive ingrates" of Aurelian's day and the leaders who, whatever faults they may have had, declared for norms of life and thought based on a specific Scriptural canon. We are their unworthy children when we opt for pan-church affiliations, based on a fashionable, universalist theology, in contempt of the Book which we still mine for right-sounding texts. We are, in fact, still concerned with "childish things" if we do not see that as the days go by we shall be sore thumbs not so much to inferior statesmen as to those men of ability most resolute in their efforts to put society back on its feet.

For Further Study

The Apocryphal New Testament: Being the Apocryphal Gospels, Acts, Epistles, and Apocalypses with Other Narratives and Fragments. Translated by Montague Rhodes James. Oxford: At the Clarendon Press, 1955. The best argument against the writings which were not regarded as inspired is to read them.

Boice, James M., ed. *The Foundation of Biblical Authority.* Grand Rapids, MI: Zondervan, 1978. Includes an important summary of attitudes to biblical reliability throughout church history (pp. 23-58; by John Gerstner).

Kelly, John Norman Davidson. *Early Christian Creeds.* 3rd ed. New York: D. McKay Co., 1972. How the early church began to summarize what it believed.

Sherwin-White, Adrian Nicholas. *Roman Society and Roman Law in the New Testament.* Grand Rapids, MI: Baker Book House, 1978. A paperback reprint of this classic first published by Oxford in 1963. A detailed demonstration of the extreme accuracy of the New Testament as regards contemporary Roman custom.

6

Fathers, Monks, and Barbarians

ISTORIANS AND INTELLECTUALS have enjoyed the leisure of centuries to contemplate the reasons for the demise of the Roman Empire. It is an opportunity unlikely to occur after the demise of present-day Western culture. So we may as well look again, carefully, as other generations have done, at the agents of the collapse of the great civilization which cradled the Gospel.

For civilizations, no less than individuals, the basic causes of failure are internal not external. We may see this by reflecting upon the crumbling society in which we now live. Internal corruption, from the bottom to the top; ideological confusion; wealth, decadence, and cynical despair; and a naivete toward hostile forces outside, inexplicable save as sheer loss of nerve. All these characteristics marked late Roman society. Political and economic corruption was rife. People lived off the state for all they were worth. And why not? Their leaders did. The populace, sophisticated and crude, was addicted to sexually vicious stage entertainment and the bloody spectacle of the arena. In certain circles it was fashionable to be unkempt and wear dirty togas.

Edward Gibbon, Samuel Dill and others—historians of Rome's decline—have emphasized the ideological breakdown. In so far as Gibbon stressed Christianity as the debilitator, the tap on Rome's will to survive, he undoubtedly prejudged and narrowed the issue. If Christians were culpable it was not so much through trusting Christ as betraying him. The Christian did not do a perfect job of balancing a proper awareness that his kingdom is not of this world with Paul's joyful identification with all men that some at least might be saved. Be that as it may, the pagan senator who blamed loss of civic virtue on a debased other-worldly Christianity was no closer to the mark than a Christian who would nowadays blame disinterest in public affairs on the influence of Eastern religions. Symptoms must not be mixed up with causes, even though they abet them.

The fact is that basic to Rome was a continuing dependence on human values. When these human values were less and less civic and more and more personal their limitations were exposed. Public interest may be self-interest only so long as the weather is fair. Then, self-interest becomes the public's interest, and people observed with some surprise that Rome was not as it had been. Where was the old patriotism? The government had, perforce, to introduce controls where once the citizens could be relied upon to control themselves. By 300, the state that presumed to regulate the gods was also fixing the tips for bathhouse attendants. And rather as Jonah was disposed to leave Nineveh to its fate, the Christian was tempted to let Rome burn. By and large, he did not. Neither must we.

If internal decline was basic, the external context was also important. Nature abhors a vacuum, they say. So does politics and so does the world of international power. The simple, monotonous and depressing fact about political history is the tendency for one power to be superseded by another. If you think of the European and Mediterranean areas as an appendage, a peninsula, of the great Asian land mass, then you can see its history as one of continuous invasion from the east, interrupted by more or less extended periods of local autonomy. In our own day, what has seemed from the eighteenth century to be the manifest destiny of an Asian power (in this case, the Eurasian power of Russia) to sweep over the entire area, has nearly come to pass. Without outside intervention, it would have. And just as the old Huns (to take just one of the older invaders) swept into the West, finally settling *Hun*gary, so the new "Huns," bringing an anti-Christian barbarism, have taken over the same European frontiers.

Our subject here, however, is the first Huns, the first Vandals, the first Goths. That all these names now have negative connotations is a reflection of the fact that the invaders were seen as uncivilized hordes or, which could amount to the same thing, enemies to Christian and Roman culture. Sensing that the Nazis embodied a similar threat to civilization, a famous English historian wrote a book in the 1940's classifying them as the latest wave of barbarians.

That Europe should have been subject to invasion is not only because there were invaders. Since the later Middle Ages, the internal divisions of Europe have hindered concerted action against outsiders. In the declining days of the Roman Empire, another factor must be borne in mind. It was simply not possible, in premodern times, to keep together such a vast empire, particularly when corruption had replaced patriotism. Increasingly, to maintain the borders, one had to make deals with border tribes, much as the West has thought to maintain its borders since 1945 by making deals with Russia. Sometimes, whole tribal armies were conscripted, with their own generals. Rome pretended she was creating more legions; actually, she was subsidizing her enemies. She pretended she was civilizing the barbarians; but they would barbarize civilization. It was left to the great Christian Augustine, in the early years of the fifth century, to wonder whether "civilization" didn't deserve it. The parallels with modern disarmament diplomacy need no elaboration.

It did not take the barbarians long to realize that Roman power was hollow. In 410, less than a century after the restorative work of Constantine, Alaric the Goth sacked Rome. The prestige of the Empire suffered a mortal blow. Without the force to back it, one could no longer borrow credit on the Roman name. In the middle of the fifth century, Attila the Hun plundered through Italy and France. As the chief success of the barbarians was in the western half of the Empire, the mantle of Rome fell upon the east where, indeed, Constantine had fixed his capital years before: Constantinople. Europe being virtually overrun by myriad tribes, her history became the history of western tribes jockeying for position. It is true that for a brief time, under Justinian in the mid-sixth century, the Roman Empire once more stretched west around the shores of the Mediterranean. But the rise of Islam in the seventh and eighth centuries definitively contained the Empire within the Balkans and Asia Minor.

In the West, the most significant power would prove to be Frankish from which France got her name. Towards 500, the dreaded Clovis became the sole Frankish king. He shrewdly adopted orthodox Catholic (as opposed to Arian) Christianity, thereby ingratiating himself with various southern tribes and identifying him with the mainstream of imperial Roman Christianity. Orthodox Christianity was thus enabled to hold the line from Italy to the English Channel and the Franks and their Carolingian successors became the key Christian political powers in a Europe struggling to find its feet. That Clovis should have driven the Arian Visigoths into Spain and that Clovis's great contemporary in Italy should have been the Arian Ostrogoth, Theodoric, shows how crucial was this moment in history for the future of the church.

Much later, the papal coronation of Charlemagne at Rome in 800 cemented the alliance of the church and the major political units which transmitted Charlemagne's legacy in medieval Europe. Together, the church and the tradition of a Christian Roman Empire, revived by Charlemagne and his various successors, provided the foundation for the cultural unity of Europe thereafter. But this is to anticipate. What can be said about the history of the church during and after the decline of Roman imperial power?

Just as the secular mind prefers to push Christ aside and talk about Paul or Augustine or Luther, so the ecclesiastical mind, the mind absorbed in the church as a mere institution, is more taken with the thoughts and deeds of churchmen than with the Word of the Founder of the Church.

This is because the only alternative to accepting the supernaturally revealed standard and future destiny of the church of Christ is to accept as a normative standard and destiny the actual state of the church at any one point in time. From this point of view, then, the life of an Ambrose, an Origen or a Tertullian, is about as significant as the life of Christ. For Christ becomes whatever these men make of him and, whether you like it or not, this is what makes the history of the church.

That the truth of the Gospel can be and has been obscured is not to be denied. Paul's letters denounce the work of the obscurantists in the very first generation. But the notion that what is most true about the church is what it is like at the moment is to be fought tooth and nail. It is the same as saying that Christ is what the Christian is like. The error is to make Christ relative to the church and the believer, instead of the opposite. The error itself springs from doubt that the church's one foundation is Jesus Christ her Lord, and that he is a *living* Lord who, by his Spirit, is inspiring his followers to those lives of holiness and godliness which hasten the coming of the day of God.

Not that the life of any believer, or any person, is insignificant. Nor that the lives of the church fathers are uninstructive. All I am saying is that one must keep constantly in view the norm of the Word of God. To be informed about the church fathers is as edifying as to be informed about church leaders ever since, neither more nor less. For all their frailties—and what would *our* lives look like under historical scrutiny?—we can give thanks for the hard labors, the aggressive defence and propagation of the Gospel, and often the eventual martyrdom, of a stream of Christian leaders from Justin Martyr in the second century to Origen in the third century.

And after toleration dawned in the early 300s, we have Jerome (died 419), great Christian scholar and linguist, whose Latin translation of the Bible was the universal version in Europe till the sixteenth century. While Jerome erred on the side of asceticism and retreat from the world, his contemporary Ambrose proved a great pastor and leader. A civil administrator whose simple piety shone through, he was raised to the office of bishop of Milan by popular acclaim in 374. He introduced congregational singing, as we have seen, and yet showed his versatility by being instrumental in the conversion of one of the greatest minds and personalities in church history: Augustine.

Augustine merits special attention as the most influential Christian leader and thinker for the next 800 years! Even 1,100 years later, Luther turns out to be an Augustinian monk; Calvin was not unsympathetic towards him; and the most vital spiritual movement in seventeenth century French Catholicism leaned on his theology. The amazing story of his early life and conversion is told in his *Confessions*. The intellectual and the profligate, son of a Christian mother, is plunged into despair from which God alone can call us. Instructed by Ambrose yet still far from hope, he suddenly caught the words of a child at play: "Pick it up and read it!" Overcome with sorrow for his life, doubtful of the extension of God's mercy to him, he ran back through the garden to where he had laid a copy of Paul's Epistle to the Romans. Opening it at random, he read from chapter 13, verses 13-14: "Not in reveling and drunkenness, not in debauchery and licentiousness, not in quarreling and jealousy. But put on the Lord Jesus Christ, and make no provision for the flesh, to gratify its desires." That was all and it was everything. He tells us: "No further would I read, nor was there cause why I should; for instantly with the end of this sentence, as by a clear and constant light infused into my heart, the darkness of all former doubts was driven away."

Augustine would become the bishop of Hippo in North Africa. He lay dying in 430, reading the penitential Psalms, as the Vandals stormed the city. For such an end he was suitably prepared. For his great work, *The City of God,* written in the years following the sack of Rome in 410, both refuted the pagan claim that Christianity had killed the Empire, and called Christians to the reality of a city made without hands.

But *The City of God* was more than this. Reflecting the intellectual energy and scope of this man, it ranged back and forth over all possible aspects of life and thought. For this reason, it could be the treasure trove of wisdom that it became for medieval Christians. Not that all of it was uniformly valuable and true. In his definite and straightforward way, he took the Platonic philosophy which had once been his lifeblood, wrung its neck of what he felt to be its alien elements, and praised those aspects of it which seemed to square with biblical truth. In so doing he was demonstrating a confidence in the Scriptures which Paul had had but which, in some quarters, had since given way to a nervous questioning of the utility of any knowledge save biblical knowledge.

Unfortunately, his intuitive sympathy for Platonism had sufficiently colored his grasp of the Gospel that his theological scalpel was blunt in places. And if his own faith was strong enough to weather minor inconsistencies, they would have a pernicious effect on later generations.

One aspect of this is clear in his interpretation of Scripture which became a model for the Middle Ages. He built on the allegorical approach developed by Origen which owed something to the Jewish Philo (an older contemporary of Christ who lived in Alexandria). Philo, in turn, was much beholden to Plato for whom the things on earth are but a shadow of the real things above. Philo had therefore tended to get away from the concrete historical aspect of Scripture, interpreting events as if they were merely stories to illustrate a heavenly truth.

In one sense, of course, events *do* illustrate such truth. But if we devalue them as history we forget the heavenly truth that God made *all* things good, even if since fallen, and that his salvation is effected in the everyday context of his creation. Now, Augustine was very far from Philo or Plato. Yet, in the wrong hands, his model of scriptural explanation could pander to man's fancy more than to his mind and will.

The most direct way of describing the model is to show it in action. Here is a famous interpretation of the taking of Jericho. (1) Joshua took Jericho; (2) The walls of sin fall before the onslaught of faith; (3) Jesus' triumphal entry to Jerusalem; (4) At the sound of the last trumpet the world of sin will fall. This really is a straightforward sermon outline, as much at home in the twentieth as in the fifth century. One danger, however, could be a slavish attempt to fit the model to every verse of Scripture. An even worse danger could be the loss of awareness that Jericho did, after all, fall and that all the extra meanings you can get out of it are no more to be subordinated to *it* than it to *them*. "*All* scripture," Paul reminded Timothy, "is inspired by God."

That Augustine himself was far from losing a sense of the uniqueness and significance of history is plain from a crucial attitude to history which he bequeathed to the West. History is linear. It proceeds from one point to another. It does not, as the Greek and Roman humanist liked to think, go round and round in never-ending cycles. God started history; he intervenes in history; he will end history. Augustine was, therefore, thoroughly biblical in this perception. He was likewise true to Scripture in that other perception for which he is famous and which he knew from experience: that God's grace is undeserved and irresistible. Luther and Calvin's respect for Augustine had much to do with their appreciation of this fact which had been half-buried by 1500.

Great as Augustine might be, he was one man in a large visible church whose spiritual history at this time requires careful scrutiny. As I pointed out in the last chapter, the difficulty of sustaining real faith, real love, real tolerance when one is not only tolerated but also in the majority, is very great. To complicate further the problem of the church (and I speak now particularly of the Western church): as the headquarters of the Empire moved east, the church at Rome was left, willy-nilly, as the last great abiding token of the vanishing Roman Empire. It had a visible, public function, even if not spelled out.

Thus, for all that the bishops of Rome purposefully built up a political power base and self-consciously arrogated themselves over other bishops, they *did* have a position of unique responsibility from which they could hardly retreat. Men looked to Rome for a lead; Rome had to give it. One is not to condone the sort of lead sometimes given. But it is unfair to forget that the bishops of Rome were saddled with awesome responsibilities which multiplied the opportunities for sin.

Save for Justinian's reign (527-565), no Emperor exerted any effective power in Italy or the West after 476. But there were several outstanding leaders among the bishops of Rome. Leo the Great was most notable in the fifth century. The title "pope" meaning father (in a spiritual sense) which was used of and by various bishops and would be claimed exclusively by the Roman bishop from 1073, was especially claimed by Leo during his tenure (440-461). In tandem with this exclusiveness, Leo would also claim to be the successor of a Peter to whom, he argued, Christ had alone granted the power of binding and loosing sin.

The heritage of this assertion was unfortunate, to say the least. Whatever the benefits—and they were many—of the impulse to good order in the church, increasingly such order fed a more and more harmfully unbiblical papal ascendancy. The outcome of this is easy to see: an overmighty, sometimes immoral, and theologically subversive papal leadership could automatically exercise power and influence through an established hierarchy throughout the West.

The hierarchy itself owed its essential form and impetus to the greatest pope of this period: Gregory the Great (590-604). He articulated a great chain of command, linking priest to bishop to pope. He was the first Roman bishop effectively to extend his control north of the Alps. It was he who initiated the systematic conversion of the English through sending Augustine (not *the* Augustine, of course, who was long dead) to England where he established the bishopric of Canterbury.

Not that England had not tasted the Gospel already. But there was a further concern of Gregory's which takes us back to the point made earlier: that at a certain level church expansion was papal expansion, or at least expansion of the church order identified with the Roman bishop. Thus, "catholic" Christianity, whose identification with Rome mirrored the Roman bishop's conviction that the church over which he presided was the truly *universal* Christian church, could not for ever exist side by side with older British and Celtic Christianity. There could be but one primacy and this primacy was settled in England in favor of Roman authority at the Synod of Whitby (664).

Yet again we must not forget the situation faced by the church, to which a man like Gregory was responding. In a day without modern communications, without the printed page, without easy means for ensuring a beneficial orthodoxy, the depths of local heresy and moral disorder to which the provincial congregations might fall were worth avoiding even if at the expense of an artificial hierarchy associated with sub-Christian views on the dynamics of church life.

Try to imagine the situation in the modern church without so many of the things we take for granted. Heresy and strange ideas are like the poor, always with us. But consider how much worse things might be without printed Bibles, or ready access, through radio, books or travel to conferences, to a host of educated, responsible teachers who serve to balance one another in the Truth.

Back in the centuries after the Roman decline which deserve, to some degree, the title "Dark Ages," there was a definite substratum of pagan survival in much local Christianity. That the situation was not worse owes much to the efforts of Gregory and his more vigorous successors to discipline and order the visible church of Christ. Gregory was not working without assistance, however.

The sort of organization that Gregory worked to establish depended not only on a chain of command but also on local bastions of belief. He was therefore a prominent sponsor of monasteries and had, indeed, before being thrust into ecclesiastical administration, formed a small community on his family properties in Sicily.

Where people are not simply apathetic about the subject, reactions to monasticism tend to swing from adulation to scorn. Let it be said that in so far as monasticism has to do with Paul's recommendation to chastity, celibacy, service to men, and freedom from concern with the world's values, it is perfectly valuable and orthodox. In so far as it tended slavishly to construct a "superspirituality" based on what the New Testament indicates as options and possibilities; and in so far as it tended to miss the wood for the trees by emphasizing the rejection of worldly values to the extent of rejecting worldly men, it very dangerously subverted the truth. Clearly, the study of monasticism requires discernment, caution and charity.

Monasticism was not new in Gregory's time, either in the history of Christianity, or the West, or the world. One thinks of the wandering monks of Buddhism or the Essene monks of Judaism around the time of Christ. And certain Old Testament prophets like Elijah and John the Baptist appear slightly monkish, while Samuel's "schools of the prophets" have a monastic air about them. What is certainly characteristic of medieval Christian monasticism is the idea of a community of celibates, male or female, bound to an agreed rule of conduct.

The central function of the monastery was prayer—prayer viewed as a social duty and a public benefit. Here, far from evading the responsibility for one's fellow men, the monk was fulfilling it at a very high level. Yet what might be a valid and specialized calling—that of an intercessor—could come to be regarded as an ideal. One therefore lost sight of the total goal of obedience to Christ through the direction of his Spirit. Only doing what *God* wants, in a body with many members, is ideal.

While there were several ongoing precedents for monasticism around 500, some of which went back to the late second century, the strongest and sanest impulse came at this time from Benedict of Nursia, a village near Rome. Settled from 529 on the famous Monte Cassino, between Rome and Naples, Benedict formulated a "Rule" whereby laymen and clerics alike could withdraw apart, vowing poverty, chastity, and obedience to ecclesiastical superiors. Each day, eight times, monks must gather together to recite the "Office"—a set schedule of prayers. The rest of the day was lived in the prayerful fulfillment of necessary duties: carpentry, cooking, farming and, gradually, learning and manuscript copying.

Education, as such, had not been one of Benedict's original aims, but as the old classical education broke down, the monasteries became centers for the schooling of society, as well as caring for the poor, the homeless, the orphaned, the widowed and the sick. Without the patient copying of texts by monks, and without their tenacious preservation of what they had copied, one wonders how the Bible, not to mention Greek and Roman classics, would have survived the savage incursions of new barbarians in the period before the year 1000 after which Europe became internally secure.

It was, indeed, not so much Benedict as a fellow Italian, Cassiodorus, who really emphasized scholarship and education and, with Boethius, in the sixth century, formulated the basic seven-part curriculum of medieval education: the seven liberal arts of grammar, rhetoric, dialectic, arithmetic, astronomy, geometry, and music.

The monks not only preserved a tradition of culture, though. They also extended the range of the church. Not content only to form those bastions of belief to which I referred above, they launched the most extensive and dynamic missionary movement since apostolic times. Irish and English monks, in particular, in the seventh century swept across the English Channel to evangelize the Continent. In the late 700s, a Frank complained that English preachers swarmed through Gaul "as thick as bees." The great and severe Boniface from England was actually murdered by Frisian robbers while preaching at the ripe old age of seventy-five (in 755). And preaching was not only to the "foreigner." Benedict himself held forth regularly to the local population at the foot of Monte Cassino.

Too often we read God's revelation in the Bible of his dealings in history as though they were limited to matters affecting the Jew. We thereby forget that he is the Creator of all men. All history is in his hands and we may be sure that, if we do not know with certainty the reason behind the great shifts in human fortunes, nevertheless God is dealing purposively with men. Empires rise and fall according to God's ordaining. The Bible leads us to assume that the judgment of God may be seen in the collapse of kingdoms. It is hard not to see God's hand of judgment humbling Rome in the fifth century. If, to return to a theme rehearsed at the beginning of this chapter, the corruption of modern Western society parallels that of Imperial Rome, are we to suppose that for some strange reason God will withhold his judgment? Civilization survived at all after the fifth century by the salt of Christianity. But it was a desperate affair. If they were reduced, as it were, to monasteries, we may be reduced, as behind the Iron Curtain, to houses and cellars.

No Other Foundation

The days are evil. We must be compassionate and we must be warned.

For Further Study

Augustine. *Confessions* (many editions). You have heard this recommended before, no doubt, so why not read it?

Clouse, Robert G., ed. *The Meaning of the Millennium: Four Views.* Downers Grove, IL: InterVarsity, 1977. When things are going downhill there is more intense (but not necessarily more faithful) interest in "last things." This useful book allows for the explanation and criticism of major interpretations.

Dill, Samuel. *Roman Society in the Last Century of the Roman Empire.* New York: Gordon Press, n.d. Vivid and authentic portrayal of a civilization in its death throes.

Rand, Edward K. *Founders of the Middle Ages.* New York: Dover, 1928. Covers some of the same material as Dill but is looking towards the life of a culture yet forming.

Smith, Michael A. *The Church Under Seige.* Downers Grove, IL: InterVarsity, 1976. Well-illustrated, intelligent treatment of this important epoch in church history.

7

The Church Renewed

JESUS PRAYED that we be in the world but not of it. Undoubtedly, it is only through continuing prayer that we can tread the narrow line. We often criticize our forebears for compromise but we should know better. Do *we* find it easy to distinguish our duty to the poor and disadvantaged when state organs and welfare programs supposedly take care of society's "underprivileged"? And if we supinely let the matter go, are we not committing the sin of becoming too far "of the world"? We know *our* contemporary paganism. What was the general environment like in the West up to the eleventh century?

I referred in passing in the last chapter to vestigial paganism in Christian Europe. Just how much paganism there was remains a disputed question. A fairly recent book on Celtic Britain (by Anne Ross) graphically portrays the survival of fertility and other cults after Britain was "officially" converted. In an imaginative vein, though based on a deep knowledge of the period, C. S. Lewis conveys something of the atmosphere through Merlin the Wizard in *That Hideous Strength*. At a later period in the history of the church, also in the British Isles, John Buchan has portrayed a resuscitation (or dark continuance?) of paganism in *Witch Wood*.

The normal form in which paganism survived was as an admixture within Christianity. This might, indeed, be in the form of a quite deliberate and official Christianizing of a pagan festival. Such is the case with the choice to celebrate Christ's birth to Mary on December 25, preempting the day of the Unconquered Sun. There would seem no special harm in this. In a more serious vein, the development of the cult of the Virgin owed much to various fertility cults in the Mediterranean world as well as farther north and west. Here, there was no exact parallel in Christianity to sustain such a cult and so it became a dangerous excrescence. When the cult really took off from the eleventh century, it penetrated the very pores of the church.

One of the best examples, frequently cited, of pagan influence, comes from the late-eleventh century *Song of Roland*. On the surface, this appears to be a great Christian epic poem. On closer inspection, it appears to glorify values far removed from the Sermon on the Mount. There is a strong underlying emphasis on irreversible fate, in which context the chief virtues are fighting well, dying well, and being loyal. The supreme vice is treachery. The mood is hardly Christian; only the trimmings.

More generally, bearing in mind that man started with the knowledge of the one true God and successively deviated from true belief into polytheism and then the worship of nature, one can see all disobedience, including one's own, as potential paganism. Paganism, in other words, is not some strange beast from the jungle; it is one of our own domesticated cats. Living as if the true God did not exist—that is paganism.

Whatever may have been happening with Bodo the peasant or Knight Roland, things were no better and, to be truthful, a lot worse, in the precincts of the priests. This was especially so in Rome where the tenth century papacy was worse even than that of the Renaissance. As long as the church thrives in the orbit of the secular power as the supplier of administrators ("clerk" was originally an ecclesiastical term) and accepts a share of the spoils in the form of gifts of land to monasteries and episcopal sees, it will tend to make spiritual values take the back seat. The church becomes a tool of social and political control instead of salt to society.

Now, in a basically decentralized society, the centralized network of the church first formed by Gregory was a unique vehicle for administration. It was perfectly natural for kings, princes and lesser rulers to seek the cooperation of ecclesiastics in governing their territories. As a result, ecclesiastics had a secondary role as secular officers and the church more and more became an automatic avenue to social and political advancement, or else a reward for those already born to power. Of course, the secular rulers themselves expected, even demanded, a say in the appointments of the men who half-ran their own government. Accordingly, spiritual reasons for church advancement tended to fade before bureaucratic ones.

83

The Church Renewed

All of this allowed for highly complex situations. When you realize that church institutions held an estimated 25 percent of all European real estate, through bequests, capital use of revenues, and confiscation, you can see why the attitude of rulers to the church was often ambivalent. When they were not enjoying ecclesiastical help, they might be placing a moratorium upon bequests or even taking over church lands outright. Kings could, on the one hand, hardly afford such powerful men in their realms and yet, on the other hand, they could not *not* afford them. Some of the great medieval warrior generals were bishops. One has only to think of brutal Bishop Odo of Bayeux, William the Conqueror's right-hand man in 1066.

It is possible to exaggerate the number of gimlet-eyed opportunists among the dignitaries of the church. But even a few would be too many. And these had unique occasion for gain. Their cooperation with the local prince frequently meant that he would turn a blind eye to their public depredations. Bishop Otbert of Liege (1091-1119) milked the parish clergy for all they were worth to purchase one property. They, in turn, had to sell church ornaments and squeeze their poor parishioners. What a scoundrel! But may one whisper that some of the exactions of modern Christian churches have peculiar destinations? And may one see in some of our hard-nosed, high-flying church officers medieval bishops in armor?

One thing that should be clear by now is that we cannot make much of a distinction between secular and religious society. When a king of France, just before 1000, for good economic reasons, appoints himself abbot of the wealthy monastery of St. Denis, we are obviously dealing with real estate, not religion.

In the ecclesiastical bush leagues, spiritual torpor was similarly evident. Men invested in parish livings, employing poor "clerks" to "work" them at a small percentage of the profits. Baptisms and burials might be sold at a fat fee. Local priests were sometimes illiterate, lived openly with women, frequented taverns and hardly constituted spiritual examples to the flock. Not surprisingly, church services fell into disrepute. The Latin service of the Mass or Lord's Supper had superseded the Greek in the fourth century so that the people of Western Europe could follow it. But by the seventh century, with the near obliteration of Roman, Latin, culture, especially among the uneducated majority, the service was almost unintelligible. Neither were the ignorant hacks

No Other Foundation

who sometimes were hired to cover a parish more familiar with Latin. They mumbled through the focal point of the church's worship, communicating the essential parts of the service by a species of liturgical calisthenics. There is an important moral here: that what in the fourth century had been a creative adjustment to assist participation in worship was allowed, by the seventh century, to become a barrier between the pastor and the flock.

This evolution is mirrored in other developments during the same period. The Lord's Table was moved from the body of the church to the east end, the congregation being cut off from what were fast becoming "holy mysteries" by a chancel screen. One of the most telling visible reforms in the sixteenth century, incidentally, was the physical removal of many such screens. This act naturally accompanied the restoration of the simple but profound Lord's Supper celebrated in the early church.

The distancing of the people from the act of worship was also reflected in the area of giving. The biblical concept of voluntary giving was gradually replaced by obligatory tithes. It was as if the clergy having made themselves professional were demanding a formal, professional fee.

What was happening? The church had assimilated itself to the mind of the "gentiles." Society is usually elitist, reeking with privilege. When late Roman society adopted the church, she began to follow suit. Whatever the theological abstractions involved, one can see all the changes in dogma and practice at this time as a logical outcome of an elitism which, proudly distinguishing itself from publicans and sinners, revealed that it had first of all rejected the mind of Christ who came not to be served but to serve. In such a weakened state, the various excesses discussed earlier appear as perfectly logical concomitants. Who could be surprised? Certainly the congregations weren't. Attendance at mass fell steadily. Church councils feebly insisted that one must attend at least *once* a year! As is always true when those officially ordained to minister fall down on the task, the most vital worship and service began to take place unofficially at the hands of those whose only calling was divine.

A renewal was imperative. It is only against this backcloth that we can appreciate the reform movement of the eleventh century.

The first stage of reform did not receive its basic impetus from

Rome. If anything, the low ebb of spirituality at Rome forced action elsewhere which only later led to changes initiated by the papacy. Considered schematically, this stage was dominated by kings, monks and laymen.

However much ecclesiastics might later inveigh against the scandal of churches under secular control, kings were often responsible for more reform than church leaders. This is a perennial situation. It is true now. The artificial life lived by a clergy out of touch with-its pastoral vocation fosters the development of ideas and practices which would curl the hair of the man in the street and alarm the secular ruler whose keen pragmatic instinct informs him of people's basic needs.

Whatever the precise outlines of their own piety, the three Carolingian kings Pepin the Short, Charlemagne and Louis the Pious, covering the years 741 to 840, were first, second and third generation sponsors of reform, good order and moral standards. The latter two put new life into the waning Benedictine rule and made it mandatory for all religious houses in their domains, in 816.

When Charlemagne's great empire was divided three ways among his three grandsons in 843 and when this division was later rationalized into a western (French) half and an eastern (German) half, the same urge for reform was present. The so-called Otto-nian emperors in Germany (named after Otto the Great who deposed one of the most scandalous popes in the late tenth century) encouraged the election of the very popes who, by their greater piety, would attack secular control in church affairs! Across the Channel in England, the famous King Alfred in the late ninth century was translating works of piety and instruction from Latin into English.

The history of Western monasticism is a history of advance and retreat, of sanity and eccentricity, reformation and deformation. Ultimately, the anecdotes about the half-crazy or the genuinely fanatic are unimportant. More basic is the fact that as each movement fell into spiritual lassitude, other movements or individuals emerged to carry on the struggle. This pattern characterized monasticism in the several centuries before the eleventh. The Cluniac movement, so-called from its parent house in Cluny, France, is a case in point.

Founded in 909, it had by the eleventh century, through gifts and takeovers, become an immensely wealthy group of over a hundred houses. Conceived in faith, it became mired in works. As

No Other Foundation

someone has very well expressed it: in the church "nothing fails like success" (Jeffrey Burton Russell, *A History of Medieval Christianity,* 1968, p. 104). Nevertheless, for a time, Cluny and other houses raised a standard of reform.

Institutions, like individuals, not only like to sin in their own way but to be reformed in their own way. It is a matter of pride: you want the credit for your own reform. Not to be unfair to the church, there is a danger that individual zeal, allowed its head, will indiscriminately remove the gold as well as the dross. The layman might sometimes be pardoned, however, for not trusting defaulting shepherds with the flock. Be that as it may, most lay reform was seen as dissent. As far as lasting and historically traceable results are concerned, therefore, spiritual revival outside official channels was destined to have little impact till political protection would allow the seed to flower in the sixteenth century.

The eleventh century saw a strong minority movement among lay people, called the "Reformists," which traced the path from legitimate protest to destructive heresy. It attacked the institution of an elite clergy; it denied the need for priestly mediators; it insisted, positively, that authority resides in the Bible alone which is opened to us by the Holy Spirit. Unfortunately, the predictably harsh response of the clergy drove the movement into radical extensions which provided a seedbed for the later Cathar heresy. Sadly, the Reformists proved the occasion for the first executions for heresy in the West since the sixth century. The burnings began at Orleans in France in 1022. Ironically, a man could be arrested at Cambrai in 1077 for preaching the same reforms currently advocated by the pope in Rome. But he was a layman and he was taken by the mob and burned outside the city.

It is significant that at the heart of the reform movement associated with the popes of the second half of the tenth century should be a contest with secular rulers over spiritual jurisdictions. If one has been accustomed by centuries to think of an official clergy having exclusive spiritual powers, then one will naturally see reform in terms of ensuring the proper exercise of those powers. There was, as we shall see, much more to the reform than that, but this aspect of it created the greatest public impact.

When we hear that popes humbled kings and emperors; that an emperor stood three days in the Alpine snows of Canossa (northern Italy) awaiting absolution from Gregory VII; that another kissed the feet of a later pope and humbly led his horse through the streets as a public sign of submission; then what manner of power are we talking about? What manner of reform? What manner of society? It was certainly closer to the scene of Saul ingratiating himself before Samuel after failing to slay Agag, than anything we can show in the modern world.

To mention the Old Testament here is apt because much papal policy in this epoch (as well as much sixteenth century reformed thinking) stemmed from a conviction that Christian society is theocratic, God is its direct head. If, further, as Pope Gelasius had put it in the 490s, there are two swords given by God, a sword of power to the emperor and a sword of authority to the pope, then the latter is superior to the former as providing spiritual direction for the exercise of power.

Under this conviction, popes had few qualms about forcibly carrying out their policies, using their own and other people's swords to do it; nor did they hesitate either to order the sword across the sea to the infidel in the Crusades which began in the 1090s.

When it came to the smouldering challenge to spiritual preeminence of the patriarchs of Constantinople, Pope Leo sent two distinguished hotheads east in 1054. The "pope" of the old eastern empire was no more happy to accept their credentials than was the Roman pope to tolerate a limitation of his spiritual jurisdiction. When the papal diplomats had the gall to place a bull excommunicating the patriarch upon the high altar of St. Sophia, the patriarch had it publicly burned. A later and unhappy result of this was the sacking of Constantinople by crusaders in 1204. It was not, in fact, till 1965 that the pope lifted the ban of excommunication. Let not the sun go down on your wrath!

I mentioned theocracy because it undergirds the redefinition of papal power which led to an ecclesiastical centralization far exceeding, one suspects, any wishes of a Gregory the Great. It is in this eleventh-century epoch that clerical celibacy is first insisted upon as an absolute, thus cementing the idea of an elite. Contemporaneously, papal elections were placed entirely in the hands of the cardinals. The immediate reason for this was to guard against secular interference, that is, nonclerical interference—a distinction which had no meaning in the New Testament as far as fellow Christians were concerned. The cardinals, who were originally

No Other Foundation

go-betweens in the dioceses between the cathedral and the parishes, were becoming purely administrative agents of the papacy and, as such, clustered more and more around the administrative headquarters, Rome. The popes were therefore in future to be elected by the leading ecclesiastical bureaucrats and then, as now, tended to come from their ranks.

Finally, it is in this epoch that previously forged documents to "prove" papal power achieved their greatest impact. The famous *Dictatus Papae* of about 1075 purported to be ancient manuscripts validating current papal claims, including power to appoint or disappoint bishops, depose kings and make princes kiss the papal pedal extremities. Ignoring the evidence of conciliar authority from the Council of Chalcedon (451) in the time of Leo the Great, no less, the documents also asserted that papal power was superior to that of councils and went back to the days of the early church.

The expert on historical attitudes can tell us that the ethos of the epoch demanded proof of authority in the form of evidence of antiquity. Thus, in a sense, one can say that the papacy, whether or not it happened to regard its authority as depending on a genuine tradition, had to provide evidence of such to satisfy the climate of the day. But apart from the incidental deceit involved, the need for validation in terms of norms actually established in the historic past happens to be at the heart of biblical religion. And so, on both counts, it is hard to find the papacy not guilty. We shall see when we get to modern times that this guilt is shared by much so-called Christian theology which attempts, in a far more dangerous way, to carry off the same sleight-of-hand. After all, the eleventh century papacy was not about to deny the Fall, the Incarnation and the Resurrection.

How did a pope like Gregory VII (the first great protagonist in the reforming efforts of the papacy) come to blows with monarchs? And how could he triumph? It is impossible to answer either question without realizing one thing: in a Europe with no effective centralized political powers, whose most successful rulers were those with territories small enough to be kept under control, the universal presence of the church, represented by those wealthy, worldly minded bishops, was a power to be reckoned with.

As we have already pointed out, kings were anxious to use and control local ecclesiastics, so you might ask how the bishops could suddenly support the pope when they had sold out to the king. But this was exactly the point: if a reforming papacy decided to be its own sovereign, to be a real monarch to its bishops, it would force the secular ruler to bargain for the support he needed at papal prices.

The papal tactic was simple: positively, to bring the bishops to heel through asserting papal powers of appointment; negatively, to deny the right of the secular prince to invest a bishop with the spiritual symbols of his office. From a purely political angle, it is also true that the pope could count on being able to use the king's local enemies against him, even if the bishops remained loyal. Against this background, the extraordinary situation that developed around 1076 is alone comprehensible.

The pope having excommunicated the Emperor Henry IV of Germany, his truculent enemies, the leading dukes of Germany, declared him deposed. After all, how could an excommunicate rule over Christians? As it happened, by an astute move, Henry was able to regain the advantage, even if at the cost of an enormously vivid display of inferiority. Recognizing the pope's obligation as a priest to grant absolution to the true penitent, he tracked Gregory VII down to a castle at Canossa and waited out three days in the snow. At this point, the pope reluctantly granted absolution, thus restoring the emperor's communicant status. Henry at once returned to Germany to put down his dukes whose position had been automatically weakened by the pope's having forgiven their enemy.

This particular incident, which was but one engagement in a long campaign which for a century was more favorable to the popes than their foes, does illustrate an important principle: that if the popes were to fight rulers their success depended on an atmosphere of spiritual respect for their office and upon the weak local base of an individual monarch. But, as time passed, respect ebbed for a papacy which continued to fight for positions when its spiritual reforming zeal was spent. And, those individual monarchs began to emulate the papacy in asserting control over their own domains. In the thirteenth century the balance was tipping decisively against the popes.

It is easy to generalize unfairly about the state of the church in the years when what amounts to a papal monarchy was being

No Other Foundation

established. The political tactics are more fascinating, make better copy, than spiritual developments. One problem for the historian is that he cannot present the evidence all at once, like a fugue. If he could, if *I* could, you would hear the somewhat more angelic strains of piety mingling with and softening the less angelic strains of backroom politics.

There was, objectively, in this epoch starting in the mid-eleventh century, a missionary expansion into hitherto barely Christianized areas of Europe to the north and east. The papacy also insisted upon far higher moral and educational standards for all priests. Teeth were put into this insistence by the papacy's growing control of ecclesiastical appointments. Genuine spiritual responsibility was required of bishops for the priests in their dioceses. A particularly hard line was taken against simony—the purchase of church office. An attempt was even made, though it sat ill with some aspects of papal international policy, to enforce the so-called Truce of God. Pioneered in Burgundy in the late tenth century, this movement threatened excommunication to any who disturbed the peace by physical attack, robbery, common injustice or resort to arms on Sundays and festival days.

But it is perhaps significant that the moral dimensions of church reform tended to originate outside Rome. Believing in the legitimacy, necessity and value of papal lordship in society, the popes drove hardest to make that a reality. In the long run, this drive would contradict and discredit the original moral dimensions of church reform. "I have loved righteousness and hated iniquity, therefore I die in exile," were Gregory VII's last words. One need not question his zeal and morality while yet perceiving that it was the papal insistence on its own central efforts which betrayed the biblical concept of a truly interdependent body of believers.

For all that the church was far from the early church in its life and doctrine, and even far from the church of Constantine's day, yet there was a distinct improvement over the touch-and-go days of Magyar, Norman, and Moslem invasions in the late ninth and tenth centuries when Christendom seemed in danger of being overwhelmed. The church also contained, whatever the doctrinal, liturgical and ecclesiological perversions, a strong remnant, as always, of determined men and women, prepared to die for their faith, prepared to defy the status quo, prepared to follow

Christ to the extent of joining a new monastic order.

We may be disposed to criticize the church of the eleventh century but perhaps we should apply on a collective level Jesus' comment on the widow's two copper coins placed in the Temple treasury: "Truly, I tell you, this poor widow has put in more than all of them; for they all contributed out of their abundance, but she out of her poverty put in all the living she had" (Luke 21:1-4). What is our abundance compared to the poverty of the eleventh century, in terms of a clearly diffused Gospel? And what is our contribution?

For Further Study

Power, Eileen. *Medieval People.* 10th rev. and enl. ed. New York: Barnes & Noble, 1963. One of the hardest problems in trying to come face to face with a vanished age is to visualize its people. These master-portraits will help.

Southern, R. W. *Western Society and the Church in the Middle Ages.* Harmondsworth, Eng.: Penguin Books, 1970. Few are so able as this author to recapture imaginatively and with full control of the facts the complex form of a civilization which was, for the first and perhaps the last time, officially and, in organization, unitedly Christian.

Two Lives of Charlemagne. Translated with an Introduction by Lewis Thorpe. Harmondsworth, Eng.: Penguin Books, 1969. Contemporary appraisals (basically "praisals") of a remarkable ruler whose reign made a Christian society seem possible.

White, Lynn, Jr. *Medieval Technology and Social Change.* New York: Oxford University Press, 1966. Some controversial judgments but that great mystery, feudalism, will make a bit more sense than it ever did in Social Studies.

8

The Church in Medieval Life

A NY DISCUSSION, at any period of time, of the church in contemporary life, should start with a consideration of the
view of faith commonly held by that church and the means
whereby all men might be saved. To explore these issues is to lay
the foundation for understanding the actual impact of the church.

If, as was the case, the church had become identified with
society through playing such a crucial role in its preservation up
to about A.D. 1000, two things may be observed:

First of all, baptism became a social as well as a religious cere-
mony in the sense that to be a citizen of Europe you had to be
baptized. Europe was, indeed, Christ's kingdom—
"Christendom." It was a *Corpus christianum*—a body of Christians. Not to be baptized was not to be a member nor even, in a
sense, a person. To be excommunicated was to be outlawed. This
was not unique in history, certainly. The same situation existed in
Athens where Socrates chose death as a citizen to a life in exile:
the first was death in life; the second, life in death. At the height
of papal power in the early thirteenth century, however, not
merely individuals but whole nations were outlawed! This is not
entirely unique, either. Is not the tendency of recent United Nations' decisions to outlaw Israel?

But the legitimacy of this socioreligious identification has to be
tested in practice. When the nonmember is ghettoized, as the Jew
was, the identification requires examination to see how far it is
society that is coloring the church, rather than the reverse. The
tendency to discriminate against the outsider is perfectly understandable, humanly, and perfectly disgraceful, spiritually.

Baptism, secondly, will tend to become a *pro forma* entry to
the spiritual body of Christ, with little or no discrimination. The

No Other Foundation

history of infant baptism in the early church and after is a disputed topic. It is fair to say that the practice is typical of the church in the second century and thereafter, whatever was the situation in the days of the Apostles. But once the church was embraced by the state in the course of the fourth century, the already growing tendency to accept some sort of baptismal regeneration theory spawned practical problems.

One may look at it like this: If all are full members of the church from infancy, how does one create the tension necessary to get people to produce those good works which demonstrate membership? Here was the natural setting for the slow evolution of that "credit" attitude to the Christian life which became the hallmark of much medieval Christianity and remains a blemish in Catholic practice. Not that the insistence on good works as a demonstration of salvation is not thoroughly biblical. Rather, that the call to good works can sound more like a threat than a promise, a heavy obligation rather than a thankful response in the power of the Spirit.

One may even trace from this the development of the idea of purgatory, officially established by Gregory the Great, where the sinfulness of the less than fully devout is purged away. Likewise, one may see the concept of the virtues of the superspiritual, the Saints, dovetailing in to provide coverage for the less than virtuous. Though not made official till a council in 787, the veneration of saints had become common practice since at least the fourth century and with it the superstitions associated with the relics of saints.

If indiscriminate infant baptism associated with immediate regeneration stimulated the idea of having to merit your salvation, it also fed the idea that the believer could be finally lost. And it now becomes obvious that hidden away behind all the ideas and practices just described is a deficient view of the scope of the grace of God in Christ. Thus, the urge to evangelize is transformed and redirected into an anxious preoccupation with the salvation of the already baptized. Missionary activity, itself, leaned toward an extremely formal and even forcible baptizing of border groups. And the missionary activity might be seen on the part of the missionaries as an aspect of their endeavor to make certain their own salvation.

Quite naturally, when all society is seen as regenerate, and when that society is manifestly full of blemishes, a spiritual elitism will tend to blossom. The agents of the body communicating regenerating baptism and administering the sacrament which is seen as the chief on-going source of grace, will be regarded as spiritually superior to the rest. We have already seen one mark of this in the absolute insistence upon clerical celibacy from the eleventh century. Another one is the exclusion of the laity from receiving the cup in the Mass (at the Fourth Lateran Council, 1215).

I stress that this development is a natural one. If there is no distinction in being a believer, because everybody is, then emphasis will tend to fall on rank (as a church official, for example) or upon particular and often stereotyped signs of exceptional holiness—hence the thirst for saints. One must also stress that none of this is a purely medieval phenomenon: it is the natural tendency of the church when it loses sight of the meaning and responsibilities of personal salvation. Whenever churchgoers use the impersonal pronoun "they" to refer to the minister and other church officers you may be sure that this tendency is present in some degree.

Dependence on priestly mediation is instinctive to the developments we have discussed above. The same council in 1215 which refused the cup to the laity also stipulated at least one confession a year to one's priest to remain in good standing. This dependence is itself echoed in the very term "Father" which was assumed by priests. The laity are the spiritual children of the Father-Priest. They are brought to life through baptism and sustained by the Mass. Laymen are only physical fathers.

The fabric of this dependence tended to inhibit common spiritual impulses among the laity. A spiritual enthusiasm outside the pattern of the regular cycle of ritual was automatically suspect. One of the few safeguards such enthusiasm might have would be exalted social status, and it is significant that most of the officially accepted reforming movements were led by men of substantial parentage. By contrast, those movements which were proscribed were far more closely identified with leaders of less social prominence.

This fact is a reflection of the way the church hierarchy tended to be the preserve of the wealthy and well-born. On one level, this is not unexpected. Leaders do tend, for obvious reasons, to come from "good" backgrounds where they have had the opportunity to develop qualities of confidence and enjoy an appropriate education. On another level, one must neither expect nor desire such a correlation if the leadership in question is spiritual.

Yet, we have a French poet around 1210 writing: *"Haute eglise requiert hautesce"*—church notables should be social notables. Canon law, in fact, forbade any man of servile origin to be ordained priest. A peasant could rise to the top occasionally. Gregory VII is a case in point. But he was an exceptional man in an exceptional age. Furthermore, he was elected by acclaim. In practice, almost all the *lower* clergy did come from peasant stock, which was fortunate because, to stay alive, the parish priest had generally to display peasant skills to farm the glebe (the lands belonging to the local church).

The elite of the living was matched by the elite of the dead. The veneration of saints and pilgrimages to see the relics of famous saints, already endemic by the year 1000, increased greatly thereafter. The three most prominent centers were St. James of Compostella (in northwest Spain), Rome, and Jerusalem. Bear in mind that there were two dimensions to pilgrimages: the spiritual and the economic. The first concerned the pilgrim; the second, the church and community in question and the places en route. Pilgrims provided a lot of revenue and prices were inflated as for modern tourists. The two dimensions of the pilgrimage combined most spectacularly in the Crusades.

The crusades (at least, the first one preached in 1095) rationalized the pilgrim motivation and fulfilled the need for land felt by younger sons who were excluded by laws of inheritance from supporting themselves adequately. Most of the leaders were such, and many of the four or five thousand knights who travelled east in the late 1090s took their families along. Many of the lesser men were also hoping to find a livelihood, if not a fortune, abroad. As has been emphasized by many recent studies, the crusades were the first Western overseas colonizing ventures.

Yet, there was also a genuine religious fervor, a sincere desire to recover the "holy places of pilgrimage" in Jerusalem. This motivation cannot be siphoned off in considering the crusades. Ventures involving the risks faced in 1095 required a spiritual component to bolster other purely egotistical ones.

Considered overall, if Jerusalem was captured from the infidel in 1099 and whole "crusading" states established in Palestine and

Syria, the next two crusades in 1144 and 1191 were miserable failures and deserved to be. Less than a century after Jerusalem was rescued it was lost again to Saladin in 1187. For all that the storied Richard the Lion Heart won Acre (a fortress town on the Mediterranean) in 1191, the fourth crusade of 1204 would achieve nothing but the Venetian-instigated sacking of Constantinople. What the pagan had so far not been able to do, the Christian accomplished!

A footnote to the crusades is the Teutonic Order of Knights who, having no employment in the east as the crusading states were dismantled, were encouraged to colonize and Christianize the Baltic lands in the far northeast of Europe. This they accomplished with such exemplary ferocity that the Slav peoples held it against the Teutons ever after. Stalin and Eisenstein could still draw on this feeling in the anti-German war film *Alexander Nevsky* (1939/40).

Driven out of the Middle East, there was always a "Middle East" frontier back home: the Jews. Forbidden to practice trade, or work the land, they were reduced to marginal occupations. Moneylending was simply the most famous of them, and the most lucrative. It was only as the laws against moneylending slackened in the thirteenth century that the Jews began to be forced out of the Western lands and move into Eastern Europe.

Jews could suffer virtually anything. Automatically, one-third of a Jew's money went to the king at death. The level of taxation was higher for the Jew. More seriously, the Jew localized in the ghetto was a sitting duck for popular violence. When the crusaders were moving south through France and Germany to the various assembly points for embarkation, there were frightful pogroms. After all, was not the Jew an enemy of the Cross nearer home? Was not his guilt greater than that of the Moslem? To be fair, men like Bernard of Clairvaux, as well as several popes and various sovereigns, struck out hard against these atrocities. But it was the start of a wave of violence which would pulsate down through the years to our own century.

The seeds of the relaxing of Jewish evangelism had borne their evil fruits. Who can say, in this century of the holocaust, in our very own 1970s when the Arab propaganda line is to brand the Jew in Palestine as the front-man for Western capitalistic expansion, that things have changed much?

So far, our discussion of the church in medieval life has been

No Other Foundation

negative. What of the positive impact? Europe, especially the towns, was clogged with churches. Around 1200, London had about 120 and Rome over 300. If the world rubbed off on the church, the church very definitely influenced the world.

Teaching, for example, for most of the Middle Ages, was either the preserve of the church or was directly carried on within a Christian frame of reference. The same church council which denied the cup to the laity also took steps to make more effective the provisions for the education of able children and youths. It also made sure that preaching would take place in a regular fashion in the dioceses.

There was far more preaching in the Middle Ages than we sometimes think. Among the most effective preachers were the wandering friars, but most of the monastic orders set aside particular brothers for this task. It is worth noting, too, that the council in 1215 underscored the need for preaching with the observation that the food of the word of God was necessary for salvation. This, again, is a dimension of medieval church thought which can easily be forgotten in the midst of negative criticism. Yes, the preaching would present opinions in conformity with church theology which were not always consonant with the word of God. But any experience in our own day with evangelism reveals how much of the Gospel manages to penetrate the most unhelpful theological screens.

There was another dimension of teaching which might be overlooked. If most people were illiterate, they were not entirely shut up to the spoken word. The great paintings which adorned most churches were a vivid Sunday school lesson to the masses. It is a fair bet that the average illiterate peasant was more familiar with Bible stories and the details of the Passion than the average twentieth-century Westerner. In another way, too, the people were instructed through the entire subordination of the whole cycle of life to the succession of Christian festivals. The medieval calendar was a mosaic of Christian remembrance. However much we may frown at saints' days, considering them incidental theological baggage, I wonder whether the medieval calendar was not preferable to our pallid, secular alternative?

As monarchies became more effective governments, reaching more surely into the lives of their subjects, criticism of the church's control of all jurisdiction relating to its own officers mounted. The complaint was part financial, because justice means money, and part juridical, because church courts tended to be more lenient than the secular.

If this leniency was a reflection of patient charity, instead of disinclination to clean one's own stables, it had a positive function in a day when sentences could be overharsh. Needless to say, it was a bit of both. That the church did have, on balance, a good influence in the area of justice can be broadly documented, however.

I have already in the last chapter alluded to the attempt in the so-called Truce of God to limit warfare and public violence. The church also intervened to drive out the blood feud and the duel in favor of trial by ordeal. Then, in 1215 again, it went a step further, condemning the ordeal in favor of trial by witnesses.

Nowadays we speak a lot about economic justice and this is an important and thoroughly biblical concept. The medieval church was in many ways far more radical in its attack upon economic injustice than the twentieth-century church with its social gospel. It insisted upon the idea of a just price which generally meant the current market value or the legally fixed rate. The church condemned profiteering in time of need or shortage. Speculation in the materials of life was strictly forbidden. Hoarding, in times of scarcity, to force prices up, was pilloried for what it was, and is: hate for one's neighbor. The secular governments were induced to forbid this, too.

Usury (interest on a money loan) was not allowed to the Christian. He was expected to loan without interest in the spirit of Christ's teaching. If loan business were necessary, it had to be handled by a non-Christian—hence the identification of the Jews with this lucrative activity. Tied up with the church's view on usury was the biblical conviction that a man should work, rather than having his money work instead, at someone else's expense.

Now, you may object, that with the development of commerce perfectly innocent forms of loan business must develop to supply needed capital and is it not better to be indebted, in this case, to a Christian rather than a non-Christian? The church became aware of this and in the thirteenth century began to allow *nonprofessional* loan activity with a strict ceiling on permissible interest rates. Calvin, later on, took a similar stance.

However quaint or impractical we may think all this, C. S. Lewis was perhaps right when he opined that Western civilization

No Other Foundation

took a false turn when, in the sixteenth and seventeenth centuries, it threw away all restraints upon usury. Nowadays we hardly think twice about it, and the church itself is up to its neck in interest rates and the esoteric theology of accountancy.

Although elsewhere I have spoken harshly about the church bureaucratic, it cannot be gainsaid that it provided the one constant source of academic and practical education and advanced job training in the West. As universities developed and branched out from the traditional subjects to give training for medical and legal careers, in the thirteenth century, there was a natural reduction in the church's contribution. But for a long time still, most literacy, most skill in administration and government, was learned from the church.

Although it deserves a long section of its own, I must quickly note, also, the unique contribution of the church in the area of hospital services, orphan care, poor relief, and every conceivable aspect of social welfare. In a day when the pendulum has swung totally in the opposite direction, we forget that, as a church, we can contribute positively to *all* areas of social need. If we don't, someone else will. It is, for example, a scandal that so many of the beneficial alternatives to modern stereotyped medical and legal practices, which victimize the patient and client, have been pioneered by humanists and people whose veneration for life derives from the ultimately deadly philosophy of eastern religions.

Because, in fact, the medieval church did make a fundamental and visible contribution to society, it could confidently call upon the ruler to purge heresy. I do not urge such influence, of course; I just want to illustrate that there was a natural alliance because of shared tasks and shared ideals.

In closing, one must stress the difficulty of using social and political influence spiritually, humbly, beneficently. We have seen, in a limited way, illustrations from both sides. What is the conclusion?

On the plus side, this was a society profoundly suffused by the conviction that this life is lived out in a cosmic, spiritual context. Superstition there was; doctrinal distortion and error; gross cruelty condoned against heretics and Jews. And yet, finally, however dark the glass had become, through a glass darkly one did look forward to a life which is far better. Undoubtedly, much of the spontaneity and freedom of the pure evangel was lost for many, and many more would be saved despite having built with hay and stubble on the sure Foundation. But saved, nonetheless.

On the minus side, the church could hardly escape being tarred with the secular brush. Likewise, today, so much church organization bears the godless stamp of Madison Avenue and Wall Street. Characteristically, the monastery was usually seen not as Benedict had seen it—a retreat from the world in order to reform it and rejuvenate it according to God's terms—but as secular rulers saw it—a retreat in order to grant wicked society a necessary conscience. As if, by establishing and funding such foundations, one could spiritually bail out the world. Indeed, the not infrequent retiring of successful businessmen to monasteries at regular intervals or before death, reminds one forcibly of modern exoduses to quiet spots in Florida and Arizona, immune to the hurly-burly of business and urban blight. Ironically, the very success of the church demanded more and more power plays, more and more forays into the Devil's world, using the Devil's methods.

All told, then as now, it was difficult to make up one's mind about the church. Significantly, if Rome had been regarded as above all a spiritual center before the eleventh century dispute between church and state over jurisdictions, it lost this identification from then on. Becoming a center of government—the most powerful government in Europe—it was too strong to venerate. Several English kings, it has been noted, pilgrimaged to Rome before 1050; not one thereafter, though several physically passed through Italy. Again, each of the twelfth century popes was a great and powerful leader. But not one of them managed to barge his way into the ranks of the saints.

The image of Rome was subtly changing. In the twelfth century one encounters anonymous satires along the lines of the *Gospel According to the Mark of Silver*. This work depicted the pope gathering his cardinals, as for a "Sermon on the Mount," but encouraging them to conduct of a different stripe. Urging them to fleece suitors at the papal court, he intones: "For I have given you an example, that ye also should take gifts as I have taken them. . . . Blessed are the rich, for they shall be filled; blessed are they that have, for they shall not go away empty; blessed are the wealthy, for theirs is the court of Rome." We also are introduced at this time to the "martyrs" Albinus (pale silver) and Rufinus (red gold). The pope solemnly placed their relics "in the treasury of St. Cupidity, beside the mercyseat of St. Avidity, her sister, not far from the basilica of their mother, St. Avarice. Here the Pope buried them in great magnificence with his own hands."

Note that this is rough and harsh satire. But satire is both an unwilling tribute to power and a recognition of the inevitability of that power.

Only one thing can transform such satire into praise: it is a life lived non-hypocritically, in the presence of God and one's neighbors. It must be a visible life and it must be an invisible one too, or else what is visible will not be worth savoring. "If the salt hath lost its savor, wherewithal shall it be salted?" No external ecclesiastical power, no membership of this or that spiritual brigade, can provide the seasoning. God's Spirit is the dispenser of spiritual salt. And he dispenses on Christ's terms, who said: "Wash one another's feet" (John 13:14).

For Further Study

Adams, Jeremy duQ., comp. *Patterns of Medieval Society*. Englewood Cliffs, N.J.: Prentice-Hall, 1969. Documents illustrating many aspects of life.

Knowles, David. *Christian Monasticism*. New York: McGraw-Hill Book Co., 1969. An overview by one of the greatest authorities. Illustrated.

Ladurie, Emmanuel L. *Montaillou: The Promised Land of Error*. Translated by B. Bray. New York: George Braziller, 1978. A fascinating study of a single community which was a center of Albigensian heresy. Describes dimensions of everyday life that one would think beyond the access of the historian. But this historian had available the incredibly full record of an exceptionally nosey member of the Inquisition!

The Très Riches Heures of Jean, Duke of Berry. Translated by V. Benedict. New York: George Braziller, 1969. Reproduced from the illuminated manuscript belonging to the Musée Condé, Chantilly, France. Adams and Ladurie open the door to common life; this famous Book of Hours introduces us to a world of wealth and sophistication. Consult this volume in a library; it is very expensive.

9

The Church and the Intellect

J AMES TELLS US in his Epistle that though the tongue is a tiny member it can, like the rudder, turn the whole ship. It has this capacity because it is the agent of the intellect. Now, it is the primary function of the intellect to inform and express our will. The intellect is inferior to the will, as such. But, taking off from the impulse of the will, the intellect can weave dazzling rationalizations of the least and the greatest of our deviations, such that one can mistakenly suppose that our problems are on the perfectly "respectable" level of intellectual disagreement when actually they are quite humdrum, backyard aberrations. The curse of the intellect, then, is that it can be used to cover up our moral nakedness, our preference for our own minds. The blessing of the intellect, contrariwise, is that it can be used to express and make clear the benefits of having put on the mind of Christ. Any discussion of the church and the intellect ranges back and forth between these two possibilities.

To make clear what I do not mean, I shall first talk about a real heresy: the Catharist. Catharism is a version of one of the varieties of heresy we discussed in an earlier chapter. It was introduced into the West in the 1140s. Cathari believed in a continuing, cosmic battle between Good and Evil, as yet unresolved. All spirit is good; all material is bad. The Old Testament God is evil because he created matter. Christ is the messenger of the good god. He was not, therefore, really of flesh and did not suffer on the cross. Accordingly, crucifixes and images are satanic, and sexual activity is perverse because it leads to the generation of more flesh. All the Christian sacraments are evil because they blasphemously make visible what is invisible. The Cathar initiate was declared pure and liberated from the flesh in a sacrament of "consolation." Thereafter, one could not sin because the sacrament, which made one perfect, was unrepeatable.

As a practical result of this teaching, Cathari naturally put off final initiation till old age, ostensibly to avoid the possibility of falling into sin afterwards. Critics saw in this an ingenious rationale for living a life of total physical abandonment. In fact, one saw both a high standard of purity among sincere Cathari and an increasingly degenerate life style among the rest.

For all its perversity, Catharism had spread widely by 1200, especially in the Netherlands, the Rhineland, the south of France and northern Italy. In France, Cathari were called Albigensians after Albi, one of their great centers. So prominent a threat did they pose that the pope called a crusade against them in 1208. The crusade ended in 1223 and substantially wiped out the Cathari, whose influence accordingly dwindled. It is an interesting fact that a predictable sourness toward the church, in view of the excessive cruelty of the crusade, almost certainly predisposed the population of the former centers of Catharism in southern France to be noticeably friendly towards Protestantism in the sixteenth century.

The evolution of Catharism is valuable as a warning, leading us to evaluate less totally heretical attitudes, for it built upon apparently innocuous deviations from the truth. In some degree, Catharism was a logical extension of a sort of superspirituality which condemned the flesh; the Reformists had also been guilty of this tendency. The same extension may be seen in our own day in groups like the Children of God.

To repeat what I said earlier, heresy comes from spiritual disobedience and marks a comfortable rationalization of it, to shield one from having to acknowledge the real moral roots of the matter. This, I think, helps explain what otherwise is puzzling: how on earth offbeat theological ideas develop in the context of apparent doctrinal orthodoxy. Jesus insisted that one's conduct bear out one's doctrine. And so if you are diagnosing spiritual sickness or trying to forestall theological declension, you should look far more closely at the conduct than at the probably quite orthodox theological exterior. It is not from the theology that the unorthodoxy develops; it is from the behavior. Of course, the behavior springs from untamed thoughts which the theology later articulates. And once the theological boat starts moving, that stimulates further distortion, till one is well within sight of the shorelines of heresy.

This discussion helps us to have a right perspective on the question of Mariology. We can be so spontaneously alarmed by the idea of Mary standing between us and Christ that we fail either to recognize her high honor or to see the natural context in which extra-scriptural teaching about her person and role evolved. This teaching had early roots in the great debates about Christ's incarnation. The insistence on the incarnation led to an overemphesis upon Mary—as if the grace bestowed on her granted a complementary relation to the Son, an idea foreign to apostolic teaching.

Some of the later roots of Mariology may be found in the medieval emphasis upon works and guilt—a guilt, that is, which is not preached as entirely lifted by Christ. Thus, to fill the gap where the undeserved grace and continuing love of God in Christ, mediated by the Spirit, should be, one emphasizes the cult of the compassionate Virgin. And, it may be that this cult was the more ready to hand in view of the ongoing fertility cults, or the memory of them.

Already by the ninth century, the Blessed Virgin Mary was seen as the mediator between man and God, praying mercifully to her Son for the sinner. Drawing upon and extending themes dating back to the second century, if Christ was the new Adam, Mary was the new Eve, who brought forth salvation on the earth just as Eve brought forth ruin. Born without sin, ever virgin and sinless in her life (incidentally here, it seems, something subtly close to the Cathar rejection of the flesh), she was the ideal of maiden purity and maternal devotion.

By the twelfth century, the cult began to strain the patience of the church authorities whose prosaic governance of the church left little room for such romantic twists. What could a papal diplomat make of a story like "The Juggler of Our Lady" where the little monk (a sort of medieval Charlie Chaplin) who is unable to write, paint, sing or theologize, juggles in secret before the statue of his heroine (Our Lady) while the other brothers are asleep. The tale ends happily ever after with the monk gaining the Virgin's special favor. More seriously, one finds pictures depicting sinners being rejected by an imperious Christ but welcomed by a compassionate Mary. And, a further step, Jesus is seen in dependence upon his Mother—the rejected sufferer comforted by Mary.

The greatest hymn to the Virgin is the thirteenth-century *Stabat Mater:*

> Weeping, the sorrowful Mother
> Stood by the Cross
> While her Son hung dying.
> A sword had pierced
> Her mourning and grieving soul
> That suffered with her Son.

But far more universal was the simple *Hail Mary* prayer (the *Ave Maria*) which was tagged on to the Lord's Prayer from the twelfth century.

One may also discover sources for Mariology in the fact that in the theological and chivalric literature of the period woman was dehumanized to the degree that she was seen as either above or below reason. She was either a baby factory or a virgin unspotted. This dichotomy is very evident in the cult of Mary. Mary is made to be both less and more than she was. It is not surprising that this cult which stressed heights of other-worldly feeling should find expression in reason-defying churches, dedicated to a Virgin beyond reason. The sheer number of churches dedicated to Our Lady in the twelfth and thirteenth centuries is, in any case, overwhelming. Notre Dame of Paris, Notre Dame of Chartres, Notre Dame of Amiens, . . . When the pendulum of thought began to swing towards practical reason in the Renaissance epoch, the cult would temporarily weaken, only to pick up again in the reaction to the Reformation in the late sixteenth century.

But to talk of the cult of the Virgin without mention of Bernard of Clairvaux would be silly and to talk of him we must say something about the monastic revival of the twelfth century.

Partly as a reaction to the increasingly governmental aspect of the church but also, perhaps, a reflection of misplaced guilt, the Cistercian Order (named after Citeaux in France) sprang up around 1100, based on a return to pure Benedictinism. Private property was forsaken; black bread, water and stewed vegetables were the extent of one's menu; manual labor took the place of study; silence was preferred to speech; and brothers slept in their clothes, on rough beds, in unheated dormitories. The fact that this regimen won the hearts of an impressive minority in an age of prosperity is part tribute to the greatest of all Cistercians, Bernard of Clairvaux. The son of a wealthy Burgundian family, Bernard forsook his possessions to join Citeaux in 1112. Three years later he left to establish Clairvaux, on the same model. At his death in 1153, he could point to 65 houses founded on Cistercian principles.

Though extraordinarily strict, Bernard could charm even his enemies. The effect of his preaching and example was so great that we are told "Mothers hid their sons from him, wives their husbands, and companions their friends"! Averse to laughter, the outspoken critic of popes, kings and ecclesiastics (he informed the famous Abbot Suger of St. Denis that his life was a disgrace), a stickler for doctrinal rectitude (he led the prosecution of the theologian Abelard for heresy and approved of his forcible emasculation at the hands of the uncle of the girl he fell in love with), he nevertheless encouraged a more subversive heresy than many whose views he attacked.

To speak analytically of anyone's spirituality is a dangerous business, implying among other things that the analyst is above it all. "Judge not that ye be not judged." If most Christians today had but a grain of the practical compassion for men which Bernard and his companions had, society would not be the same. If most of us shared a little more of the devotion to Christ expressed in the hymn written by Bernard or one of his followers, there would be a greater depth to our worship:

> Jesus, the very thought of Thee
> With sweetness fills the breast;
> But sweeter far Thy face to see,
> And in Thy presence rest.

Few have meditated so deeply on Scripture and expressed their insights so poetically, as Bernard, and yet?

And yet, for all that he spoke powerfully about the love of God, it seems that he strove more for kindling in himself a love *for* God, than for a positive and dynamic recognition of the love *of* God. I say this because otherwise it is hard to explain the constant harping upon guilt. As I said earlier, I believe that it is in the context of deep guilt and a failure to see Christ's work as totally complete that the cult of the Virgin is able to flourish. It is hardly surprising, then, that this gigantic personality—for such Bernard surely was, this terror of kings—should himself in his own dwelling upon personal failing have the most fully embraced the cult of Mary

No Other Foundation

and preached it with unexampled fervor and insistency to the men of his day:

> Dost thou fear the divine Majesty in the Son?
> Wilt thou find an advocate before him?
> Flee to Mary; in her, humanity is pure.
> The Son will listen to the Mother, and the Father to the Son.

To read Bernard's devotions is to be simultaneously stimulated by his imagination and depressed by his apparent "slowness of heart" to share the Apostle's joy in "the earnest of our inheritance."

There was another side to monastic reform, though, which leads us toward the greatest intellectual movements of the thirteenth century.

Roughly contemporary with Bernard was Norbert who founded the Premonstratensian Order (named from Prémontré, near Laon in northern France; Prémontré itself is an artificial name indicating, in the original Latin, that the location was "pre-shown" to Norbert by an angel). The Premonstratensians were especially dedicated to learning in preparation for teaching, in order to evangelize the growing numbers of people in the towns who were, as later in the Industrial Revolution, more and more out of touch with the Gospel and Gospel living. Over two hundred houses were founded by 1200. But both the Premonstratensians and Cistercians, strict and devout as they were in origin, were so successful by 1200 that they contradicted the aims of their founders and lapsed into luxury and moral flatulence.

The history of monasticism, as I remarked in a previous chapter, is one of advance and retreat. The two great orders which picked up the slack in 1200 were dedicated to teaching and preaching, and both made enormous intellectual contributions: the Dominicans and the Franciscans. The Spaniard, Dominic, founded his order in 1215. Its greatest ornaments would be Albertus Magnus who died in 1280 and his younger, greater contemporary, Thomas Aquinas (died 1274). The Franciscans, the other order, derived of course from Francis of Assisi (died 1226), son of a wealthy cloth merchant. He gave up his inheritance to devote himself to poverty and preaching.

What is so attractive about Francis is that he did not lose the openness of his preconversion personality. A sparkling joy contrasts greatly with the introspective spirituality of Bernard. Forsaking the world, he rediscovered it as God's creation. Overzealous critics might find a vague pantheism in his love of creatures and flowers. But I find this love to be the fruit of his overflowing awareness of God's loving and saving presence in all that he has made. Incidentally, the sometimes maligned Bernard once called the oaks and beeches under which he meditated, his "friends."

Distinctive again of Francis was his great reluctance to institutionalize what he stood for. He said: "I strictly command all brothers never to receive coin or money, either directly or through an intermediary." He knew the downfall of the other orders. But the Franciscans, officially established in 1223, after Francis had already himself given up the formal leadership in 1220, were already grieving the founder at his death a few years later. Indeed, within a century his closest followers—the so-called "Spirituals" or Fraticelli—would be banned as heretics. Harshly dealt with by ecclesiastical authorities, they were laid open to the dangers of an unbalanced pursuit of their particular distinctives—illustrating a recurring turn of events in church history.

Francis's mission had been to bring all men, all nature even, to a recognition of their true nature as God's handiwork and hence to a Christian understanding of the implications of this fact. This powerful and universal mission was, in a different key, echoed in the great intellectual and artistic undertakings of the day.

One cannot begin even to summarize the intellectual endeavors of an epoch which produced men of the stature of Anselm, Abelard, Albert, and Aquinas. I wish simply to look at the inspiration for their work, as this may be perceived from the output of the greatest of them, Aquinas, and even in his case glance but briefly at a single aspect of his thought.

Frequently referred to simply as Thomas, hence "Thomism," Aquinas was a large, slow-moving Italian born of a good family south of Rome. An accomplished poet and a man of holy life, he is yet primarily famous for his total systematization of Christian theology. This work of synthesis evokes the first thing I want to say about him: that he typifies an age seeking to harmonize Christian theology with the growing knowledge of Greek, and particularly Aristotelian, thought and philosophy.

No Other Foundation

This entailed both an attempt to state the Christian answers to questions not always directly dealt with in Scripture and, in so doing, to measure the possibilities of agreement between, chiefly, Aristotle, and the Bible. This brings me to the second thing I want to say about his system in particular. For Aristotle was, above all, the philosopher of nature, of the world as it is. He stands for the power of the mind to reason accurately and fruitfully about nature and human problems. Aquinas did not, by any means, accept Aristotle uncritically, nor did he dismiss Plato whose influence till the eleventh century marked the rough limit of Greek input to medieval thought. But his preoccupation with Aristotle is paramount, reflecting in philosophy a climate of experiment and assimilation which marked all contemporary fields of endeavor, from commerce to statecraft.

In harmonizing Aristotle and the Bible, Aquinas undoubtedly took a step towards driving the thin edge of a wedge into Christian thought—the wedge which divides faith from knowledge, experience from doctrine. It would be wrong to say that Aquinas saw it so baldly. He did not. But in his famous saying, "Grace does not abolish nature, it perfects it," he gave a special place to reason (that is, nature), independent of God's intervention (that is, grace), which would help launch the whole emphasis upon human self-help in the Renaissance period, and which continues right down to modern times.

Simultaneously, he opened the door to according faith a special place beyond the questions of reason. In this respect, the earlier thought of Anselm came into its own. Anselm said: "I believe that I may know." He overemphasized the other side and yet is echoed by Aquinas in the sense that he tends to put belief and knowledge into separate, watertight compartments. It is not surprising that Karl Barth in our own day, who is so identified with defining a faith beyond the shock of human events and human knowledge, should have devoted a very large book to Anselm. Just as Thomism could open the door to an emphasis on the physical, the visible, as in the Renaissance, so the modern distinction between faith and everyday life can encourage an abandonment to crude technology and sensuality. Oddly enough, the drift of Thomism or Renaissance thought or much modern theology might seem on paper to be contrary to the heresy of the Cathars. Yet in practice they yield the same results: uncontrolled physical freedom within certain bounds.

I was, however, supposedly talking about Aquinas. And I want to add that his brilliant theological and philosophical system, his consideration of every conceivable human question—economic, political, artistic, metaphysical, whatever—this system became the accepted orthodox theology of the Roman Catholic church in the late sixteenth century when Rome was determining her position as against the ideas of the reformers.

The other major dimension of the systematizing intellect to which I wish to pay lip service is the Gothic cathedral. The body of Aquinas's writings and thought has often been compared to a cathedral. Having glanced at his work, we may now compare the cathedral to it.

I am speaking not of any sort of cathedral but of the Gothic cathedral. The adjective "Gothic" which derives from "Goth" was a term of abuse applied to medieval thought and its monuments by an eighteenth century culture which considered itself vastly more civilized. "Gothic" is, therefore, not originally a technical word describing what was distinctive about a certain phase in cathedral architecture. But, just as the terms "Whig" and "Tory" were at first meant as insults but later developed a respectable meaning, so "Gothic" respectably refers to the most highly developed and sophisticated forms of medieval art. Finally, seeing as the cathedral, in a society dedicated to the proposition that God exists, was the most important public building, it came to embody the most daring and substantial examples of Gothic art. Hence, Gothic has become synonymous with medieval cathedrals at the highest stage of their development, from about 1200 onward.

The Gothic cathedral was a symbol in stone and glass of spiritual mysteries. Its entire structure was based upon a few simple geometric organizing principles. All beauty, it was theorized, must conform to geometric principle, for beauty is the embodiment of perfect harmonies and proportions. Thus, Notre Dame in Paris which, along with Notre Dame of Chartres, is the best known example of Gothic architecture, is constructed entirely according to a sequence of four squares: a square; a diamond in a square; a square in a diamond in a square; a square in a square in a square.

These perfect and perfectly interlocking proportions evoke the supreme symbolic meaning of the cathedral: the church as an image of heaven where perfection reigns. Gothic cathedrals were

No Other Foundation

not the first to be designed to illustrate this idea. The oft-depicted sculpture of "Christ in Majesty" in the earlier, Romanesque phase of medieval cathedral architecture, a sculpture which was placed over the entrance to the nave, beckoned you into the sphere of Christ's kingdom, the church. Gothic architecture brought the idea to a triumphant conclusion, projecting the idea of the church beyond immediate physical and temporal reality into a realm spiritually transcendent and remote.

On the level of spiritual perception, then, the cathedral purveyed the mystical experience of a heavenly court which is not of this world. If successful, the cathedral should make us forget our actual location in space and time, as we are transported into the mansions of the spirit. It is in this context, quite apart from the fact that the great cathedrals were enormous community projects sacrificially but often warmly supported by the populace, that we can soften our criticism of the vast expenses required in building. A town was proud to have a church embodying beauty and all harmony, bespeaking the sphere of God's perfection.

Bernard was perhaps the greatest single inspiration for the Gothic cathedral, insisting that all art be attuned to religious experience and arguing that art can only be justified if it guides the mind into an understanding of ultimate truth. It was Bernard, also, who insisted on the two components fundamental to Gothic: proportion and light. Of proportion we have spoken; light is also crucial. The windows were thought of as transparent walls, allowing you to envision the interior as a vessel of light. Here, the analogies are obvious. Christ is the Light and his Church embodies his Light. Christ's Light shone in darkness and the cathedral towered above the roofs and fields, sending its signal far and wide. Yet more specifically: the congregation observing the celebration of the Mass would see the single candle left burning at the end of the service while the priest would follow the thirteenth century custom of reading John 1:1-18. Finally, now risen and ascended, reigning with God in heaven, Christ the Light illuminates God's perfectly proportioned cosmos. The Gothic cathedral is God's order suffused with Christ's Light.

The major and serious gripe I have with the Gothic cathedral and the aesthetic and theological ideas behind it is the same as the one I have with the tendency of Bernard's thought and that of Anselm and Aquinas. There is, however one wishes to look at it, a downgrading of the material and physical (as something evil) and the separation from it of what is spiritual. This would be the neo-Platonic, Augustinian, Bernardan stance. Alternatively, emphasizing natural reason as good in itself, there is nevertheless a dissociation of the human from the spiritual. This would be the link with Anselm and Aquinas.

The cathedral builders very deliberately chose the square ratio of 1:1 over the rectangular ratio of 1:2. Why? Because the number two was considered from the twelfth century to be the symbol of sin, the symbol of material reality over against number one which was the symbol for the Godhead, spiritual reality. What is inevitably lost here is the fact that God made all things good, even if now deformed, and that if heaven is the realm of spiritual perfection it will contain solid physical bodies. Christ's resurrection body, John's awed sentences at the start of his first epistle, Paul's driving argument in chapter 15 of First Corinthians, all alike emphasize this. The Church *is* a vision of heaven, it *is* the City of God. The church of the thirteenth century, like the church of today, was in danger of abstracting and de-materializing the concept of spiritual purity to such a degree as to lose touch with the more and more brutal and go-ahead society in which it existed.

To come down to earth, the fate of a certain Peter Valdes deserves a lone comment as we close. If you intellectually emphasize the separation of the spiritual from the material then you will already and increasingly emphasize in daily life the separation between spiritual ideals and actual living. We have seen that Francis of Assisi's followers were not tolerated by the institutional church.

The fact that Francis was made a saint is partly explicable in terms of his avoidance of official confrontation and his geographical closeness to Rome. I say this because his older contemporary, Peter Valdes of Lyons (France), in the 1170s was very much a pre-Franciscan and yet was hounded down and excommunicated, his followers being persecuted as were Francis's followers. What was the difference? Well, Peter Valdes fell foul of a nasty local bishop and was humiliated by a supercilious council at Rome when appealing the bishop's ruling. It has been suggested that, in a way, Valdes was a trial run for Francis. The hierarchy was more diplomatic when it came the turn of Francis.

No Other Foundation

Peter Valdes, the former merchant, dedicated to poverty and preaching, not unnaturally turned more and more against established hierarchies and practices. He and his "Poor Men of Lyons" became hunted men. Interestingly, however, having escaped institutionalization (the "kiss of death" to the Franciscans) the Waldensians survived as a far more effective and long-lasting presence than the Fraticelli who were even disowned by the order supposedly identified with their founder.

The different histories of Valdes and Francis and the movements they started underline an old debate in Christian living for which there is no blueprint answer. What is the justification for obeying or disobeying the authority of those ordained to pastor the flock? Under what circumstances is schism necessary? One thing is certain: the resolution of such questions cannot be delayed for the sake of a stained-glass window. Further, if the resolution does not flow from and generate a life of genuine beauty and harmony in Christ, one may question whether it was worth it.

For Further Study

Lewis, C. S. *The Allegory of Love.* Oxford: At the Clarendon Press, 1936. A book as beautifully written as it is informative. A whole mentality is recaptured.

The Political Ideas of St. Thomas Aquinas, ed. D. Bigongiari (1969). You need to read Thomas to get an idea of his systematic approach. The ideas he deals with here are concrete enough to give you a sense of contact. Notice, incidentally, that there was, and quite correctly, no incongruity in a theologian being an expert on political systems.

Sayers, Dorothy L. "The Lost Tools of Learning." In *A Matter of Eternity,* essays by Miss Sayers edited by Rosamund K. Sprague. Grand Rapids, MI: Wm. B. Eerdmans Pub. Co., 1973, pp 107-135. A description of the basic medieval curriculum which will make you wish you weren't so lucky as to live in the 20th century.

Simson, Otto von. *The Gothic Cathedral: Origins of Gothic Architecture and the Medieval Concept of Order.* Princeton, N.J.: Princeton University Press, 1956. The classic work on the symbolism of medieval architecture. Illustrated.

10

The Church Betrayed

S WE WALK THROUGH the twilight of the Middle Ages, 1300-1500, we are reminded of the early centuries of Christian Europe, 250-600. In those days the church was moving out of pagan Roman society into Christendom. From 1300, the church was in danger of being enveloped in a new paganism. In the long run, taking the story right down to our own day, it has largely succumbed. A well-known book which discusses a key phase in this process in the eighteenth century is entitled, significantly, *The Enlightenment: The Rise of Modern Paganism.*

Without a vital grasp and experience of what made and makes the church truly Christian, we are tempted in modern times to lapse into nostalgia. In the nineteenth century, as Enlightenment paganism more and more had its way, there was a romantic attempt to recapture the faith of one's medieval forebears. One of the most evocative lines written in this spirit was by the English historian Froude. Distilling the essence of a solitary hour in a country churchyard, he spoke of "the sound of church bells which falls on the ear like the echoes of a vanished world."

He was, of course, historian enough to know very well the day-to-day realities of that vanished world. Vanished, however, it certainly is and the task of the next two chapters will be to describe how and why. In this chapter, I shall deal with the negative factors which contributed to profound spiritual uncertainty and the positive factors which marked a secular reaction away from older Christian values.

However monolithic and powerful a church organization, it eventually faces the effects of its spiritual treachery. If you live by the rules of politics, you have to survive by the rules of politics. Furthermore, the outside world will demand that you return to

No Other Foundation

your supposed spiritual commitment and will take crude steps to ensure at least a formal religiosity.

The pontificate of Innocent III (1198-1216) which saw the Fourth Lateran Council (1215-16) and an exercise of power unexampled in its boldness ("bad" King John and his entire kingdom of England were interdicted by Innocent!) marked the zenith of church influence. If the thirteenth century seems the golden century of the church it was becoming an Indian summer by 1300. Pope Boniface VIII who tried to emulate the tactics of Innocent III, this time towards France, was summarily treated by King Philip. Manhandled by French knights in 1303, Boniface died soon after. Between 1200 and 1300 the balance had tipped: the spiritual debasement of church leadership had coincided with the first flush of confident royal power.

In 1305 a willing tool of Philip was elected pope, Clement V, and he was set up in Avignon, beginning the so-called "Babylonian Captivity" of the papacy (1305-77). It would be wrong to jump to too many conclusions, however. For one thing, although most cardinals and all the popes appointed in this time were French, the papacy was not unduly francophile. For another, the move from Rome was more striking in consistent duration than in simple fact. After all, from 1100 to 1300 nearly two-thirds of the time had been spent by popes away from Rome.

Truth to tell, the popes were usually safer away from the barbarous and vicious Roman nobility than close to them. In addition, at Rome the pope was far more susceptible to the power-plays of a marauding German emperor than in Avignon. This being acknowledged, including some positive religious reform, the fact that appraisals of the Avignonese papacy are normally couched in political and administrative terms indicates how low the level of discussion has become. Rome or Avignon, this was no apostolic order directing the church.

The tension between a regularized Avignonese papacy and the general feeling that the Roman bishop should reside in Rome erupted in 1378, one year after a pope had indeed transferred back. The death of this pope required a new election; rival proceedings saw the election of two popes, one in Avignon, one in Rome. From 1378 to 1415, accordingly, Europe was treated to the farce of two popes—between 1409 and 1415, even three popes—alternately excommunicating one another. Exactly who was validly baptized, validly married, validly confessed, validly given the last rites, when the church could not decide who exercised valid authority?

Apart from general disgust and bewilderment, there were two specific results of what is called the "Great Schism." Local control of the church once again became pervasive as the secular ruler had to deal with the church more in terms of local bishops than dubious antipopes. And, another revival of a development halted since the eleventh century, there was an impetus toward the old conciliar theory of church government where authority is said to reside in a council of bishops, rather than a pope.

Conciliarism was attractive to rulers because it allowed them to express their own preferences through their own bishops and therefore influence church policy to some degree. At the same time, it must be underlined that the papacy had learned to make deals with kings and princes for quite a long time, and what was chiefly at stake in conciliarism was whether a theoretical boost might be given to this de facto breakdown in centralization. Naturally, if practice is awarded theoretical support it does also gain extra strength.

It is an interesting fact that conciliarism as a theory parallels the idea of popular monarchy, the council being the equivalent of a sort of parliament to which the king (or pope) must listen because it represents the people's will. In other words, the church not only gave the secular world a model for effective monarchy in the papacy; it also gave a model, even if largely theoretical, for parliamentary development in conciliarism. Needless to say, neither in councils nor parliaments was one really talking about *popular* power; it is still a question of elites.

Conciliarism did, in any case, receive a boost from the Great Schism. For how could you end the Schism, how could you decide between rival popes, without invoking a body superior to the papacy? Thus, the Council of Constance, which met with the strong backing of secular rulers in 1415 and restored a unitary papacy, took the opportunity to declare: ". . . that it is a General Council . . . and that therefore it has its authority immediately from Christ, and that all men, of every rank and condition, including the Pope himself, are bound to obey it in matters concerning the Faith, the abolition of the schism, and the reformation of the Church of God, in its head and its members."

118

No Other Foundation

Unfortunately, these brave words were effective for the duration of the council and not much longer. More concerned for order than for the things of the spirit, once order was restored the rulers who had provided the muscle were content to make their own private arrangements with the church. Thus, the kings of France were ultimately more concerned with the practical advantages of the Pragmatic Sanction of Bourges in 1438, which guaranteed considerable control over the church, than with a theological argument between ecclesiastics about church government. Thus, the papacy was confident enough by 1460 to issue a bull (called *Execrabilis* from its opening word) which condemned the idea of a council's being superior to a pope as "rebellious, poisonous, erroneous, and detestable."

Yet, papal prestige had not been helped by all these events. The popes ruling the church, including the one who issued the bull, were a study in contradiction: humanists before they were Christians, libertines before they were celibates. That Rome a century later, in 1560, should have lost over a third of Europe to the wave of reform need not surprise us. If church reform could not be achieved from the inside, it had to go outside.

It is customary to denigrate the morals of the clergy in the late Middle Ages. There had, after all, been criticism before, in the twelfth and thirteenth centuries, not to mention criticism thereafter. One famous earlier satire (*The Council of Remiremont*), features a group of nuns debating the relative sexual prowess of a layman and a priest. On a more elevated level, but no less telling, the ethic of courtly love had glorified the adultery of the noble woman, and praised her in terms bordering on the blasphemous. If this sub- or anti-Christian comment was a defiant reaction to church power, the real decline in the clergy's morals after 1300 simply opened the floodgates.

Some of Balzac's nineteenth century *Droll Stories* are set in this epoch and explore the same sort of subject as contemporary writers. But he hardly upstages writers of the power and subtlety of a Boccaccio in Italy, a Chaucer in England, or a Villon in France (all writing between about 1350 and 1450). Boccaccio's famous *Decameron,* which is typical enough, depicts ecclesiastics, male and female, in all manner of compromising situations. Far more pervasively than ever before, the priest and monk become the universal butt of all jokes. Rather than elaborate on a secular caricature of the clergy, I would like to document the condition of the church in terms of its own sober appraisals.

From a series of orders issued at a provincial synod at Paris in 1429 (from Denys Hay, *Europe in the Fourteenth and Fifteenth Centuries,* General History of Europe Series [New York: Holt, Rinehart and Winston, 1966], pp. 304-5) one may draw the following conclusions about clerical conduct: there was gossip and laughter during church services; failure to turn up for services for which one received a share of the collection; hasty running from one church to another in clerical garments in order to hold several jobs at once; inability to read and/or understand the Epistles, Gospels and the rest of the church service; involvement in such "secular" pastimes as pub-crawling, and commerce in wine and cereals; blasphemy and perjury; extortion and other irregularities in church law courts; and finally, a direct quote: "Concubinage is so common among the clergy that it has given rise to the view that simple fornication is not a mortal sin. No bishop will tolerate any clerk living in concubinage, still less will he allow his connivance to be purchased."

As I say, this is the church talking about itself. No further comment is required.

On the theological and spiritual level during this same time, there was a similar lack of touch with the simple, direct Gospel. A dangerous game of extremes was played between barren intellectualism and a totally rarified, abstruse mysticism. The intellectualism is usually summed up in the word "scholasticism" and generally caricatured as armchair theologians debating minute points of doctrine. But, for one thing, scholasticism was broader than this, and the use of this term in a negative sense is no more fair than the way we ignorantly employ the word "puritan." For another thing, debating minute points of doctrine may not, in itself and in the right context, be at all bad. I do not see much difference between long debates over the substance of angels and long debates nowadays over the details of the Second Coming.

What is important is whether such debates take the place of and smother the fulfillment of Christ's commissions to us. Ultimately, what we mean by the barren intellectualism of the church in the late Middle Ages is the tendency for theological debate to be carried on outside the flow of life and with little regard for men's living souls.

No Other Foundation

As for the mysticism, devotion was turning more and more in upon itself. In the process, it was ceasing to be prayer and becoming mere meditation. Its relation to the work of God in everyday life was being lost in favor of individualist piety. It is not surprising that the anonymous *Cloud of Unknowing* (late fourteenth century) should insist that the mind can tell us nothing about God; that only mystical, inner experience is worthwhile. When we lose touch with God's active work through us in the world around, we naturally lose touch with any firm biblical sense of his objective existence. He quickly becomes our own spirituality and St. John's declaration that he has heard, seen and touched the Word of Life becomes meaningless. Ultimately, the mysticism of which the *Cloud of Unknowing* was an extreme example and which is gaining more and more sway today, covers deep theological scepticism. It is a world removed from the New Testament.

A further aspect of late-medieval spirituality which deserves mention because it was much more common was a morbid preoccupation with death and self-punishment. In this case, a particular circumstance played an important role. In the mid-fourteenth century, Europe was visited for the first time by a major attack of bubonic plague which produced the so-called Black Death that wiped out anywhere from a third to a half of the entire population. It was called "black" because in its advanced stages it produced a severe discoloration of the flesh.

Now, one may plot all sorts of reasons for the decimation by plague—a decimation, by the way, which continued off and on till the late seventeenth century, though never again with such overall ferocity. For example, an economic boom led to relative over-population which led to malnutrition, which exposed masses of people to disease to which otherwise they might not have succumbed. Surely, this is true. At the same time, knowing that God is the Lord of history, I am struck by the coincidence between a church in such open decline and a natural disaster of the magnitude of the Black Death. I cannot help feeling that at some point the pattern of God's judging those cultures to which he has given so much is visible here.

In these circumstances, the preoccupation with death is a morbid, rather than a spiritually healthy, reaction. It is a reaction not of true repentance but of superstition; not of dependence on the mercy of God in Christ's finished work, but on the lacerations of the priests of Baal on Mount Carmel. Contemporary art forms are a grisly study in what was going on in people's hearts and minds at this time.

The dance of death or *danse macabre* dates from this period. Festive processions in the streets were salutes to the powers of evil more than expressions of an eternal hope in Christ. Most vividly, tomb sculpture, a favorite prerogative of the wealthy and well-born, lost its character as a proud glorification of the deceased. Marble corpses are sculpted in which the body is invaded by worms and toads; or the body is depicted as a hideous skeleton; or there is a two-story contrast between the traditional body in repose, hands crossed in pious prayer, and a grinning corpse below.

What is almost stunning to realize is the haunting similarity between this sort of pessimistic devaluation of the body and, on the one hand, the gaunt, terror-struck faces which stare at you in the sculpture of the declining Roman Empire, and, on the other hand, the trapped, insane, screaming figures painted by Munch and Francis Bacon in our very own twentieth century.

To return to the late Middle Ages, a diseased spirituality brought forth a diseased church and an ailing society. But if, in addition and in reaction, society were to depart formally from the church's teaching, would not that deliver the final blow? The answer is yes, but in the circumstances described by Paul in Romans chapter 1, where he observes that God gives over men to the willful enjoyment of their own passions. Only later do they taste the bitter fruits. The process is long. Let us look at its beginnings.

A good test of the church's losing touch with its mission is when its members quite naturally talk more about the things of mammon than the things of God. As the church loses its grip, the outside world becomes more gripping. The stock market, sports results, business concerns, children's education—all these become more substantial to the spiritual mind which is atrophying.

To contemporaries in the late Middle Ages, the things of the world must very often have seemed much more substantial than the things of God. After all, the reign of King Ahab in the Old Testament is, from the point of view of secular history, a great success. But we know what God thought of it. I wonder what God thinks of our age? I wonder what he thought of the epoch which

No Other Foundation

modern man regards proudly as his own cradle, the Renaissance?

Contrary to what is normally said on the subject, societies do have a distinct idea about themselves. In periodizing the past, we may indeed "artificialize" it by quoting dates and naming centuries. But there are, nevertheless, epochs in the past with a distinct character of which contemporaries were aware. The fact that we can discern in the history of art, for example, very clear manifestations of the "spirit of the age" tells us that this is so.

No doubt, most of the people condemned to a marginal existence were not so aware of change as others more privileged. Yet, ultimately, no part of society can remain forever untouched by a major displacement within society. And no major movement in the arts can be separated from a consideration of other aspects of life, economic, social, and political, which underpin it. This is a way of saying that, in the last analysis, there is no such thing as cultural history, economic history, church history, from a narrow point of view. Just as the artist nowadays is as interested in income taxes, elections, and the price of bread, as any one else, so these mundane facts of life impinge upon the history of whole artistic movements.

It is particularly important to bear this fact in mind when considering the Renaissance because it is usually seen in terms of the visual arts and nothing else. "Renaissance" means rebirth—a rebirth of values and a way of life which had been submerged during the medieval period. The values and way of life were those which had flourished in classical Greece and Rome and, but this was less emphasized, had been baptized and confirmed by Christianity. This idea of continuity with the civilization which had preceded the break-up of the Roman world is not a theory of historians; it is explicit in the writings of fifteenth-century thinkers. If these fifteenth-century thinkers were usually Italians, the same ideas would be expressed by other Europeans in the following generations. The Renaissance is first of all an Italian movement because the conditions which gave rise to it had developed more precociously there.

What were these conditions? A pattern of life had developed in, was indeed identified with, the great medieval towns which had mushroomed into prominence with the economic boom from the eleventh and twelfth centuries. This pattern was crucial to the Renaissance later on.

Negatively, it represented a tradition of life alien to the medieval mentality. It was free of the traditional dependencies of the land where a man's identity and social value seemed fixed forever. It denied that what was true yesterday had to be true today. "City air makes you free," ran a German proverb. Anyone capable of making a living and who, by whatever means, had liberated himself from personal, legal obligations outside, was eligible according to the particular rules of the city in question to become a citi-zen.

Positively, city life placed a premium upon personal prowess. If, on the land, time-bound methods of agriculture supported time-bound social hierarchies, in the town there was an accent upon initiative. Men were made and unmade before one's eyes. Life was full of human success and human failure. Even when all the exceptions are counted, even when we admit that the everyday ties between town and countryside were very close, it remains true that the town was an island in a rural sea.

What was the spiritual potential of the new life in the towns? Much good, for a start. If traditional medieval Christianity tended to downplay the body, as if the word "flesh" in the New Testament usually meant literal flesh instead of the unrestrained ego, then one sees in the towns an affirmation that the body is not of itself bad. Extending this farther, there was a strong tendency in the towns to take the things of the spirit into the market place. In addition, the awareness of the significance of individual effort in daily life made townspeople more sensitive to the biblical emphasis upon personal responsibility and more susceptible to the Gospel appeal to individual commitment.

Although a mature theological framework for this would not be forthcoming till Luther in the early sixteenth century, the evolution of informal groups of lay people in the towns for purposes of prayer, worship, and charitable works is impressive. It is worth noting here that if mere lay people were taking upon themselves such spiritual responsibilities, the traditional elitism of the clergy meant somewhat less than it did in the countryside. No townsman needed to think of himself as a second-rate person, and so there was not the same room for a spiritual pecking order.

The so-called rediscovery of individualism in the Renaissance is basically related to all these circumstances. Projected onto the level of intellectual concerns, the hard-hitting, fact-oriented mentality which informed commerce and city government introduced a healthy spirit of criticism. Thinkers would tend to accept statements more on the grounds of their conformity to known facts than because of the word of a venerated, long-dead philosopher. A positive result of this attitude, which came to fruition in the sixteenth century, was a preparedness to question whether every doctrine and practice of the church was biblically authentic.

These were the good things in town life. The bad were simply the other side of the coin. Awareness of personal responsibility could overbalance into self-dependence. "The self-made man" comes into focus. The yardstick of success becomes purely human. In fact, success is relative to the greater or less success of others, which is the foundation for bad-neighborliness. In this mentality, a great gap is opened between the concept of God's grace to needy men and the self-sufficiency of the self-directed, hard-working townsman.

Intellectually, the spirit of criticism becomes an end in itself, dominated by pride in the unaided powers of mind. Used aright, the spirit of criticism is the mind, though not the heart, of systematic reform. Misused, it devolves into total skepticism. Sometimes the two possibilities can be observed side by side, as in the warm-hearted, devout, pioneer educator Vittorino da Feltre, and his vicious, brilliant, but cynical pupil Lorenzo Valla. At its most self-confident, the Renaissance sought to tune the universe. Whereas Augustine had tried to Christianize Plato, and Aquinas had tried to Christianize Aristotle, the Renaissance tried to Christianize both. The result was disastrous; it ended up Platonizing and Aristotelianizing Christianity. The human gives value to the divine, instead of vice versa.

In a vivid way, you can see this in certain paintings of the Virgin from fifteenth century Florence where the model turns out to be the painter's mistress. A critic might say, "Yes, but there are thirteenth century Virgins who are just as sensuous and unholy." To which one must reply that the crucial difference is that whereas, arguably, in the thirteenth century the Virgin gave meaning to one's mistress, in the fifteenth century, one's mistress gave meaning to the Virgin.

At this point, one's misgivings begin to take over. Perhaps the relative independence from ecclesiastical control which the towns achieved was at too high a price. For while it gave access to great freedoms, it also meant that when freedom became license there was no structure of spiritual authority, however oppressive that might be, to check the drift into total unbelief. We have, in fact, broached one of those perennial questions to which good and godly men give opposing answers.

It seems to be a fact of spiritual life that there is no free-flowing Christian community without accompanying risks. For Christian discipline and admonition is conceived in a context of love and, too often, men forget that in Christ love and justice have kissed each other. At all events, as the Renaissance came to its height in Italy around 1500, ideas about life and society had come to the forefront which owed very little to a strictly Christian instinct.

Nowhere is this better exemplified than in political thought. As secular political power began to overshadow the power of the church hierarchy it developed its own rationale, its own "theology." Marsilius of Padua in the fourteenth century, in the title of a famous book, saw the secular ruler, not the pope, as the *Defensor Pacis,* the Defender of the Peace. When we come to Machiavelli, just after 1500, he does not even consider religious authority an issue. Spiritual things have become entirely unreal to him. The state is autonomous, a law unto itself. Like the state of Ahab, it reckons itself beyond the criticism of the prophets.

This is not to say that governmental power need be an enemy to true religion. Many times, in fact, as the history of the Reformation would show, it could be a greater friend than the established church. But when the state ceased to be at all serious about spiritual values, then its structures (as now) would increasingly delimit the life of the population to one of purely secular dimension. The thought and practice of Renaissance Italy would, in this case, anticipate the thought and practice of the entire West in the following centuries. There were to be some prophets, however, before this came to pass and in closing this chapter we should glance at their precursers in the late Middle Ages.

In speaking of the towns I have alluded to a grass-roots spirituality, a spirituality which helped prepare the ground for the Reformation. It would also be a continuing inspiration in the Roman Catholic fold after Rome's rejection of Luther drove a wedge into Christendom.

Perhaps the most famous example of this spirituality is the

No Other Foundation

Brethren of the Common Life in the Netherlands. The Brethren could sometimes lapse into a morbid piety, such as we have already decried. Normally, it is far healthier, more down-to-earth, given to practical deeds of love. The classic devotional to come out of the Brethren is Thomas à Kempis's *Imitation of Christ*. It would be presumptuous of me to note that it still bears thoughtful and prayerful study. Though the Brethren could be, as the young Erasmus found out, somewhat dour, there was a sound connection between love of God and care for one's fellows. If it had a weakness, it was one which it shared with most of the other movements of the time: a lack of doctrinal rethinking. For that, we must look at two remarkable figures, in England and Bohemia, respectively.

In England and Bohemia (part of modern Czechoslovakia), significant popular movements heralded a new age in which secular powers might choose to tolerate and protect religious movements proscribed by the pope. Wycliffe (died 1384), an English priest, attacked papal supremacy, denied transubstantiation, refused to see the Mass as the absolute center of worship and expressed doubts about the legitimacy of the priesthood. He encouraged a translation of the Bible into English, hoping that men would read it for themselves. His followers were such persistent open-air evangelists as to be dubbed "Lollards"—a Dutch-derived word meaning babblers. Though driven underground for most of the time in the fifteenth century, the Lollards provided an English seedbed for the Reformation.

If Wycliffe managed to die in his bed, the Czech Huss was fortunate to win the martyr's crown. The conciliarist Council of Constance showed itself more political than spiritual in its impetus when it broke its word to Huss in 1415 and burned him at the stake as a heretic. But, strikingly, the Hussite movement which owed some of its inspiration to the Lollards and stood for similar convictions, survived the betrayal of its leader. Granted protection by local rulers, it enjoyed a relatively peaceful development till the sixteenth century when it flowed into the great reforming tide.

The varied fortunes of Huss and Wycliffe and their followers foreshadowed the varied fortunes of their great sixteenth century successors. And the ambiguity of the secular response to their convictions prefigured similar ambiguities in the age of Reformation which would play such a role in shaping the religious map of Europe thereafter.

For Further Study

The Cloud of Unknowing. Translated by C. Wolters. Harmondsworth, Eng.: Penguin Books, 1961. An extreme of medieval mysticism but not discontinuous with contemporary spiritual developments.

Hartt, Frederick. *History of Italian Renaissance Art*. Englewood Cliffs, N.J.: Prentice-Hall, 1969. Whether by use of this volume or others, the best way to sense the changes taking place at this time is to *see* them. For example, compare the early illustrations in Hartt with the later ones.

Miskimin, Harry A. *The Economy of Early Renaissance Europe*. New York: Cambridge University Press, 1975. Sounds academic but is a very clear and interesting account of how people got along in times of change.

Pius II, Pope. *Memoirs of a Renaissance Pope: The Commentaries of Pius II, an abridgement*. Translated by Florence A. Gragg. London: Allen & Unwin. This will give you a far better insight into the character of the papacy at this time than technicolor accounts of womanizing, and so on.

The Seraphim Guide to Renaissance Music. A three-record set which effectively, if sketchily, lets you hear the changes in sound between 1300 and 1600.

11

The Reformation: Revival and Reform

WHEN WE THINK about the Reformation, we often forget its dimensions as a great spiritual revival. We identify the Reformation with reform of doctrine.

When we think about revivals—the eighteenth-century ones, for example—we often forget their dimensions as important returns to doctrinal rectitude. We think of them as movements of spiritual power, remote from the world of doctrinal statement.

The reason for this false distinction is our habitual failure to plumb the meaning of Jesus' teaching that the truth can never not be done. When we see that Jesus is the Truth; that Paul says that for him to live is Christ who works good works in the believer—then we can begin to sense the degree to which truth, or doctrine, is right living, and right living is living according to the Truth.

There is no revival without painful reexamination of the Truth, without a preparedness to obey the Truth. And there is no true Reformation unless accompanied by the reviving work of the Spirit of Truth within us. The only reason why the doctrinal element is more obvious in the sixteenth-century Reformation than in other works of spiritual renewal is that a great deal of theological ground had to be reclaimed in 1500. Less doctrinal brush had to be cleared in subsequent revivals; the part played by formal doctrinal confessions was thus minimal. But make no mistake: whatever doctrinal misconceptions or exaggerations there may have been in the revivals (and the Reformation was not perfect, either) there would have been no working of God's Spirit whose sword is the Word of God if the Word of God had not been honored and obeyed. We forget this at our peril. There are no spiritual shortcuts.

No Other Foundation

As we saw in the last chapter, while the final drift of the Renaissance was towards a non-Christian humanism, it contained elements which were biblically wholesome. One important facet of the Renaissance mind which would be very influential in the Reformation was the urge to open one's eyes and mind to see things clearly as they are. Despite his personal scepticism, Lorenzo Valla (to whom we referred) expressed this urge in his painstaking study of old texts according to the principles of sound scholarship.

Valla was a great pioneer in what we call philology—the study of words to determine their meaning. By asking commonsense questions about a word or a statement in a document, and applying his knowledge of history and language, he could decide whether the document was likely to be genuine. In the same way, to take a simple example, a philologist in the year 2000 might evaluate a document purporting to date from 1945 which included a sentence that presupposed the existence of the United Nations. Knowing that the United Nations did not exist in 1945, his respect for the document's claim would be destroyed. The most famous exposé perpetrated by Valla was his demonstration that the "Donation of Constantine" was a forgery of the eighth century. This document had bolstered papal claims to land in central Italy by purporting to be a contemporary record of Constantine's "donation" of the land in the fourth century.

But Valla's demolition job here is not the best possible example of philology, for it emphasizes too much the negative side of the discipline. Valla himself, though he liked destroying sacred cows, made far more important positive contributions. Utilized by men of faith and good will, like Erasmus, Luther, Colet, and Calvin, philology provided a tool for studying the Bible in a new way. One could get at the heart of the original meaning of a passage and thereby, in some cases, show a contradiction between the practice of the New Testament church and the church of the early sixteenth century. Doctrinal and liturgical accretions could then be exposed for what they were.

If the first utterly outstanding biblical exegete was Calvin, it was the man who died the year that Calvin's *Institutes* were first published, in 1536, who set the pace for the Reformers. Erasmus of Rotterdam was the most prestigious scholar and writer of his day. He was the first best-selling author to come along since the development of modern printing in the mid-fifteenth century, a development which played a notable role in disseminating new ideas during the Reformation. With a vigorous style, pungent wit, and overwhelming erudition, he educated, cajoled, and amused an entire generation.

Yet no work of his was more significant than an apparently innocent publication in 1516 which had taken more of his time in preparation than anything else he ever wrote. It was his version of the New Testament in Greek, printed with the commonly accepted Latin version of the church in parallel columns. This major scholarly labor won the unusual honor of being placed first in the list of prohibited books by the Roman church when its "Index" of forbidden works was introduced some years later.

What was wrong? Quite simply, by displaying for educated perusal the two versions of the New Testament, he was able to demonstrate the errors in the official text. To Erasmus, this was a wholly beneficial aid to knowing better the Gospel. To the church's rather defensive leaders, it was an open invitation to dangerous private interpretation, followed by destructive criticism of doctrine and practice.

Poor Erasmus, faithful to the Roman church to the end despite his acid comments on her refusal to reform herself, told the story of a Catholic doctor in Constance who kept Erasmus's portrait on the wall in the hallway so that he could spit on it as he passed by. And poor Erasmus, who could not see his way to joining his many followers who turned into greater and lesser Reformers, complained that he was sharing the fate of an old classical teacher who was stabbed to death by his pupils' pencils.

What in fact separated Erasmus from the Reformers? What was lacking in the philological antecedents of the Reformation? To be most direct, a truly confident spiritual experience of the Truth was lacking. The intellectual preparation was there but it was weak in spirit.

In the fourteenth and fifteenth centuries there was, in the midst of great spiritual depression, a deep undercurrent of spiritual longing which led to all sorts of local, and frequently non-clerical, movements of piety. The weakness of these movements tended to be lack of intellectual or doctrinal focus. This was an exact contrast, then, to the weakness of the philological movement. The latter lacked spiritual commitment, the former was in need of intellectual formulation. In effect, followers of groups like the Brethren of the Common Life thought that spiritual reform could come without a serious spring-cleaning of theology. They were just as mistaken as Erasmus who thought that theological spring-cleaning would be sufficient to revive the church without deep spiritual struggle.

Oddly enough, Erasmus was trained by the Brethren of the Common Life, so it might seem that he should have been the "Luther" of the Reformation, rather than the Saxon monk. But Erasmus, son of the illegitimate union of a priest, had lost both his parents by his mid-teens and suffered deep emotional wounds. Were it not for the warm influence of Colet and Thomas More in England he might never have got over a spiritually crippling resentment against the Brethren of the Common Life. As it was, he never allowed anyone to penetrate beyond the shield of his dazzling conversation. Keeping his emotions and intellect in watertight compartments, he lacked effective spiritual power and impact. He did not allow his heart to know the earth-shaking consequences of sins forgiven. And he did not let his mind know that his feelings could be released because of the freedom we have in Christ. Perfect love casts out fear.

By the early sixteenth century, then, we have the potential for a great spiritual revival: a serious concern for truth and a serious concern for right conduct. But the two hemispheres have to be brought together till the critical explosion point is reached. Looking at our own day in the best possible light, we might say that a similar situation exists. There are those who press for an authentic spiritual experience and there are those who call for real doctrinal purity in the midst of profound theological betrayal. We must pray for God's grace to raise up more men and women, starting with ourselves, who have reached the critical point of explosion; in whom the passion for biblical truth is married to a passion for Jesus Christ.

Yet, as we look back to the period of the Reformation, we must note that there was one other crucial ingredient over which Christians had little or no control.

Why did the Reformation not take place with Wycliffe and Huss a century earlier? After all, they were both close enough to Luther's insights. Well, in England, the Wycliffites were forced underground by hostile secular and ecclesiastical authorities; in

Bohemia, lack of effective leadership, especially theological, after Huss's martyrdom in 1415, meant that although Hussitism was tolerated it did not develop the implications of Huss's thought for the state of the church as a whole.

The question of God's timing is, of course, a mystery. The first century world was ideal for the coming of Christ and the spread of the Gospel, just as the time will be "full" for Christ's return. But few were ready for the first coming and few will be ready for the second. The same may be said for the situation around 1500. A combination of unlikely circumstances played into the hands of reform to facilitate its survival, spread and consolidation.

We have seen that the spiritual movements of the time were spirituality in need of a theology and that the intellectual movements were theology in search of spiritual power. On the level of politics and society, we see newly mature and developing regional sovereignties in need of a cultural, religious identity. The pope's effective control of the local European churches was severely curtailed, producing a vacuum in the sphere of creative spiritual direction.

Not that anyone was likely to seek spiritual insight from the Renaissance popes. They were better at interior decorating. Ecclesiastical appointments were, to all intents and purposes, made by regional kings and princes who had reduced to a dribble the flow of church taxes to Rome. Why allow the money of one's subjects to support the military and diplomatic postures of a pope who might even be allied against you? No wonder papal income had to be drawn from less and less legitimate sources: 25 percent of it was now coming from the sale of church office! No wonder the pope drove a hard bargain when selling licenses to local ecclesiastics for the sale of indulgences.

Indulgences recalls a further evidence of the regionalization of the church. When the infamous Tetzel sold indulgences in 1517 near the borders of Saxony, thus arousing Luther's ire, he was careful not to set foot over the border. For his license to hawk these credit coupons for Purgatory covered only the territories of the Prince-Bishop of Mainz. Was not the pope the head of the church? Yes, but he could not in practice proceed without local political cooperation. This was a "universal" church politically contained.

If we bear in mind the degree to which the papacy was spiritually discredited, as well as politically shackled, it is not hard to imagine a prince like Luther's Duke of Saxony being prepared emotionally, politically and theologically to challenge papal power by protecting and encouraging a native Saxon church reform. When papal prestige was high in the Middle Ages, when theology was less brittle than it had become by 1500 under the impact of the incipient humanism of the Renaissance, such action was beyond contemplation. In the sixteenth century, it could seem so natural that men caught up in the reform might unjustly criticize their forebears with the exclamation: Why did this not happen before!

There are two other general circumstances that require elaboration, however, in order to understand the success of the Reformation. The first concerns the opposition to Luther's eventual overlord, the Emperor Charles V. Although under the influence of Erasmians early in his reign (he became Emperor in 1519), and never a friend of the papacy, Charles would later seek to stamp out reform because of its partial identification with political opposition within his German lands.

In any case, without external hindrances, it is inconceivable that Charles would not have dealt firmly with Lutheranism. After all, he was the mightiest monarch Europe had seen since Charlemagne in the late eighth century. And his lands far surpassed the Carolingian's. Owing to accidents of birth and inheritance, Charles was the king of Spain; the Emperor of the German lands along with modern-day Austria, Czechoslovakia and Hungary; the Netherlands (Holland and Belgium); the lands along France's eastern flank bordering the Rhine and Switzerland; more and more of Italy and, finally, more and more of the New World in the wake of Pizarro and Cortés.

But this empire was unmanageable and, by its threatening extent, provoked continual opposition from nervous neighbors and from imperial princes who feared the centralizing efforts of Charles. Thus, the very power that must surely crush a reforming effort in Saxony was frustrated by the consequences of its own greatness. The moment of supreme climax came around 1550 when, with the Lutheran princes apparently at his mercy, Charles was suddenly betrayed by the Catholic German princes who were afraid of the general results of an outright imperial victory.

Charles abdicated a few years later, retiring to a monastery—broken in body and spirit.

The second general circumstance that indirectly aided the Reformation was the threat of Turkish power. Historically, the ebb and flow of Turkish power has followed the emergence and disappearance of dynamic leadership. Under Mohammed II the Turks had taken Constantinople in 1453, removing the one last buffer to the West. Under Suleiman the Magnificent, whose reign coincided with Charles V's, the Turks mounted a terrifying offensive by land and sea. And whether they advanced by the Mediterranean or the Danube, the Turks were always faced by lands controlled by Charles V. That is another way of saying that it was always Charles V who had to face the engulfing tide of rampant Moslem power.

Not that other Europeans were not concerned. It is rarely appreciated that Luther's great hymn "A mighty fortress is our God" was penned under the shadow of a Turkish assault upon Vienna. The enemies against whom Luther invokes God's protection are more Moslem than Roman. It is nevertheless true that Luther and the movement he began were protected by the Turks because when Charles was not dealing with European enemies he was trying to stave off disaster to the east.

With all this explained, the intellectual, spiritual and political background, the Reformation is still not accounted for. God chooses specific men to work with, and his particular man to stand in the breach and recall Europe to truly biblical religion was Martin Luther.

Martin Luther (1483-1546): The son of a well-to-do, self-made Saxon mining entrepreneur, Martin was intended for the law. As a young man he already took seriously the unseen spiritual world, even if in an unhealthy way. Caught one day in a terrifying thunderstorm, he vowed to become a monk if his life were spared. He was barely twenty.

To get any sort of accurate picture of Luther we must at once forget the image of a loud-mouthed, beer-swilling "Orson Welles," trotting around in *lederhosen*. He *could* drink beer, which was a bit safer than water; he *could* talk in strong, boisterous accents—witness his table-talk which is available in several trans-

No Other Foundation

lations. These characteristics do not explain, however, a literary production which fills well over a hundred big volumes in the English edition. They do not explain a man who could turn out on average a serious pamphlet every two weeks for the rest of his life when he sprang to fame around 1520.

The fact is that Luther was a man with immense powers of concentration who had learned the secret of godly discipline. He also had a first-rate mind. We can underrate his intellect by comparing him with a Calvin. But the man who could hold his own with Erasmus in a debate on free will was no run-of-the-mill university professor. Only an academic would even dream of discounting Luther's mental powers!

As an Augustinian monk, Luther quickly impressed his superiors with his spiritual devotion. As a professor of theology in the new University of Wittenberg (a cultural showcase beloved of the Duke of Saxony), Luther rapidly proved himself a star. But external success and the respect of the devout were incapable of mastering the spiritual integrity which told Luther that his "righteousnesses" were as "filthy rags."

He could not accept the well-meaning assurances of confessors that his deep-rooted sense of guilt was purely emotional or the product of a warped sensitivity. He was sent to Rome but the change of air and theological climate made things worse. Fresh from doing all the good things pilgrims were expected to do in the Eternal City, he was more despairing than ever. After all, if Rome could not eradicate his guilt, where could he find help?

It was here that the vital training in studying the Bible without blinkers, which he had learned from Erasmus, came to his aid. Appointed to lecture on the *Epistle to the Romans,* he found himself grappling with what at first seemed a mere textual, exegetical problem. Its resolution would revolutionize his life and his world.

Luther's confrontation with Paul's words in Romans, chapter one, verse seventeen, reminds me of Nicodemus in John, chapter three, puzzling intellectually over Jesus' replies and then later, no doubt, receiving Spirit-given understanding. Romans 1:17 was used by God's Spirit to reveal to Luther his real dilemma and real salvation. These are the external facts with which most people are familiar. If we wish to comprehend the internal process that went to making this verse so crucial we must take a step backward into Luther's thought-world.

"For in it [that is, the Gospel] the righteousness of God is revealed through faith for faith; as it is written, 'He who through faith is righteous shall live.' " Righteousness implies a standard and a standard implies justice. It was Luther's assumptions about justice which made it hard to understand Romans 1:17.

Less than a century before, the Netherlands painter Roger Van Der Weyden had produced a great work called *The Last Judgment*. A detail of this, showing Michael the Archangel weighing souls, is a vivid illustration of the medieval view of justice under which Luther was laboring. Like modern figures of a blindfolded "Justice" atop court buildings, Michael is remote from the scales he holds, in whose pans one soul is weighed down, his sins too heavy, another soul elevated, his credits sufficient. In medieval theology, justice had become a question of the scale of merits outweighing the scale of demerits. The "merit" of Christ was there as a foundation but, rather like a matching grant, one had to merit it by one's own conduct.

Luther's personal problem begins to come into focus here. For by any normal standards he had a very good spiritual record and his confessor was there to prove it. But an unusually acute spiritual sensitivity, allied to a dogged but keen intellectual faculty, would not allow him to accept either that he was pure of heart or that the accepted theory of righteousness was correct.

Faced with Romans 1:17, the essentially punitive nature of the medieval view of divine justice was exposed as false. What staggered Luther was that Paul should identify God's righteousness with good news (the gospel). He had been taught to identify righteousness with a severe judge. How could a standard of infinite perfection be anything but a nightmare? Yet Paul goes on to explain that dependence upon, faith in, God is equivalent to righteousness and therefore gives life.

What an astounding revelation! As Luther wrestled with the concept he saw indeed that faith is righteousness for the simple and profound reason that it means a trust in acts that God has performed which are, by definition, righteous. God's acts were to judge our sin in the person of his Son, who thereby bore the just or righteous penalty; and, since his Son was without sin, to restore him whole by the resurrection to his heavenly estate. He thereby promises to those who participate by trusting acceptance in his death the matching purity, or righteousness, of the risen Christ. Neither the death is ours, nor the righteousness. To put it crudely, by cornering sin Jesus also cornered righteousness. We cannot say that "he became sin for us" without adding that he also became our righteousness (2 Corinthians 5:21).

As God's Spirit opened Luther's eyes to these truths (because he did admit his blindness unlike the Pharisees and many a contemporary of Luther who claimed to see well enough) he realized that since God had judged his sins in Christ he no longer had a judge but a heavenly Father. The full beauty of being an adopted son of God dawned on him. Without fear of unknown reprisal he could now joyfully and determinedly bend his energies to doing his Father's will. He could now tell the world that the gospel is the message not of condemnation but of life: "For God sent the Son into the world, not to condemn the world, but that the world might be saved through him" (John 3:17).

Just as the finest evidence of Christ's resurrection is the impact upon his disciples, so the finest evidence of Luther's rebirth is the floodtide of activity into which he now felt capable of entering. Imagine the depth of his outrage at the indulgence racket which betrayed the gospel, denying the common people a knowledge of the truth. It was like confronting men selling spiritual thalidomides just after you have discovered they cause destruction.

The challenge of his ninety-five theses of 1517 fits in here. To circulate statements as a basis for debate (which is what the theses were) was, incidentally an accepted academic custom of the time. Soon after come his famous tracts written for a wider and wider audience—the *Address to the Nobility of the German Nation,* for example. Then his translation of the Bible into German, a version which has a similar place in German culture to that of the King James' version in the English-speaking world. Then a stream of commentaries and his voluminous correspondence.

We can also understand now the source of the immense courage whereby he could stand in the physical presence of Charles V, the greatest German princes, and hostile theologians, and affirm in the face of Charles's call to recant: "Here I stand. I can do no other." Did he utter these words? It cannot be proved. That he did stand is beyond question.

The response to his stand astonished him. Had not Huss been burned for less? But God had work for him. Forestalling any repetition of Huss's betrayal, the Duke of Saxony kidnapped him and spirited him away into the Wartburg Castle where he spent a dizzy year translating the New Testament and responding to letters from everywhere. Erasmus, above all, sang his praises. Only when the reality of a break with Rome became apparent did Erasmus draw back, fearful that reform was a fragile vessel that could not survive conflict and division. Erasmus was not entirely wrong. Yet his failure to appreciate the issues is apparent from his cool counting of the odds; the reformers were more intent on following the plow, not looking back.

The response which must have warmed Luther most, however, was the response of a whole generation of men and women waiting for the man of God's choosing, at the moment of God's choosing, to publish once more the good tidings of "release to the captives, recovering of sight to the blind, liberty for those who are oppressed."

Not that all was "roses, roses" for Luther thereafter. The fuller our apprehension of the grace of God, the more acute our awareness of the ungracefulness of men. Luther was forced to make choices, public choices, for which he was neither trained nor fitted. His acquiescence in the bloody repression of the Peasants' Rebellion in the mid-1520s is a sad chapter, reflecting oddly upon that "liberty for the oppressed" promised in the gospel. Yet, even here, the picture is extremely complex and most historians would agree that any black and white judgment is out of place. Luther died a disappointed man. Not disappointed in his Savior; disappointed in men—disappointed in himself. "Enter not into judgment with thy servant; for no man living is righteous before thee" (Psalm 143:2).

Luther's career and impact raise the fascinating and serious question of the role of the individual in history. Are great men important? Are individuals crucial? Or would the Reformation have taken place with or without Luther? On one level this last question may easily be answered by saying: "No, because it happened the way it happened, and you cannot remove even an insignificant link in the chain without breaking the continuity of cause and effect."

No Other Foundation

Granted this fact, we may still reflect intelligently upon Luther's place. Just as the Reformation would not have been what it was without the interrelated themes of intellectual, spiritual, and political preparation, equally it could not have happened without Luther. The fact is, that God is a person who works with persons to revive persons. The great moments in biblical and church history are marked by great men and great women of faith.

We can most usefully ask what made these people usable. Their preparedness to be what God wanted them to be, despite the opinions of believers and unbelievers alike; to be fools for Christ's sake. To endure as seeing a city which is invisible. To believe that God's power is unchanged and unchanging. How often do we read with approval and awe the life of a Hudson Taylor or John Wesley or Las Casas, while yet nurturing that pathetic reflex which draws our feet back from the path of faith and kicks at those who walk it? Nothing ventured, nothing gained. "If God is for us, who is against us?"

For Further Study

Atkinson, James. *Martin Luther and the Birth of Protestantism.* Baltimore: Penguin Books, 1968. With good use of Luther's works, this is an excellent "theological" biography.

Erasmus. *Christian Humanism and the Reformation: Selected Writings of Erasmus.* Edited and translated by John C. Olin. New York: Fordham University Press, 1965. Gives you a feel for the man and his thought.

Harbison, E. Harris. *The Christian Scholar in the Age of the Reformation.* Philadelphia: Porcupine Press, 1978. The best, clear guide to the intellectual underpinnings of Reformation.

Manifestations of Discontent in Germany on the Eve of the Reformation: A Collection of Documents. Edited and translated by G. Strauss. Bloomington, IN: Indiana University Press, 1971. Gets down to the grass-roots social, economic and political grievances which accompanied the religious ones.

12

Catholics, Protestants, and Skeptics

Then Pharisees and scribes came to Jesus from Jerusalem and said, "Why do your disciples transgress the tradition of the elders? For they do not wash their hands when they eat." He answered them, "And why do you transgress the commandment of God for the sake of your tradition? For God commanded, 'Honor your father and your mother,' and 'He who speaks evil of father or mother, let him surely die.' But you say, 'If anyone tells his father or his mother, "What you would have gained from me is given to God," he need not honor his father.' So, for the sake of your tradition, you have made void the word of God. You hypocrites!" (Matthew 15:1-7).

O NE OF THE WAYS we make void the word of God is by automatically identifying ourselves with God as judge, over against what or who is being judged. In this passage we may comfortably identify ourselves with Christ against the Pharisees and scribes, till the Spirit reveals to us our own inner hypocrisies. We can do the same thing historically, as we judge the past.

Applied to the separation of Christendom into Catholics and Protestants in the sixteenth century, we can easily see the Catholics as Pharisees, intent upon outward observance, while inwardly being wolves. But we need to remind ourselves that all were sinners and, if saved, then saved by grace, "lest any man should boast." We do not sin as Catholics, or Protestants, or sceptics. We sin as men and women before a God who is no respecter of persons or party labels.

142

No Other Foundation

It is important to be clear that Luther had no intention of starting a new church. Like any devout member of Christendom, he desired that all should taste the freedom of the Gospel as he had and that the Body of Christ be united in a life of active worship. This is a thoroughly biblical aspiration which we can stress too little because of the mockery of twentieth century ecumenism.

Even when Luther had been censured by the Emperor after the Diet of Worms (1521), where he made his famous stand, and even after he had been duly excommunicated by the pope, he still had no idea that in thirty years Europe would be deeply divided into two major religious camps. After all, men had been censured and excommunicated before. It had happened a century earlier to John Huss. At worst, he might be executed and the movement of reform he had set under foot would have only local influence like Hussitism in Bohemia and Lollardy in England.

As it happened, the political situation hampering Charles V, the independent stance of European princes toward the church, and the natural appeal Luther's doctrine had in intellectual and spiritual terms, all guaranteed a future to Lutheranism, pope or no pope. Indeed, this being the case, it is important to search for factors in Catholicism itself to explain the unique split which would gradually come in Christendom. Otherwise, it is hard to understand why *more* of Europe didn't become "reformed." Most of the factors contributing to Luther's success existed elsewhere. After all, reform in the past had never been a German or north European prerogative. And there were genuine spiritual stirrings in those parts of the church which ultimately remained faithful to Rome.

In the late fifteenth and early sixteenth century we find in Italy, for example, many groups springing up, dedicated to prayer and acts of charity. The most famous, perhaps, was the Roman "Oratory of Divine Love," which stressed personal obedience to God's will and service to others. Lay people were in the vanguard of these groups and it was they, interestingly enough, who gave the first and strongest stimulus to several official orders of reforming, pastoral priests who sprang up in the first half of the sixteenth century, the Theatines and Barnabites, for instance. In a similar context, the Capuchin Franciscans in the 1520s managed to revive something of the spirit of Francis of Assisi's original intentions.

Catholics, Protestants, and Skeptics

Certainly, among the people, lay and clerical, who sought a closer walk with God, were a number who embraced Lutheran ideas and, in process of time, had to choose between obedience to papal dictate, discretion, or exile. The Italian community at Geneva, numbering some very substantial families and impressive individuals, was a product of such choices. Even in high church circles in Italy, a Cardinal Contarini could plead openly on the highest levels for a modified version of the doctrine of justification by faith. In 1537 he headed up a papally appointed commission to recommend reforms which came to the conclusion that the abuses under which the church labored derived from the secularization of the pope's spiritual office.

Unfortunately, as this finding suggests, the commission managed to skirt the issue of basic doctrinal and ecclesiological distortion in Roman Catholicism. It stressed a purely "spiritual" adjustment and, as we saw in the last chapter, such was not enough because structural dogmatic questions would always prevent a truly biblical reformation. One is reminded a little of Jeremiah's anguish at the reforms of Josiah which went so far but not far enough.

Nevertheless, the vigor of charitable works, in the best sense, in southern European Catholicism was very imposing. No one better exemplifies this vigor than Carlo Borromeo, Archbishop of Milan in the late sixteenth century. He was a model pastoral bishop: tireless, selfless, uncompromising with the secular authorities, insistent on clerical discipline, given to much prayer and more and more ascetic in his private life as he grew older. The best testimony to his life is the fear among high church officials that he might become pope and force them to live likewise!

The chief thing I find suspect in Catholic spirituality, then and now, is also perhaps the secret of its appeal to many men and women of genuine stature: it is the paradox of unswerving devotion to the organization (in Borromeo, as in his younger contemporary Francis de Sales, this meant harsh treatment of Protestants or suspected heretics), combined with an insistently individual, personalized, verging on mystical, spiritual life. There is lacking the community sense, which one finds in Paul's epistles and in those bodies of believers at any time who have tasted the full meaning of the oneness in Christ of those freely open to his Spirit. To some degree one can see that the intense individualism of the personal devotion is an inevitable reaction to the stern loyalty to an organization whose machinations are spiritually unsavory. It is a case of letting the Holy Spirit rule in one's closet but not in one's "boardroom."

Yet, then as now, one does well to emulate the charitable concerns of the Catholic which lead his spirituality into the mainstream of the Gospel. However ascetic or extreme one may sometimes adjudge individual Catholics to be, their record of consistent care (for example, in Biafra or the Congo or Vietnam) frequently puts Protestants to shame. And over one half of the Rumanian Catholic bishops chose jail and torture to compromise in the 1950s, as Wurmbrand has testified.

Thus, to get back to the sixteenth century and to the question with which we began this section, one reason for the splitting of Christendom was a strong, buoyant, spiritual minority which made *some* headway in official circles, such that it could not see its way to leaving a church that it felt would reform itself in time. There was, furthermore, no political leader in Italy or Spain who might conceivably foster radical protest. Charles V, and his son Philip II more so, were wedded to traditional medieval orthodoxy when it came to the push. They ruled Spain from 1516 to 1598 and, thanks to Spanish success in Italy, they were the major power there for most of the same period. They had no love for the popes but, as established rulers in an age of civil conflict, they wanted nothing to do with the religious version of political heterodoxy. None of the circumstances is entirely novel.

The reluctance to desert a church that one feels is still receptive to reform is a common theme in twentieth-century denominational history. To speak of but one of these denominations, the Roman Catholic church, there are fascinating parallels between the circumstances it faces now and those faced by the church in the early sixteenth century. Now, as in 1500, the authority of Rome has come into question. A certain lack of nerve has allowed ideas and practices to mushroom which were formerly well contained. These are, on the one side, a selling out to humanism (Renaissance humanism in 1500; theological liberalism and neo-orthodoxy now) and, on the other side, a proliferation of predominantly lay groups seeking a deeper spiritual life (the groups we have described in Italy; nowadays, "charismatically" oriented fellowship meetings and Bible studies).

Out of these lay groups there have been spinoffs into Protestantism but, as in sixteenth century Italy, most have stayed within the orbit of Rome, hoping and praying for a reform which will, in effect, bring the church as a whole the refreshment they themselves enjoy. What happened in the late sixteenth century was a severe tightening of the hierarchical reins which dissolved the freedom that had originally allowed the groups an independent evolution. Whether this is the future of the Roman Catholic church in the late twentieth century remains to be seen. For now, however, we must pay some attention to the organizational crackdown in the Reformation era.

The management of the church has to be seen as a further important cause of the split in Christendom. Negatively, the church's devolution into bureaucracy symbolized, encouraged and put into practice those abuses which left Europe bereft of spiritual leadership for so long. Positively, the sheer decadence of the church was the inducement for a permanent reform in those parts of Europe where the various conditions were favorable.

The particular organization of the church to which I am referring in these paragraphs, however, was more a reorganization to meet the challenge of the day. As the reform movement spread in the 1530s, as even faithful old England under the unusual circumstances of Henry VIII's succession problem broke away from papal rule, men still obedient to Rome were nearly beside themselves in frustration with the pope's refusal to act positively, by calling a council.

Pope Paul III (1534-49) was, personally, far too concerned with enriching his own Farnese family to lead an effective, sincere reform. Apart from Paul's own corruption, the papacy's diffidence is easily understood. Recalling the papacy's past experience of reform by council for which men had begun to clamor once more (including Luther and Erasmus), and appreciating that the more corrupt the pope is the less likely he would be to survive intact the proceedings of a council, then one begins to see what a tight spot the popes felt themselves to be in. Not to call a council was to risk seeing Europe drift inexorably away into the Protestant camp. Yet to call a council might result in a radical reduction in papal powers.

But something had to give and by waiting desperately late (1545, in fact), the pope was able to buy terms which would guarantee a council subservient to his wishes. The Council of Trent, as it is called, which convened off and on from 1545 to 1563, met at Trento in northern Italy—friendly soil. The voting by head rather than by national body favored the huge Italian delegation. The pope won the right to fix the agenda: doctrinal clarification first and only then specific talk of reform.

The success of Trent in restoring coherence to Catholicism—which it is from now on proper to call Roman Catholicism—made permanent the existing split in Christendom. Not that Trent marked acquiescence in the great losses to the reform. Indeed, it provided guidelines for a major offensive to win back Protestant Europe. It helped define the areas of future operation for the new order which would epitomize what is often called the "Counter-Reformation"—the Jesuits. It emphasized a vast educational program in which the Jesuits would play a crucial role. And if implicit in Protestantism, as in conciliarism before, was a tendency towards constitutionalism, explicit in Roman Catholicism was an absolutism which joined hands in the Counter-Reform with secular absolute monarchs to uproot religious and political heresy wherever it could be found. A revived Inquisition in Rome; the Index of Prohibited Books—these also were pressed into service.

It is not often realized how much of modern Catholicism, as we know it, springs from no farther back than Trent. Paradoxically, in view of what I said about the isolationist spirituality of the Catholic saint, Trent gave the impetus to that hallmark of modern Catholicism: an almost ritualistic attendance at weekly Mass and confession. The church must be seen to exist.

There is not space to discuss the developing "heresy" of Protestantism in any detail. There is, after all, no lack of good, readable accounts. Luther's ideas spread quickly because they answered a genuine need in the right way. As with many crucial events in history, circumstances anticipated what was coming to pass.

Printing, for example, was not an accidental shot in the dark in the mid-fifteenth century. It represented an ingenious and logical response to a need. The same was true for the teachings of Luther and the other reformers. It is, for instance, an old question whether Zwingli in Zurich arrived at Luther's articulation of the doctrine of justification by faith through Luther's influence or entirely alone. There is evidence both ways, and he himself claimed not to have been influenced while acknowledging the encouragement that the news of Luther's stand and writings gave him. Probably, this is how it was. Zwingli had stumbled to the same conclusions, and yet one wonders whether things would have evolved as they did at Zurich without the example of events in Luther's Saxony.

In Zurich, the town council gave its official backing to reform in 1523. It is worth pausing to see what this meant because it will tell us how "protestantization" took place. Usually, as in Zurich, it entailed the abolition of the Mass and therefore the abolition of the priesthood as formerly understood. In other words, under the conviction that in Christ the great sacrifice for sin is completed and that there is, therefore, no question of the Lord's Supper being a fresh sacrifice attended by an Old Testament-style priesthood, reformation always involved clearing away doctrine and liturgy which denied this. Positively, it was accompanied by regular and systematic teaching from the Bible with a carefully planned program of adult and child catechism.

The Reformation penetrated all levels of the population. It cannot be "explained" economically or socially although, as one should expect, the total condition and circumstance of a person will play a unified role in the total surrender of himself to Christ. The despair of the poor as well as the rich man's perception that wealth does not give happiness may equally and properly produce repentance. Long lists of refugees to Geneva from France, which give clues to occupation and social condition, reveal a fair cross section of society. If the impact of the Reformation was especially strong and well organized in towns (matching, therefore, the particular coherence and dynamism of town life), it is not true to say that it could not reach the conservative rural peasant. The Swiss mountain cantons remained generally loyal to Rome, but the mountainous Cevennes in southern France turned strongly Protestant, as did parts of mountainous Savoy, bordering on Lake Geneva.

This being said, it is yet obvious that the towns being route centers they should play a rather special role. The Gospel of our justification by faith in Christ's work first came to Geneva through enthusiastic south German merchants. Tyndale's con-

No Other Foundation

traband English Bibles were smuggled into England from the Netherlands in bales of merchants' goods. It is natural, therefore, to find new ideas entrenched early in the towns.

But there was, also, an added factor. The "priesthood of all believers" acted like a leaven in the towns because it revived ideas of community which had been steadily dying all through the fifteenth century. In other words, the Gospel which gave a body blow to spiritual elitism and by so doing enlivened the church, also reinvigorated the theory and practice of the town as a shared community by hacking at the roots of social elitism.

The manner in which the reformation was frequently accepted in the towns in fact presaged a return to more "democratic" ways. The urban authorities would arrange for a public debate in the local cathedral between theologians from the two sides, followed by a vote as to the preference of those present. Empowered to introduce the reformation to town life, the council would accordingly take the appropriate steps.

It is in this context that we are able to gain insight into a phenomenon which is frequently misunderstood or exaggerated—the breaking of statues and stained glass in churches. The statues and the ideas expressed in the windows stood for doctrines publicly repudiated—the intercession of the saints, for example. Their public destruction went along, therefore, with the reforming of the town. In cases, we even have evidence of the participation in such destruction of people who had originally paid for the works in question. We may now regret the demolition on aesthetic grounds while yet remembering that art does have a meaning and some of the demolition "crews" took their art a bit more seriously than we do. I say some because it would be silly to deny that there was, in many instances, a greater or less degree of sheer philistine vindictiveness involved.

By the time the Council of Trent was ready to mobilize the Roman church for action, the attrition wrought by Protestantism was enormous. All of Scandinavia gone; much of Germany and modern Czechoslovakia; Scotland; England by default; France, shaky; the Netherlands, shaky; Switzerland, fifty-fifty; nearly 100 percent of the great Imperial Free Cities of Germany, the commercial backbone of the Empire; much of modern Austria; and dangerous cancer spots in Italy, Hungary, and Poland.

Ultimately, Rome would, by sheer force in many cases, win

back Austria and Poland, and gain official victories in Czechoslovakia, Hungary, and France. But she lost much. At the same time, the Protestants lost much. Both camps lost two things, quite apart from territorial considerations: they reacted against each other too far; and they silently gave momentum to a movement of skepticism which fed off the fires of religious conflict. Let us look at both types of loss.

The Catholics lost very serious doctrinal emphases by seeking to avoid the contamination of Protestant "heresy." Justification by faith, for example, was not so heretical an idea as to be carefully circumscribed. Historians who like to downplay the revolutionary nature of the Reformation can easily find medieval expressions of it. As we have seen, of course, to find theological expression of an idea is not the same as to "find" a reformation. There are other things involved in a combination and at a time brooded over by God's Spirit. Justification by faith is, in any case, very close to classic Augustinianism. It was the identification of this idea with a movement which attained independent ecclesiastical status which led the Roman church authorities to play it down so much.

The same goes for the priesthood of all believers. The implicit drift of those lay piety groups, in Italy and elsewhere, was to affect the balance in the church beneficially in favor of the laity by questioning the spiritual uniqueness of the clergy. But after the Council of Trent came a sudden overemphasis on the sacraments as administered by the priests, and upon obligatory attendance at weekly Mass and confession. Ironically, the Mass which should be the heart of fellowship, came to be such a rote affair that an even stronger emphasis was generated upon the individualistic mysticism of the elite few and the good works of the zealous. Indeed, just as Catholicism was identified with monarchy, so (as in the monarchical state) welfare tended to be less a congregational matter than the concern of a few.

In another notable way Rome reacted to the Reformation and all its works—in this case, its art works. There was a grand extravaganza in painting and sculpture, emphasizing all those ideas and symbols rejected by the reformers. If, in the hands of great artists, the glorification of saints and the insistence upon depicting stories deriving from the Apocryphal books (rejected as uncanonical in the Reformation) produced art of a high order, in the hands of lesser men a sickly sentimentality took over. In comparing a Saint Sebastian, pierced by arrows, from the Renaissance and from the seventeenth century, one is struck first by the loss of vigorous realism and second by the loss of taste.

At the same time, in its endeavor to go on record as the only authentically Christian church in Christendom, the Roman Catholic church raised the single greatest ecclesiastical edifice since the Gothic cathedrals—St. Peter's in Rome. No "puritan" inhibition was allowed to stand in the way of making Rome the greatest church capital, if not the capital of the church.

Referring back to the monarchical impulse within Catholicism, Protestantism, by contrast, stood much more for a constitutional position. In terms of church practice, good works were seen far more as a congregational responsibility. But, when in good order the congregation handed over authority for implementing its corporate responsibility to a board of deacons, it could very quickly wash its hands of the business. Here, the Protestant church tended to mirror the dilemma of the constitutionalist state whose emergence it encouraged. In other words, we trust the state's welfare system for which we pay taxes to do our good works for us, thus insulating ourselves from the possibility of more active public obedience to the Sermon on the Mount.

Clearly, the answer to elitist monarchy does not lie, *per se,* in a constitution; and the answer to a "monarchical" church order does not lie, *per se,* in some form of congregationalism. These answers are structurally beneficial but they still must rely on active personal and corporate obedience to the Word of God. If one general problem for Protestantism was a tendency to suppose that having cleared the Augean stables theologically all was well for ever and ever, there were also specific difficulties.

For example, Protestants overreacted towards the issue of the confessional. Whereas we cannot accept the shortsighted view of some modern Protestants that the Reformation made a great mistake in eliminating a regulated confessional, we can see that there was a culpable tendency in Reformation churches to make nothing whatever of the New Testament injunction that we "confess our sins one to another."

Again, and this hits hard at most Reformed churches, the evidence from the New Testament and from the history of the early church is overwhelming as regards a regular observance of the

Lord's Supper on a weekly basis. Yet, in overreaction to the false doctrinal use of the Mass by the Catholics, Reformed Protestantism limited its observance to four times a year, or, at most, once a month.

Calvin, in fact, who also showed a keen understanding of Scripture over the practice of confession, was strongly against such a crippling reaction. He warned his fellow pastors and the Geneva Council to judge acceptable practice by the Bible, not by a species of ecclesiastical expediency. One must wonder at suggestions for changes in the church which are either clearly contrary to New Testament practice or else quite peripheral: Why don't critics take a look at something which is obviously debilitating to the church, such as infrequent celebration of the Lord's Supper?

One might also say a word, in terms of Protestant self-criticism, about the relative lack of a missionary impulse. Sometimes, one can read too much into this. The fact that colonization overseas was predominantly in the hands of nations loyal to Rome meant that there would tend to be a greater activity overseas of Catholic rather than Protestant missionaries. When, in the context of the great missionary movement of the nineteenth century, one sees a preponderance of Protestant missions it is only fair to note that by this time it was Protestant nations which were most active overseas. It may, however, also be true that other factors were at play in the missions history of early Protestantism.

For one thing, much effort was devoted to consolidation of the movement of reformation—Europe itself was something of a mission field. For another, against the onslaught of a revived Catholicism from the late sixteenth century, Protestants were sometimes fighting a hard defensive action. It may also be possible that the individualistic, somewhat heroic, piety that mainline Protestants criticized on the Catholic side, and the seemingly rootless piety that they criticized to their "Anabaptist" left, was a more fertile soil for mission effort. Until, that is, the self-conscious quest for stability, that was sadly followed in the seventeenth century by a lapse into dead orthodoxy, was at last succeeded by Protestantism's very own revival! It would be this revival, this call to first principles, which would most fully establish the necessity of personal spiritual responsibility and spawn an epoch of missionary expansion notable for outstanding individual pioneers.

No Other Foundation

There is one last subject that I must touch in passing. I alluded in the last paragraph to the "Anabaptist" left. In recent years more and more careful and sympathetic study has been devoted to those elements in Protestantism which were not only treated in a gingerly fashion by what I refer to above as "mainline Protestants" but even suffered severe physical persecution from them. It is customary to refer to these elements as "Anabaptist" because they shared a rejection of infant baptism (the title means "rebaptism"), a person of this persuasion undergoing an adult baptism despite previous infant baptism which was regarded as invalid.

Apart from this conviction held in common, the so-called Anabaptists were actually a highly diversified series of small groups, ranging from the downright crazy to believers of the utmost sobriety. It used to be popular to get as much mileage as possible out of the more technicolor practices of the more technicolor groups. Suffice to say that any release of spiritual, social and intellectual forces as mighty as those of the Reformation epoch is bound to produce peculiar side effects. At the same time, there were certain restraints built in to the major Protestant churches to guard against disorder, precisely because the Reformers were afraid of being branded as fanatics or enemies to all tradition, social as well as religious.

One such restraint is summarized by an adjective often used nowadays for the mainline Protestant churches: "magisterial." This adjective derives from "magistrate" and conveys the fact that these churches, like the Roman church, expected to work closely with secular government. They saw society as a unified whole, expected government to be conducted by Christians in a Christian way, and were not about to hive off into a corner just because social and political amelioration was longer in coming than the preacher expected. Their reaction to splinter groups which proposed to wash their hands of public life because it was not sufficiently regenerate was two-fold: a vigorous theological assault and a refusal to tolerate religiously or civilly what seemed a fundamental threat to all civil and religious order.

I deal with this subject in the context of the Protestant reaction because I think much of the more intemperate and, to say the least, uncivil, conduct towards the Anabaptist groups was fostered by a tendency to lapse into a negative definition of truth.

The truth is what your opponent does not believe. When the opponent was as known and as well understood as official Catholic theology, this outlook, so expressed, comes off as dry humor. When the opponent was a series of propositions alien to the main line of debate, the outlook was dangerously obscurantist.

To be fair, most of the Anabaptist groups died not from persecution but from lack of substance. Born of the moment, they merited no continuing influence. The chief heritage of the Anabaptist experience would be the survival of the most moderate group, the Mennonites, and the intrusion into theological and ecclesiastical vocabulary of ideas and practices which would surface again in the seventeenth century—this time for a more permanent stay. At their best, the Anabaptist groups were like the Mennonites at their best: orthodox by any reasonable standard and, while refusing to work through other agencies, exemplary in their active concern for the world round about.

While skepticism was stimulated by the prospect of Christendom religiously torn asunder, it was not produced by it. It was the natural result of Renaissance humanism reaching its logical, atheistic conclusion. When you have attained your goals and still have not arrived, what gives? In terms of classical perfection of form, the visual arts (to take the most obvious example) had matched the highest achievements of Greek and Roman art by the early sixteenth century. Thereafter, a self-questioning sets in, already heralded in the experiments of the early Mannerist painters around 1500. Not only in art, but in politics and manners, one had supposedly reached the end of the rainbow and—it wasn't there.

Two very great figures express the dilemma. Michelangelo hoped to find his peace in the exaltation of soul over matter. His famous "unfinished" statues, symbolizing the soul imprisoned in matter, portray his failure. Leonardo da Vinci, for his part, trusted to reason and the senses but gradually came to a full stop before the evident impossibility of a finite mind's grasping and controlling a seemingly infinite world. The very last man of the Renaissance, the arch-skeptic Montaigne, summed up the state of the quest towards the end of the sixteenth century in a famous answer to Pontius Pilate's question of long ago: "Truth is opinion nailed to the cross of custom."

No Other Foundation

When we remember that Pilate was confronted by the one who is the Truth when he asked "What is truth?" we realize both the responsibility of men for their decisions and the Christian's responsibility to be, by the Spirit, the embodiment of the Truth to his neighbor.

All in all, the profound spiritual revolution of the sixteenth century must be regarded as having considerably delayed the onset of paganism in the West. At the same time, there was unbalanced teaching and unbalanced living which did feed the fires of skepticism. Just as the thinkers of the Enlightenment would later discredit all religion by pitting one form of it against another, so the doubters of the sixteenth century would try to discredit Christianity by pitting one denomination against another.

I do not here enter a plea against denominationalism in itself; it springs up when the form of society allows it. Rather like the kingship in Israel, it is not ideal but, under certain conditions, God is still able to work with it.

Denominations must be appraised in terms of relative hindrance to the indiyidual's and congregations' knowledge of, and obedience towards, God. At their worst, denominations may reflect the human tendency to major on minors; to strain away a gnat and swallow a camel, as Jesus caustically put it. At their best, they challenge any universalism based on the particular ideas and practices of any one group. In so far as Protestantism stressed the binding and ruling authority of the Word of God, in so far as it continued to be judged by that Word, it expressed that challenge in the only acceptable way. When it ceased to be judged by the Word it naturally diluted that challenge into a mere principle of negative criticism—what some in our own day have described as "the Protestant principle." As if the critics who called the early Reformers "protesters" were right—that they had no vital biblically based beliefs of their own but were simply demonstrating against corruption.

Let it be said in conclusion, that when the Body of Christ is most healthy it can most afford to break down denominational barriers. Contrariwise, when it is least healthy, those barriers serve an incidental purpose in preventing an epidemic. How can one tell when the removal of barriers is a sign of health or the onset of contagion? When the church feeds on "the sincere milk of the Word," it is healthy. When it does not, it is not.

For Further Study

Dickens, A. G. *The Counter Reformation.* New York: Harcourt, Brace
& World, 1969. Very helpful though overly self-conscious attempt by
a Protestant scholar to get to the heart of Catholic spirituality in the
sixteenth century. Beautifully illustrated.

Great Debates of the Reformation. Edited with commentaries by Donald
J. Ziegler. New York: Random House, 1969. Very convenient as-
sembling of the crucial Reformation debates, starting with Luther's.
Not only "Catholic" versus "Protestant" but also the disagreements
among the latter.

Montaigne, Michel de. *The Autobiography of Michel de Montaigne:
Comprising the Life of the Wisest Man of His Times.* . . . Selected,
arranged, edited, prefaced, and mostly translated anew from his essays by Marvin Lowenthal. Boston and New York: Houghton Mifflin
Co., 1935. This is out of print but either in a library edition or by
consulting an edition of Montaigne's *Essays* you can gain a good
impression of late-Renaissance scepticism. The tone is similar to Lucretius's whose essay on the universe was mentioned at the end of
chapter 3.

Williams, George H. *The Radical Reformation.* Philadelphia: Westminster Press, 1962. A huge book but the most authoritative analysis and
description of the radical "Anabaptist" wing of the Reformation.

13

Religion and Society: The Puritan Problem

N O ONE WILL DENY that if Christian faith is real, it will affect society. If, as Jesus said, the truth is something that we do when his mind is in us, then visible changes in conduct are not options but inevitabilities. And if a large number of people in society—even if still a minority—seek to live Christ, then we can expect to see important changes in society at large.

This, however, is where a problem arises, and it is not a uniquely Christian problem. If provisions are made for moral and spiritual discipline among Christians, in the Christian church, then what if all society is deemed Christian? May one exercise, in good faith, the same discipline for everybody, with the reasonable aspiration to protect and preserve society from decadence? That is to say, may one make spiritual rectitude a civil affair? Or, better still, may one so define "civil" that it is synonymous with "religious"?

This is not, as I say, just a Christian problem. Americans, especially, with a constitutionally guaranteed separation of church and state, but also the whole Western world in general, regard any confusion of function or idea as dangerous, if not neanderthal. Yet, in upholding this emphasis, Western society is flying in the face of the entire weight of Western history before the eighteenth century and the entire weight of experience in all other cultures in the world.

In other words, it is the rule rather than the exception for societies to insist openly, if not on certain religious observances, then at least on certain very clearly specified ethical ones. And I am not here talking about matters dealt with by the law, such as murder, robbery or assault, but rather about the things which are more insidiously destructive and yet not actionable—for example, malicious gossip, breaking one's word, or being systematically unpleasant to family and neighbors.

The reason why past societies have been deeply concerned about these extralegal offences is that they have been seen, quite correctly, as barometers of a general mentality upon which the law itself is founded. That is to say, a legal system is based upon popular habits of mind and if these habits change the law will change. And if one deems the law good, if for instance, the popular habits of mind reflect religious convictions which undergird the law, one will take great care to nurture those habits of mind which are its sole, eventual underpinning. Not to do so is to allow what is good to evaporate by default, much as failure to discipline a child is to allow positive potential to be dissipated.

In our own day, we see the erosion of the law with regard to pornography, abortion, parent's rights over their own children, and marital privacy. In all these areas the ground was prepared by the rapid evolution of popular conduct and conviction towards sexual laxness, loss of respect for authority, loss of respect for man because no longer seen as God's creation, and rejection of the insistence that the family unit is more basic than the social unit. Thus, ironically, in a society dedicated to a separation of church and state where, nevertheless, humanistic concepts are fed to our children in the public schools with inadequate channels for counter-response, one finds in the largest American city, New York, that parents try desperately to get their children into parochial schools!

Society is not able, therefore, to operate according to its own rules. Or perhaps we should say that, rather naively, the Founding Fathers were so sure that the values of their day would forever subsist or even get better that, in the name of toleration, they set up barriers which now inhibit the formal access of the essentially religious source of these values into the public process. Thereby, in effect, the way is opened for the triumph of utterly contrary values.

Short of popular agitation and pressure upon elected officials, there is no recourse in this situation. Other societies were better equipped, for they never for one second assumed it either wise or possible to separate the so-called secular, governmental realm from the ethical or religious one. Thus, in ancient Rome, through the powerful office of the Censor, one had a way of dealing with types of behavior which could not be dealt with by law. If a rich sadist went through Rome punching people in the nose, while his servant handed over to each bleeding victim the cash penalty specified by law, the Censor could intervene to enforce an exemplary punishment.

When, for various reasons, the values on which the Roman republic was founded were diluted, the Censorship became much more lax, turning a blind eye to conduct previously not tolerated. Similarly, nowadays, with the change in values in the West, a degree of exposure of the body that would have been punished as a form of suggestive exhibitionism in the past is now commonplace on our living-room television screens, not to mention elsewhere.

When we turn to the Bible, specifically, we find that this general subject is dealt with very fully in the context of the fact that man is God's creation and owes obeisance to him. Outside of man's own regulations, which echo, however distantly, the fact that we live in a moral universe, there is a cosmic justice of God partially enacted during our lives but mostly to be completed in the hereafter.

In the theocratic society of Israel—and by theocratic I mean what the Bible means: not ruled by priests but rather recognizing God actively as the creator, sustainer and leader of society—in this society, laws were given and enforced which reflected God's desire to guide Israel into right paths. But what happens when the law of God, through the New Covenant, is extended to all men, most of whom are not living in states which are submitted to Jehovah?

The first point to make is that in the New Covenant the Spirit is given to each believer, the law being now inscribed not in stone but on the heart. The disobedience of the believer is taken care of by the principle of mutual discipline which is defined as an aspect of mutual love. The second point is that Jesus and the authors of the epistles (Paul and Peter, notably) distinguish between what is due to Caesar and what is due to God but insist that paying our dues to Caesar is an aspect of our obedience to God.

So far, so good. But what if the state becomes officially Christian? Is it then a theocracy and do the laws given to theocratic

No Other Foundation

Israel obtain for "theocratic" Geneva? I think the secret to this perennial question is in recognizing clearly that the Old Covenant, with its privileges and penalties, was given to a physically identifiable people which became, by birth, in each succeeding generation, a party to that covenant. Even if it was not in the heart of an individual Jew to obey the covenant, he could yet legitimately be held to it because in any case, willy-nilly, he enjoyed its privileges through living in a promised land, through being, indeed, a people at all by God's mercy to Abraham.

By contrast, the New Covenant is given to individuals of whatever nation. They do not enter into it by blood birth but by spiritual birth. The rules of the Christian life are only for those who are thus reborn and they are "enforced" not by outside pressure but by a basic inner response which is the work of the indwelling Holy Spirit who has written the law on their hearts. Provisions are set up whereby the congregation of believers may exercise the mutual discipline in the context of mutual love, to which I have already referred. And if a person is obdurate then, as James would emphasize for us in his epistle, we have to assume that, most likely, the law is not written on that person's heart. And such a person must be separated from the assembly in order that the cause of Christ be not brought into disrepute.

However, this is the extent of the discipline, although one would agree that, in spiritual terms, it is decisive and awesome because it implies that the individual is not a child of God. It does not extend to "legal" reprisal or retribution. Indeed, what could be the point of any discipline beyond excommunication for a person who does not share in the New Covenant? In the Old Covenant, discipline was relevant even for the obdurate because, through birth, he stood within the Covenant, enjoying its privileges. In the New Covenant this is not the case.

There is yet a further problem to consider, however. Or, rather, a key area in which we have to apply all this. Assuming that the *civil* consensus is Christian, that a majority of the people and the leaders of the people are Christian, thus meaning that Christ is the head of most people, are non-Christians to be judged and disciplined by those Christ-like values which are presumably basic to the law? I think the answer has to be that if a person opts to live within such a Christian state, partaking of its benefits (like the stranger living with the Old Covenant Jew), he must either accept retribution for such offences as murder, injurious dishonesty, assault, and the like, or become an exile and join a society more to his liking.

As for which offences are to be written into the law, and in what way, some distinction would need to be made between discipline proper to the believing church member and discipline proper to the population as a whole. In other words, a citizen is not answerable for those basic values which undergird the law if he does not believe in the God whose character they express. He is responsible—and otherwise he can pitch his tent elsewhere—for the written law which, in broad, societal terms, depends on those values. Meanwhile, the church would not expect types of retribution to be meted out by the state which go beyond the spirit of Christ's teaching. For example, the woman caught in adultery would, under the old law, have merited death but Jesus forgave her and commanded her to sin no more. The same would go, presumably, for offences like blasphemy or fornication.

No society ever stands still, of course. When John Milton and John Locke wrote against the detailed application in law of values accepted by Christians they assumed that it would be a confession of weakness to proscribe, let us say, a book expressing non-Christian views. Surely, they supposed, truth will always defeat error in the marketplace?

Truth will, of course, defeat error but not always in the marketplace. Societies always have and always will run down. As they do so, shifts will take place in the values people accept and, as a result, the form of the law will change. In this situation, a tension is bound to develop between the living embodiments of Christian values and those who reject these values. The Christian has a perfect right to argue for laws which reflect Christ's teaching because he knows that they are far better than other laws.

At the same time, if and when his representation within the society has shrunk to that of a minority group, he must expect that the values of the majority will slowly begin to color the law of the land. That he himself when he was in the majority made a distinction in practice between the values, exclusive to believers, which undergird law, and the law itself, should allow for a natural though sorry transition to a different legal atmosphere accompanying a different "value atmosphere" and should, hopefully, allow him to benefit from a similar distinction by the upholders of the new values.

All of these seemingly abstruse issues are most relevant not

No Other Foundation

only to the epoch of the Reformation to which we shall soon turn but to our own day. For example, we are all perfectly familiar with the idea of voluntary exile on behalf of convictions and involuntary exile decreed by a state against dissidents. No state will tolerate everybody. John Locke would not extend toleration to Roman Catholics and atheists, the former because their prior commitment was to a foreign potentate, the pope, and the latter because, owning no supernatural sanction for their actions, their word could presumably not be trusted.

We have seen the United States draw a line at Communists as far as potential immigrants are concerned, on the same arguments advanced by Locke against Catholics. The United States itself is the greatest living monument to groups who have voluntarily or involuntarily become exiles for reasons of conscience. We complain about the Soviet Union refusing exit visas to Jews or anybody else, for that matter, while forcibly exiling special cases like Solzhenitsyn.

One could multiply the examples. Basic to most people's feelings on these matters is the dual conviction that individuals are personally responsible for their own beliefs and actions and that the state, representing the ideas and wishes of most of the population, in theory, has a responsibility to safeguard those ideas and wishes up to the point of exiling serious dissidents. If the dissidence has resulted in personal harm then, of course, sanctions have to be exacted on the spot: for murder, robbery, fraud, and so on.

Christians in the West are now in a considerable minority and in most places have seen the law changing to accommodate humanistic values. Capital punishment, abortion on demand, these are but two clear areas where drastic shifts have occurred, shifts which, to the Christian mind, well illustrate the basic egocentrism of humanism which, by taking life lightly, will sentimentally preserve the murderer's life and callously commit a million fetuses to the hospital incinerators.

In this situation, the Christian must exercise his right and responsibility to campaign for laws which, through drawing on God's law, will best preserve the fabric of society. Meanwhile, for all that the law of the land may separate church and state, may exact a formal standard of conduct by law on all citizens leaving other areas grey, the Christian is called to apply only *one* standard for business, politics and the like: that of Christ. "Whatever

your task, work heartily, as serving the Lord and not men . . .''
(Col. 3:23).

All of the foregoing may seem a needlessly long discussion of a
side issue. I hope, however, that on reflection you will see that it
has a direct bearing on the Christian's position in the world today
and that, as you continue to read, you will see that it lays an
essential foundation for comprehending the dynamic experiments
in Christian living which took place in the sixteenth and
seventeenth centuries. It should also allow us to be sympathetic
to different conclusions drawn at that time, because we have
forced ourselves to face the same knotty issues. In fact, only now
are we really in a position to look intelligently at the Puritans and
at Calvin whose ideas were a major influence upon them.

There are many interesting things one could say about this
French lawyer, intellectual and theologian from Noyon in
Picardy. Born in 1509, Calvin was still a boy when Luther had to
take his stand. He grew up in the atmosphere of theological dispute. He never knew an undivided Christendom even though he
would take far more seriously than most theologians on either
side of the divide the hope of restoring church unity.

A precocious devotee of the classics and the whole world of
humanistic scholarship, he had the nerve before his twenty-third
birthday to take on Erasmus in his very first published work, a
commentary on the Stoic Seneca's *De Clementia (On Clemency)*
which disagreed with Erasmus's standard edition in various ways.

Quietly converted to a living faith while studying in Paris,
shortly after, this man of iron resolve and exemplary rectitude
suffered the consequences of politic exile in Strasbourg and
Geneva. It was in Geneva—a city he never really gave his heart
to; he preferred Strasbourg—in 1536, en route elsewhere, that he
let himself be persuaded by the fiery and forceful older reformer,
Farel, to settle down and take charge of a systematic reformation
of manners and church life in the newly reformed town. Why
should Farel have vested such responsibility in a mere twenty-
seven year old? Because he was the author of the recently published book which, more than any other work of the Reformation
era, provided Protestant Europe with a clear statement of its
biblical convictions: *The Institutes of the Christian Religion*
(1536). The edition we now read is the much expanded last edition

of 1559 but the first edition was impressive enough.

Calvin's vigor, resourcefulness, clarity and lack of compromise were too much for the city fathers of Geneva, however, and in 1538 he left when the preconditions for fulfilling his commission were denied him. He only returned (and reluctantly, because he was in Strasbourg with his friend and mentor Bucer) when, in 1541, Geneva granted him his preconditions in the face of the need for a firm, directing hand in church affairs.

What were they? Simply put, they were the freedom to catechize the population and exercise proper spiritual discipline. These preconditions strongly reflect the best insights of Renaissance humanism as they intersect with New Testament Christianity. They represent the wedding of theory and practice, knowledge and experience. How can a person live aright if he has not been taught aright? And if he has been taught aright should not his life match the Gospel teachings? Catechism provided for systematic Christian education in Geneva; spiritual discipline made certain that those who profess the truth should not live hypocritically.

Now Calvin's program must be related to the historical context. The establishment of the Reformation at Geneva had been a civic act, an open, majority decision by the citizenry. In proposing a program of wholesale catechism and discipline, therefore, Calvin was not being overbearing; he was pursuing the logic of the town's decision. Furthermore, it was proper for the council in 1538 to block Calvin and in 1541 to assist him because, as elected magistrates, they had this right. Indeed, it is worth noting that at no time was Calvin more than the first pastor of Geneva. This was an immensely influential position, of course, but the council of Geneva contained powerful, intelligent and headstrong men, too, and the degree to which Calvin was able to mold their actions was only the degree to which by word and deed he was able to impress them as a voice to be heeded.

In following out his program, Calvin displayed great practical genius. Incidentally, too, he showed that he could learn from others, for the imprint of practices in Strasbourg associated with Bucer is quite definite in the arrangements set up at Geneva. Because the town's acceptance of the Reformation was an official act, Calvin had every justification for assuming that the values to be inculcated and protected in Geneva were radically biblical.

Religion and Society

While honoring the functional distinction between the office of magistrate and that of pastor, Calvin sought to establish spiritual institutions which would honor the idea of the town's being a unified whole. Thus, the lay eldership in the churches provided a direct link between civic leadership and church leadership because the sort of able men who became elders were precisely the sort of men who led the town's public life—whether in business, the professions, or politics. At the same time, an agency of communal moral discipline dealing with such issues as blasphemy, drunkenness, adultery, fornication, malicious gossip, and domestic discord was led by the elders and pastors together, the elders being in the majority.

An agency of this type was by no means unique in Reformation Europe and the name of the Geneva one (Consistory) was a carry-over from prereformed days, when the bishop had likewise (more in theory than practice) sought to direct moral conduct. What distinguished sixteenth century consistories from their prereformed antecedents was that they meant business. What distinguished Geneva's Consistory from others was that it had the power of excommuniction; elsewhere, this power was exercised by the civil government.

In other words, Calvin was insisting that it was as elders rather than as magistrates, along with the pastors, that the members of the Consistory should make such a spiritual decision as to exclude someone from the sacrament. This is not separation of church and state; it is preservation of the integrity of the church. If civil government wishes to present itself as Christian, then it should defer to a church agency rather than a civil one to decide what is Christian. Otherwise, the name "Christian" may be dragged into disrepute.

Meanwhile, true to the twofold balance in Calvin's program, a generation of Genevan youth was being educated according to a rigorous catechism devised by him in the 1540s. If it was not till the mid-1550s that Calvin's dominance in Geneva was fairly established, one factor in that dominance was that former catechumens had reached the age of responsibility in public life.

The influence of Calvin's church order for Geneva was felt far and wide. He hoped to purify Geneva, to make it what, indeed, the admiring John Knox and many Englishmen judged it to be: "The finest school of Christ on earth since the Apostles." The distinctive outlines of Calvin's program may be discerned not only wherever presbyterian church government prevails but even in such nonpresbyterian churches as the Anglican church, some of whose members had weathered out the Marian persecution of English Protestants, in the 1550s, at Geneva.

Not all who were influenced by Calvin necessarily followed him in everything, however. If we can admire the wisdom with which he brought church and state together in creative unity while yet preserving the church's integrity, we can also question the assumption that underlay the imposition of penalties for blasphemy or for the retention of Catholic practices.

To be fair, the Consistory (like the Inquisition) did not punish. It remonstrated, sought repentance in the wayward, and otherwise passed over to the jurisdiction of the civil government any whose persistently offensive public behavior merited sterner measures. This was the case with the well-known but not typical burning of the heretic Servetus in 1553 who had escaped the Catholic Inquisition and ill-advisedly came to Geneva to stir up trouble. The assumption we may discern behind certain of the Consistory's judgments was some sort of direct parallel between the theocracy of Old Testament Israel and that of New Testament Geneva. The objections to such a parallel we have summarized earlier in this chapter.

In Calvin's defence one might point out two things. Firstly, the parallel as such was not new. It had characterized much medieval thinking on the subject. Furthermore, it was a mirror image of a similar parallel pressed in current civic humanism between former classical Greek and Roman ideals and the conduct appropriate to a city like Florence or Venice. Indeed, it has been suggested that some at least of the attraction of Geneva to former humanists was that Calvin was seeking to put into practice there, in a Christian framework, what had never quite got beyond the utopian drawing-board stage in the Renaissance.

Secondly, by throwing the onus of specific punishment, as opposed to stern remonstrance, upon the government, Calvin was allowing that important space between what the church holds advisable and what the state does. If the values of Genevan society evolved away from those upheld by the church, the failure of the government to heed the Consistory's advice would quite naturally, in time, produce changes in church and state such as to match the new frame of reference. This is, more or less, what happened. Councillors, then elders, then pastors, became less and less insistent upon those things which were life and death to Calvin and his contemporaries. But this evolution did not mature till the eighteenth century. It was preceded by the inevitable phase of hypocrisy where the old standards were selectively imposed upon one's enemies or social inferiors.

Nevertheless, this was in the future as far as Calvin's day is concerned. Most of the time under Calvin (died 1564) and his successor Theodore Beza (died 1605), genuine zeal and honesty won out over hypocrisy and cynicism. We may quote a shrewd Venetian ambassador of 1561 who reported:

Your Serenity will hardly believe the influence and the power which the principal minister of Geneva, by name Calvin, a Frenchman and a native of Picardy, possesses in this kingdom. He is a man of extraordinary authority who by his mode of life, his doctrines and his writings rises superior to all the rest.

A modern historian of Geneva has observed that without the discipline Calvin brought "Geneva could not have managed her unique achievement as a sixteenth-century revolutionary commune that maintained her independence until the French Revolution. Without Calvin, Geneva would have been nothing more than an economically decaying Alpine town that revolted against the House of Savoy. . . . With Calvin, Geneva has earned her share of attention in world history" (E. William Monter, *Calvin's Geneva* [New York: Robert E. Krieger Pub. Co., 1967], pp. 236-7).

But I mentioned Knox before, who tried to establish a sort of "national" Geneva in Scotland, and I should like to look in more detail at Calvin's influence in Europe. For, not only ecclesiastically, but also politically and socially, Calvin's Geneva had a great impact. As a famous historian once pointed out, in its insistence on a quasi-republican form of church order and in its stress that no political or social distinctions could have any meaning at the Lord's Table, Geneva played an important role in the development of representative democracy. Authority there must be, but participation, too, Calvin taught. His own personal stance backed up his teaching: never permitting willful flouting of his legitimate authority and yet, for example, refusing money for better clothes from the council till the poorest Genevans should be clad as well.

No Other Foundation

Calvinism was easily the most dynamic force in Protestantism after 1550. While Lutheranism settled down in Germany and Scandinavia, Calvinism forged ahead in Hungary, France, the Netherlands, Scotland and, in special circumstances, England. Although Queen Elizabeth was anything but an orthodox Calvinist, the pope nevertheless excommunicated her as such, testifying to an identification in his mind between the rejection of Rome and the teachings of Geneva.

Europe in the late sixteenth century was a scene of almost cataclysmic strife. If the first half of the century saw great international conflict, between France, Spain, the Empire, the Turks, and assorted allies, the second half saw deadly civil struggles. These struggles are commonly referred to as "the religious wars," but most modern historians agree that they were more than that. If genuine religious difference gave a special dynamic and direction to them in many instances, they were also a vital stage in a continuing battle between centralizing governments and elements in the state which resented the steady assault upon provincial rights. In religious terms Calvinist presbyterianism dovetailed into the provincial, antimonarchical fight for a measure of popular control.

Thus, in France, the official opposition to a growing and very powerful Calvinist minority (the Huguenots), fused religious resentment with provincial, noble distrust of royal power. In the context of a succession of weak rulers from the early 1560s, a serious threat was mounted to the king's authority. The best known single episode in this bloody and not always creditable conflict was the Massacre of St. Bartholomew, August 24, 1572. The queen mother, Catherine de'Medici, took advantage of a great princely wedding in Paris, involving one of the leading Huguenots, Henry of Navarre, who was in line for the throne, to initiate an awesome slaughter of the Calvinist leaders who had gathered as guests. Spreading to the provinces, something like seven thousand Huguenots, including a disproportionate number of the most prominent, were liquidated.

Not surprisingly, the Protestant movement in France became distinctly more radical thereafter. Through its pamphleteers, it advanced and refined theories of representative government and governmental accountability which anticipated the more devel-

oped theories of John Locke a century later. At the same time, by
becoming so radical, the Huguenot movement tended to sacrifice
the support of the more traditional social and political elements
who had given it its broad-based support and military muscle in
the past. In 1598, when a peace was arranged, the Huguenots won
two or three generations of toleration till, in 1685, Louis XIV felt
secure enough to abolish their civil rights. The Calvinist
movement which in France was numerically stronger than anywhere else in Europe and probably had a greater leadership tal-
ent, having bid fair at one point to change the complexion of
French religious practice, ended up as the officially designated
"so-called reformed church."

Meanwhile, in the Netherlands, a similar scenario was being
played out but with different results. The people of the Netherlands, under the sovereignty of the King of Spain by an accident
of birth and inheritance, reacted violently to the economic and
political high-handedness of Philip II in the late 1570s. Striving for
the uniformity dear to the hearts of all centralizing bureaucrats,
Philip also set about to wipe out Protestantism by use of the
Inquisition. What was at root a secular quarrel was therefore
given wings by religious fury.

When, by 1609, a truce was declared, the seven northern provinces that had managed to maintain their independence became a
natural asylum for all Protestants in the Spanish-dominated south
(modern Belgium). Because Belgium is strongly Catholic now we
forget that in the late-sixteenth century there were far more Calvinists there than in the northern Netherlands. It was an accident
of conquest that made the area we now call Holland the final
bastion of Netherlands Protestantism. The republican form of
government that developed in Holland was a natural counterpart
to the Calvinist presbyterianism of her churches.

The big difference between the Netherlands' revolt and the
movement in France was that, despite the assassination in 1584 of
the great Protestant leader William of Orange, the moderate leaders managed to retain control, thus preventing a release of exag-
geratedly fanatical or radically political forces. Moderation pre-
vailed and moderation reigned in this republic which, in the
seventeenth century, evinced more ideological and religious tolerance than any other state in Europe.

Holland, of course, is first cousin geographically and religiously to England. We must now cross the Channel to examine the situation there.

The Reformation came to an England whose soil had been prepared by Wycliffe. Before Henry VIII needed a divorce, the Reformation was already penetrating English society. It was, nevertheless, the political accident of Henry's requiring a divorce (in his search for a male heir) at precisely the time when the pope was unable to grant it, that caused Henry, in good autocratic style, to declare the English church a law unto itself under the king's headship and therefore able, through the offices of the Archbishop of Canterbury, to annul Henry's marriage. This politico-ecclesiastical event provided the same sort of umbrella for effective articulation which Lutheran ideas had enjoyed on the Continent.

It is to be noted that Henry himself never embraced the Reformation. Indeed, he had at one point written a learned refutation of Luther for which a grateful pope had awarded him the title *Fidei Defensor* (Defender of the Faith) which title, by a choice irony, has continued to be employed by the formally Protestant monarchy of Great Britain and may be seen on the coinage to this day!

Because England never underwent a truly radical upset, save for the reversion to Catholicism under Mary Tudor in the 1550s, the evolution of English doctrine and church practice was more calm and measured than elsewhere. In a sense, what happened in England is what might have happened all over Europe, if the Reformation could have been received along the lines optimistically envisioned by Erasmus.

When Elizabeth, the daughter of Henry VIII's second wife, Anne Boleyn, came to the throne in 1558, after the terrors of Mary Tudor, religious refugees flooded back from exile abroad. Having "wintered" in such spas as Geneva, they returned full of enthusiasm for a rather less casual reformation of church and society than England had so far enjoyed. It was in the context of Elizabeth's deliberate conservatism, deliberate compromise, aimed at binding up wounds and keeping the ship-of-state together, that Puritanism as a conscious force was born. As a famous historian of the Puritans has put it: "Elizabeth, to their dismay, did not reform the Church but only swept the rubbish behind the door. The Puritan movement may be said to have sprung out of the shock of that disappointment.'' (William Haller, *The Rise of Puritanism* [Philadelphia: University of Pennsylvania Press, 1957], p. 8)

As elsewhere, however, the Calvinist, Puritan, presence in England was political as well as religious. If Puritans longed for what they felt to be a more biblical, a purer (hence "puritan") type of church, they soon were quite naturally identified with political elements disgruntled over the monarchy's attempt to establish a firmer foundation for itself, at the possible expense of Parliament. Thus, Puritanism became synonymous not only with a purified church but also a purified politics and society.

Some idea of the spunk of the Puritans is vividly conveyed by a short extract from a sermon preached by one Edward Dering before the Queen in 1570. Having criticized the impurity of the church and the lack of firm direction from the Crown, he addressed himself personally to Elizabeth:

And yet you in the meane while that all these whordoms are Committed, you at whose hands God will require it, you sit still and are carelesse and let men doe as they list. . . . I tell you this before God . . . : amend these horrible abuses and the Lord is on your right hand, you shall not be removed for ever. Let these thinges alone, and God is a righteous God, hee will one day call you to your reckoning.'' (quoted in Haller, p. 13)

Some idea of the patient tolerance of which the fiery Elizabeth was capable is conveyed by the fact that Dering was merely forbidden to preach for the rest of his life—a sentence which she allowed to drop two years later.

Forty years after Elizabeth's death (1603), a unique opportunity was given to the Puritans to experiment in the uproar of the English civil wars, the beheading of the king in 1649, and the ensuing Commonwealth epoch. But after spearheading a generally approved constitutional limitation of royal powers, they began to outstrip general opinion. Radical elements produced all sorts of radical programs. The "Diggers," for example, asserted universal property rights and began to dig up a hillside in Surrey. The Fifth Monarchy Men, for their part, expected the Second Coming in 1660. But only the licentious Charles II came back in 1660, and the real achievement of political Puritanism would come in 1688 when moderates of many stripes would join forces to effect the abdication of the Catholic James II and establish the

No Other Foundation

principle of limited monarchy and responsible government.

Before closing this chapter, let us look briefly at Puritanism in the New World. The singular characteristic of the founders of Massachusetts is an almost hair-splitting concern with technicality joined to an almost unexampled courage and power of decision. They were congregationalists who disbelieved in the efficacy of bishops but believed in the importance of "state accreditation" on the basis of Romans 13:1. They could not remain in England with a good conscience, because the only church accepted by the state had bishops; yet they could not set themselves up independently without forfeiting a sense of due order and obedience. They cut the Gordian Knot by setting up as a trading company (the Massachusetts Bay Company) and emigrating to America.

As an official company with a royal charter to make a settlement overseas under the titular religious authority of the Bishop of London, they could satisfy their consciences on the score of subjection to the powers that be. Separated by three thousand miles of water, they could meanwhile enjoy virtual immunity from either Crown or episcopal interference in ecclesiastical matters. In effect, they set up in 1630 their own Geneva, their own "light set upon a hill which cannot be hid," confident that they would show the world what a godly commonwealth is really like.

Although critics have often harped upon their failures, what is most immediately impressive is their success. The extraordinary leadership of an absolutely extraordinary man certainly helped. John Winthrop was a sort of layman's Calvin. His authority sprang from inspired commonsense, an indomitable will and great personal integrity. But I have no space to discuss the Bay colony in detail. Rather, I wish to look at it in the light of the problem which we are trying to confront in this chapter: the church in society.

The Massachusetts Puritans were striving for a Christian society and therefore the crucial social membership rite was not baptism as in the Middle Ages, nor possessions, as in the secular city, but a "credible profession of Christ," credible because of a worthy life such as should befit anyone who would partake of the Lord's Supper. Civil and religious life met at the communion rail.

So far, so good. But what if one's sons and daughters who have not had to leave Haran are behavioral heretics? Or one's grand-children? Civil leadership depended upon communicant status in the church and communicants were, of course, baptized persons. But one did not expect to baptize the child of noncommunicant parents, of parents, that is, whose life did not appear to fulfill the covenant made on their behalf at baptism. Within a generation, Massachusetts had to face the inexorable logic of spiritual declension. If more and more sons failed to become full communicant church members, fewer and fewer children would be baptized, yielding yet fewer communicants in the ensuing generation. In a short time, the church and the government would be a tiny island in an ocean of unbelief.

At this point, Massachusetts took a fatal step down the road to the Middle Ages, as it were. By the so-called Halfway Covenant of 1662, it was decreed that the children of baptized but noncommunicating men could be baptized. Thereby was guaranteed an at least vestigial investment in the church for the generations to come. And who could know, perhaps the grandchildren would be better than the children? But thereby, also, were sown the seeds of formalism, of "generational" belief, of mere churchianity. In effect, family name became the qualification for baptism.

This is, in a sense, the natural dilemma of all churches, of all groups of believers, of all families of believers. It is very particularly the dilemma of believers who are so serious about social purity as to limit social leadership to themselves. When the condition of purity becomes a mouthed formula, when the condition of purity ceases to be a direct and manifest experience of the living Christ, hypocrisy is unavoidable. All families, all groups, all churches which have crept into this hypocrisy have spiritually died. If there is any empirical rule about Christian families in the church, it has to be that thrusting the sons of elders and deacons into the same offices without regard for the normative New Testament standards is folly. And this is not always because of declension; it may be a simple question of aptitude. Consider the sons of Eli, and Samuel. Consider Ham. Consider Absalom.

The only antidote for the winding down of the church has been the one Jonathan Edwards sought to apply in the second century of New England's history: a genuine return to dependence on the grace of God, by which alone we shall want to and be able to obey his commands. We must, like Paul, forget what lies behind and

174

No Other Foundation

strain forward to what lies ahead, toward the goal for the prize of the upward call of God in Christ Jesus (Phil. 3:13-14).

For Further Study

Haller, William. *The Rise of Puritanism*. Philadelphia: University of Pennsylvania Press, 1957. Classic study, documented from sermons and much else. Delight to read.

Mattingly, Garrett. *The Armada*. New York: Houghton Mifflin Co., 1959. Using one focal event the author draws together the strands of international politico-religious conflict in the late-sixteenth century.

Moeller, Bernd. *Imperial Cities and the Reformation*. Translated by H.C.E. Midelfort and M. U. Edwards, Jr. Philadelphia: Fortress Press, 1972. Brilliant studies which penetrate to the ideas behind local circumstances and enable us to see Geneva, for example, in its own setting.

Wendel, Francois. *Calvin: The Origins and Development of His Religious Thought. Translated by P. Mairet. New York: Harper & Row*, 1963. Self-explanatory. But go on to read, or at least sample, Calvin's *Institutes* or his excellent Biblical commentaries in which his gift of commonsense is so marked.

Winthrop's Journal, History of New England: 1630-1649, 2 Vols. Edited by James K. Hosmer. New York: Barnes and Noble, 1959. No better way to appreciate the calibre of the Puritans, their confidence, and the real-life problems facing them.

14

Orthodoxy, Pietism, and Latitudinarianism

THE SEVENTEENTH CENTURY is not an easy century to discuss in terms of church history. But perhaps this should remind us that, in fact, all ages are complex and that the labels "Reformation" or "Great Awakening" which simplify our task in the sixteenth and eighteenth centuries actually do the disservice of making us oversimplify matters.

Be that as it may, there is no one convenient theme which we can follow for the seventeenth century. As in our own day, against a backdrop of cataclysmic events—war, famine and disease—men oscillated between unbelief, disbelief and overbelief. A mere remnant, it seems, preserved a balance between God and Caesar, repentance and guilt, joy and euphoria, doctrine and life. The one area which would run exceptional to this analysis is England and her Massachusetts dependency where, for reasons discussed in the last chapter, there was a period of extreme creativity.

Let us look, first, at the external circumstances which confronted people in the seventeenth century.

This century has been the focus of great dispute among historians. Until fairly recently it could also be said to be understudied, compared to the periods preceding and succeeding it. Certainly, it is far harder to find assured textbook treatments of this epoch than for any century since the Renaissance. All of this should warn us that a great deal of importance must have been going on if the historians cannot quite put their fingers on it.

Looked at from a great distance, the seventeenth century forms a deep depression in an otherwise continual upward movement from the fifteenth century to the First World War. I hasten to add that I am not speaking of the history of the human mind but the history of things like population, prices, and industrial development. All show stagnation in this era, with few exceptions. And then affairs resume their upward way in the eighteenth century. The last stand of the great killer disease, bubonic plague, takes place before 1700. If, in the middle of the century, over 50 percent of the population dies in some areas, from about the 1660s the plague fades out to return only once more to mainland Europe: to Marseilles in the 1720s. But one thing which greatly exacerbated and partly caused these multiple cancers was war.

As we have seen, the second half of the sixteenth century was largely taken up with civil conflicts having strong religious overtones. In the seventeenth century, in the momentous Thirty Years War (1618-1648), many of the strands of earlier international conflicts of the sixteenth century were picked up, woven together with some of the civil issues, and fought to a finish. The classic international rivalry was between France and the Hapsburg family which controlled Spain and the German Empire. Into this overarching rivalry, which saw France emerge supreme by 1659, were fitted three other struggles.

The first was the defence by the Dutch of the independence from Spain which they had managed to carve out by 1609. While it is true that the northern provinces of the Netherlands could never have fought off Spain without the coincidence of events which hampered Spain's offensive, it is also true that Dutch success was founded on immense courage and tenacity, very able local generalship and an economic stability and prowess which was the envy of Europe. Dutch courage, which carries a negative meaning now only because of England's later war propaganda against the Dutch, is nowhere better illustrated than in the moving inscription on a house in Haarlem built soon after 1600: "To the dear Netherlands. I shall be true. I shall not waver" (cited in Johan H. Huizinga, *Dutch Civilization in the Seventeenth Century,* ed. Pieter Geyl and F. W. Hugenholtz, trans. A. Pomerans [New York: Frederick Ungar, 1969], p. 105 and n.). Dutch commercial success is briefly conveyed by the simple statistic that about 75 percent of all shipping in the Channel and the North Sea in the period of the Thirty Years War was operated from the northern Netherlands. When I add that this particular shipping lane was the most lucrative in Europe, the statistic takes on extra meaning.

The second was the bloodily contested independence of the German princes, especially Protestant, over against Imperial sovereignty. In the mid-1550s a truce had been declared in the political and religious struggle in Germany which would have been satisfactory if times had been stable. In brief, it stipulated that within any one principality of Germany the state religion should be that of the ruler. An important qualification of this was the added provision that as of the magic date 1552 no further depletions could be allowed of Roman Catholic church territories. This qualification expressed the real fear that a political desire to obtain the lucrative lands of the church might tempt rulers to "reform." Such a movement could seriously upset a delicate internal balance between Catholic and Protestant forces in the Empire.

I say "Protestant" forces: actually, one problem about the truce was that it narrowly defined Protestantism as Lutheran at just the time when the most dynamic force within the Reformation was Calvinism. In the next half-century more than one prominent ruler would embrace the Calvinist version of the Reformation and thus, by the letter of the truce, disqualify himself from benefiting from the religious choice allowed. The Elector of Brandenburg, the nucleus of the future Prussian state, was one such. Because, in fact, the times were not stable, the viability of the truce became less and less apparent as 1600 approached.

Both the Catholic and the Protestant standpoint may be appreciated. No new Protestant ruler relished the thought of the Catholic church retaining its lands within his own state because they amounted to a sort of fifth column. Accordingly, Protestant rulers broke the truce flagrantly. On the other side, one could hardly expect the Catholic church (and, in sympathy with them, Catholic rulers) to take kindly to the loss of valuable lands and revenues just because a local ruler had a religious change of mind. Needless to say, the only way to deal with the impasse was by the more and more open use of force. It was only a matter of time before a circumstance would develop to ignite the powder keg. That time came in 1618. The circumstance I shall have to leave to your curiosity to find out. The overall result by 1648 was to give virtually unqualified sovereignty to each unit in the Empire.

No Other Foundation

The third struggle saw the emergence of Lutheran Sweden, under Gustavus Adolphus, as "Mistress of the Baltic." The seventeenth century is not only the golden age of the Dutch but of the Swedes, too. Sweden's prominence is related to a line of very able rulers, chief of whom was Gustavus, and several circumstances from which she was able to profit. These were a monopoly of copper supplies, essential for armaments in an age of war; a good supply of ship-building materials to export all over Europe; and the protection of the Baltic Sea against enemies who would dearly have liked to limit Sweden's participation in German affairs by bringing war to her own doorstep.

One might also add that the need of embattled Protestant princes for an ally, plus France's desire to pay Swedish armies to fight her Hapsburg enemies, induced Sweden to play a role in German affairs which both prevented the Hapsburgs from imposing their will on Germany and gave Sweden a valuable footing on the German shores of the Baltic. A curious footnote is that Gustavus Adolphus, a brilliant general and tactical innovator, became a sort of Protestant hero, and an English country gentleman called Oliver Cromwell imbibed basic rules of the new warfare through avidly reading a paper called "The Swedish Intelligencer" which provided the latest news of the great conflict on the Continent.

Mention of English concern can remind us that although the purely religious aspect of the Continental struggles can be exaggerated, it is nevertheless true that if the Hapsburgs had had their way in Germany, not to mention the Netherlands, Protestantism would have been snuffed out there, just as it was snuffed out or driven underground in Czechoslovakia, Austria and Hungary. That the struggles were not entirely religious, however, is vividly illustrated by the fact that if it had not been for the powerful intervention of Roman Catholic France, the Protestant powers would hardly have held out.

While all this was going on, a remarkable revolution was taking place in England which would perhaps not have been able to develop so freely without the protection of the Channel and the absorption of the rest of Europe in its own battles. A virtual constitution was forced on a king in the early 1640s; the same king was beheaded in 1649 because, unwilling to accept a permanent limitation on his powers, he stood in the way of any possible restoration of order; a republic followed, degenerating into a sort of oligarchy, giving place finally to the restoration of the monarchy in the person of the son of the late beheaded king.

The original constitutional revolution was not, however, lost. In 1688, in the face of a determined effort by James II, a self-confessed Roman Catholic, to re-Catholicize England and establish a thoroughly absolutist monarchy, the same moderate elements which had brought change in the early 1640s guaranteed its legal permanence thereafter. The abdication of James was forced by the invitation of the Dutch leader, William of Orange, to England. A king established by legal act is under the law. Thus was born the "limited monarchy" which would be the envy of European liberals in the eighteenth century. Yet it is ironical that the stability and assurance which seemed to characterize English affairs thereafter came out of a cauldron of events in the seventeenth century which had caused Europeans to shake their heads at such anarchy, such tampering with "the powers ordained of God."

The mention of William of Orange brings us to Louis XIV and France, however. For if Spain, the greatest power in the sixteenth century, had been the terror of Holland till 1648, the new European leader and the new scourge of the Dutch was France.

The great remaining wars of the seventeenth century were, indeed, occasioned by the ambitions of the "Sun King," Louis XIV. Generally speaking, Louis was expanding France's frontiers at the cost of his neighbors till the late 1680s. From then on, through having stirred up too great a hornet's nest, he was busy defending his aggressions till his death in 1715. It was in the context of this great drama of French containment that Churchill's great ancestor, the Duke of Marlborough, came on to the stage, and England gained a Dutch king.

It was here that English and Continental affairs meshed, because the Dutch badly needed positive English aid and the English, as we have seen, required an alternative to James II (William of Orange was James's son-in-law, actually, hence the legality of his becoming sovereign derived from his wife who reigned jointly with him). It was a tactical mistake of Louis XIV in withdrawing troops from the Netherlands frontier, and the so-called "Protestant wind" which enabled William's fleet to evade the waiting English fleet, penned up in its own harbors, that permitted William's successful invasion. The total commitment of

No Other Foundation

England to Continental affairs thereafter was the major factor in France's containment.

There is one last, but very important matter we must investigate before we may pass on to the history of the church. And this does not involve wars and politics.

The seventeenth century was marked by many revolutions only one of which, the English, was truly successful. These revolutions were related to the expansion of central authority; they reflect a dying attempt by essentially provincial interests to stem the flood of royal power. There was, however, another quieter revolution going on which would have a far greater impact on human life than any civil strife in France, or the Ukraine, or Catalonia. It is sometimes called the Scientific Revolution but its scope was much broader. Its heroes are men like Galileo, Descartes, Kepler, Pascal, Harvey, and Isaac Newton.

To summarize as simply as possible what the revolution was about: it marked on the one hand an application of those Renaissance/Reformation principles of objective enquiry to all aspects of the physical universe; it marked, on the other hand, the birth or rebirth of a humanistic self-confident dependence on the power of the mind to explain everything. After all, if Newton, reaping the harvest of the work of his scientific predecessors, could tell us the simple formulas which held the universe together, perhaps other "Newtons" in other fields of endeavor would soon be able to tell us the formulas behind human society.

Basically, this has been the hope of Western man ever since. The entire history of the church since this epoch has been played out in the context of this hope. In so far as the hope has seemed possible of realization, the relevancy of the church's message has been discounted by the world.

The irony is that the intellectual revolution depended very heavily on fundamental biblical ideas, such as the fact that the Bible assumes a world of order in which mathematical calculations and empirical observations make sense. Without such a backing, how could one be sure that two plus two will always equal four, or that organizing principles might be anticipated in the study of the endless variety of natural things? The greatest living expert on Chinese science has noted that it was precisely the absence of this backing which robbed the Chinese of the possibility of capitalizing upon their own very impressive investigations into the physical world. It is not, however, unprecedented for man to take God's gifts and use them to build a world to his own liking. Life itself is a gift of God. It is for the church to show the meaning of this gift when transformed by the spiritual new life given to us in Christ. What was the church doing about it in the seventeenth century?

The sixteenth century was a period of deep religious and theological upheaval; the seventeenth century, by and large, was one of consolidation. "Confessional Orthodoxy" is how one church historian characterizes the age and, whether in Catholicism or in the major Protestant denominations, one also sees a hardening of the theological arteries. Let us glance at the positive and negative aspects of the church's experience.

To enunciate clearly what is normative for Christian belief is a positive service. On an inspired level, the New Testament epistles perform this sort of function, applying the Gospel of Jesus Christ. But it is also worthwhile to spell out the Gospel in brief, in order to guard against current distortions and the tendency of the Christian to neglect whole areas of biblical concern.

As far as Catholicism is concerned, doctrine was effectively settled by the Council of Trent (1545-63), and no significant restatements were made in the next century. As far as the Protestants are concerned, also, most of the key confessions were formulated before 1600: for example, the Belgic Confession of the Netherlands Calvinists in the 1560s and the Heidelberg Catechism of 1563. The use of the first person singular in the latter makes it peculiarly warm and penetrating. On faith, for instance, we read:

It is not only an assured knowledge whereby I hold as true all that God has revealed to us in his Word, but also a hearty trust, which the Holy Spirit works in me through the Gospel, that not only to others, but also to me, forgiveness of sins, everlasting righteousness and blessedness are freely given by God, of mere grace, only for the sake of the merits of Christ.

Such, in fact, was the number and variety of confessions, that out of Geneva in 1581 came a *Harmony of Confessions* which was an answer to the strongly anti-Calvinist Lutheran "Formula of Concord" of 1580. The Genevan work was more conciliatory than the Lutheran. The best known confession to Presbyterians, a classic of confessions in its own right, was the Westminster Con-

No Other Foundation

fession of 1643-47 along with the Westminster Shorter Catechism with its timeless statement: "The chief end of man is to glorify God and to enjoy him forever." Perhaps the superior quality of the work accomplished at Westminster in the 1640s is a mark of the fact that the Scots were hoping to persuade the English to accept a Presbyterian church order and so were careful to produce as solid and balanced a statement of doctrine as possible. The English were to prove obdurate, however.

Mention of the *Harmony of Confessions* evokes the negative aspects of orthodoxy, to which we shall now turn.

These negative aspects are *both* the ossification of church leadership and life, such that the truth is no longer lived and if not lived then essentially not believed, *and* the harsh repression, even persecution, of even the mildest deviations and variations.

In the context of the Roman Catholic churches, the forced and often brutal re-Catholicization of territories like modern Czechoslovakia and parts of Hungary and Austria leave a black stain. In Czechoslovakia, it was not only a de-Protestantization but also a systematic attempt to Germanize the land, the Czech language being outlawed for all public purposes. In Prague, where in 1600 the English traveller Fynes Moryson saw a Hussite servant conduct his Catholic master to church and then cross the street to worship in his own assembly, the heavy hand of the Jesuits took over in the 1620s.

And within the Catholic church proper, reactions to a growing deadness and coldness were harshly dealt with. In France, especially, the ideas of the Belgian Cornelius Jansen, a modified sort of Augustinian Lutheranism, were viciously proscribed. Even the graves of a famous group of nuns of Jansenist persuasion were desecrated, in the first decade of the eighteenth century, and that by a plow team! It was in France, too, that the most famous example of intolerance took place when, after eight decades of grudging toleration, the Protestant Huguenots were officially declared dead and buried. It is possible that Louis XIV may actually have thought that only a handful of Protestants was left. In any case, in 1685 he revoked the Edict of Nantes which, since 1598, had been the statute of toleration. He thereby unleashed open and savage persecution which led to a major emigration from France of up to a quarter of a million valuable citizens.

On the Protestant side, there were no comparable outbreaks of savage proscription of Catholics. The treatment of Irish Catholics by Cromwell's troops in several special cases was barbaric but the situation was complicated there by the fact of long-standing racial antipathy which continues to be mirrored in the Irish problems of the present day. One is also talking about a military operation, not a peacetime policy. More obvious in Protestantism as befitting, perhaps, a movement divided into multiple theological options, was the ominous hardening of lines against deviation, against the attempt, in some cases, to recover the sense of freedom which we may expect when the Holy Spirit is truly the leader of the church.

This is the epoch of hyper-Calvinism, an exaggeration of Calvin's theology which many people imagine to be the real thing. It was as if theologians forgot that systematic theology depends upon biblical theology, and that biblical theology must be judged by its fruits—if of the Spirit, good; if not, then let us return to first principles and examine ourselves. Too often only the theological textbooks, as it were, were consulted and many an anguished believer, seeking greater reality in the middle of dead orthodoxy, was unlovingly humiliated or cast out and thereby encouraged to bitterness or real heresy.

I think it is in this context that it is proper to speak of Arminianism. For one tendency of hyper-Calvinism, or Calvinistic scholasticism as it is sometimes referred to, was to so rationalize the order of salvation and God's dealings with man as to rob of their meaning such texts as "Have I any pleasure in the death of the wicked, says the Lord God, and not rather that he should turn from his way and live?" (Ezekiel 18:23; cf. 2 Peter 3:9). Cut-and-dried theologizing which tended to reduce man to a cipher found its natural opposite in an equally rationalistic interpretation of Scripture which reduced God to a cipher. The tendency of the theology of Arminius was to rob of their meaning such texts as "No one can come to me unless the Father who sent me draws him" (John 6:44). What is rarely appreciated is that theological hyper-Calvinism and Arminianism cannot be separated from their behavioral correlates; and that Christians ill-advisedly accept party labels which do not really define their knowledge and experience of the Word of God.

Within Reformed Protestantism one celebrated case of extreme insistence upon a too tightly regulated theological confession was

No Other Foundation

the expulsion of many ministers in French Switzerland in the
early eighteenth century. Their crime was a refusal, in good conscience, to swear by a rather extreme doctrine of predestination
spelled out in the Helvetic Confession of 1675 in reaction to rampant Arminianism.

This expulsion took place despite pleas from Reformed
churches elsewhere in Europe. It played into the hands of an age
already tending towards humanistic rationalism which would
exhibit a form of religious toleration based less upon love than
upon simple lack of strong conviction. But it also played into the
hands of the theology of pure experience—Pietism in the worst
sense. It is reminiscent of the hard-line, over-rationalistic reaction to tongues speaking in our own day. When guardians of
orthodoxy declare categorically that certain gifts of the Spirit
were exercised only in the Apostolic age and that their manifestation now must be satanically inspired, they engage in extrabiblical
theorizing. But they also tend to make the subjects of their criticism wary of substantial doctrinal commitment. Both sides lose.

Having just spoken of Pietism in the worst sense, I should note
that the label usually connotes such an emphasis on experience
that doctrine is slighted. Pietism is not necessarily like this but it
tends in that direction. If, for the first generation pietist, the insistence upon a godly life and good works is a beneficial response to
barren repetition of doctrine, for the second generation, lacking
the doctrinal framework which, willy-nilly, its fathers had enjoyed, pietism will become mere experience unchecked by reference to God's Word. That is to say, the biblical norm is the
truth lived and known. The error of dead orthodoxy is to separate
truth from life; the error of pietism is to separate life from truth.
This said, we must now pay attention not to the errors of Pietism
so much as to the positive elements of a movement which, in the
seventeenth century, was still mostly true to the Word.

Within Catholicism, there has always been a pietistic inner
core: the largely subjective approach to the Mass, the confessional and charitable works. And these in the context of an
indulgent priesthood happy to tolerate or encourage such pietism
which is much less obviously dangerous than an emphasis in the
opposite direction. Apart from this constant, however, there were
quite specific movements in the seventeenth century which managed to combine both a deeper spirituality and a questioning of

accepted doctrinal formulations. I shall mention two which are particularly associated with France.

I referred earlier to Cornelius Jansen who represented a strong reaffirmation of Augustinian theology in the Catholic church. Emphasizing certain issues, reminiscent of Luther's use of Augustine, Jansen's theology was frowned upon and ultimately condemned by Rome. Nevertheless, Jansenism, with its insistence on a life of godliness to match true belief, attracted to the ranks some very impressive people. Foremost was one of the greatest Frenchmen who has ever lived: Blaise Pascal. A writer among writers, a scientist of genius in an age which abounded in genius, one of the most acute ethical thinkers who have ever lived, it is no wonder that Voltaire in the next century went out of his way to try to discredit the ideas of this embarrassingly eminent Christian.

Most people know Pascal from his published *Pensees (Thoughts)*. Here are a few:

We make of truth itself an idol; for truth apart from charity is not God, but His image and an idol, which must not be loved or worshipped; still less must we love or worship its opposite, namely, falsehood.

There are only two sorts of men: the righteous, who believe themselves sinners; and sinners, who believe themselves righteous.

Christianity is strange. It bids man acknowledge that he is vile, even abominable, yet bids him desire to be like God. Without such a counterpoise, this dignity would render him horribly vain, or that humiliation would render him terribly abject.

The second French strain of pietism is associated with the name of Madame Guyon (1648-1717)—so-called Quietism. Literally, Quietism was what it sounds like: the conviction of the quietness of the saved soul, as a result of an inner light granted by God. Quietism, though, was much closer to pietism in the bad sense than Jansenism. Perhaps for that reason it suffered less at the hands of the church hierarchy, finding a notable protector in Archbishop Fénelon whose practical charity makes up for his approval of the papal assaults upon the Jansenists.

What is disturbing in Quietism is the stress on a type of piety out of touch with biblical holiness. It glorifies self-punishment; prayer becomes meditation; any vital sense of the wholesome, visible Body of Christ as evidenced in the Acts of the Apostles is lost; it places an unhealthy stress upon obedience to a spiritual

No Other Foundation

superior who fulfills the function of a *guru*. It is a sad testimony to the drift into a formless Christianity within Protestantism that Madame Guyon's influence was perhaps stronger there than within Catholicism. Judging by modern reprints of her writings, this may still be true.

Classic Pietism is associated not with France but with Germany. I have not emphasized German Pietism, however, because pietism properly understood is a perennial phenomenon within the church. To underline the particular contributions of seventeenth and eighteenth century German Pietists, as if pietism began and ended with them, is to miss the wood for the trees.

Yet, we must not neglect to mention the truly impressive lives and works of men like Jacob Spener (1635-1705), August Hermann Francke (1663-1727) and Count Zinzendorf (1700-1760). In their outlook there is a beneficial union of teaching, study and charity. They insist on the necessity of regeneration, even if sometimes defining too closely the process of conversion. In a marked way, they provide a stimulus toward dynamic missionary activity. If they have been criticized for a tendency in some quarters to become group oriented, it may be said in their defence what one says about the later Methodist groups in England, that the dullness and coldness of the state church, combined with official opposition, left little alternative.

A word is in order about England. Later we shall speak of the Methodist revival in which the influence of German piety, mediated through Moravians, was important in the early stages, just as Methodism would return the compliment in its later stages by invigorating the Germans. Here, I wish to mention the Quakers and their founder, George Fox (1624-1691).

Whatever may have been true of Fox's personal commitment and determined effort to reach common people through unorthodox preaching efforts prophetic of the style of Wesley and Whitefield, he led the way to a dangerously free-floating, experiential, and ultimately formless piety. What perhaps helped to prevent the Society of Friends from the silent death of similar movements was Fox's personal gift for effective organization. To a considerable degree, the structure Fox imparted helped maintain also a genuine substratum of orthodox commitment, sufficient to nurture Christians of the calibre of Hannah Whitall Smith in the nineteenth century.

It is, however, instructive to place alongside Fox his contemporary Richard Baxter, or John Bunyan, the tinker of Bedford. Baxter, especially, knew Fox and insisted, from a standpoint no more officially popular than Fox's, upon the biblical norms as universal. Fox argued with him that his own personal experience of God transcended the biblical record and, in effect, became a commentary upon it. He claimed in his *Journal* that he had actually, not just theologically, been "renewed up into the image of God by Christ Jesus, so that I was come up into the state of Adam, which he was in before he fell."

Ultimately, all actual or potential distortions of the truth tend to join hands. In the sixteenth century it is fascinating to observe how the most radical wing of Anabaptism drifted into what we should call Unitarianism.* Thus rejecting Christ as the Son of God and only Savior, the Unitarians linked up with the skepticism of late-Renaissance humanism which had arrived at the same opinion by a different route. When Pietism lost its biblical bearings, it drifted very rapidly into freethinking. As has been often pointed out, many of the freethinkers of the eighteenth century were, in effect, the Pietists of the late seventeenth century. And freethinkers in the church, with no doctrine to provide an imperative for good works, sometimes added up to Latitudinarians.

As the word implies, Latitudinarianism stands for latitude of belief. And because belief is inextricably linked to conduct, this latitude extends to personal behavior. The emergence of a clergy, a church leadership, latitudinarian in thought and conduct, as the eighteenth century dawned, is not surprising. Where, either because of skepticism or myopic superspirituality, the Bible is taken selectively or discounted altogether, there is bound to be great latitude to determine one's fate, great interest in personal affairs, and a corresponding boredom with doctrinal issues. If dead orthodoxy went to one extreme, Latitudinarianism went to the other. If one had to choose between the two, the clear advantage of the former over the latter would have to be the retention, at least in principle, of the authoritative Word.

Wherever one looks in Europe around 1700, one sees the

---

*A recent study of some dimensions of this drift is provided in R. J. W. Evans's book *Rudolf II and His World: A Study in Intellectual History, 1576-1612* (Oxford: At the University Press, 1973).

No Other Foundation

emergence of what in England is the marriage between the fox-hunting country squire and the port-sipping country parson. The squires and parsons of Jane Austen's novels soon after 1800 are only a stiffer, more dignified, duller version of their ancestors of the previous century who are caricatured in *Tom Jones*. Neither version would be at home in the pages of the New Testament. To be fair, would we? There *is* a question of aspiration, however.

Bernini's Rome is a splendid Latitudinarian showcase, a triumph of seventeenth century baroque. More than any other style of art and architecture, perhaps, baroque is a self-conscious exercise in controlled "carelessness." It is the gesture of the patrician hand. Splendid yet awful. Who can stand in a baroque courtyard or a baroque church and not feel diminished? and by man, not God.

The painstaking methods of twentieth-century historians sometimes yield fruit: what does one make of a French episcopacy which, the statistics-conscious historian tells us, was drawn almost 100 percent from the highest aristocracy of the land? This is not perhaps what Paul had in mind when he wrote: "The saying is sure: If any one aspires to the office of bishop, he desires a noble task" (1 Timothy 3:1).

The seventeenth century closes with the search for religious unity. The great German intellect Leibnitz devoted years to fostering schemes for international, interdenominational accommodation. The new church in Mannheim, in the lands of the—Calvinist, did we say?—Elector of the Palatinate, was called *Sancta Concordia,* "Sacred Harmony." The dedication service featured a Roman Catholic priest, a Calvinist minister, a Lutheran pastor. Against the backcloth of the sorrow and bloodshed and hypocrisy that more than one generation of people had experienced before this late-seventeenth century service, we are not to throw stones too quickly. But can harmony ever achieve harmony?

John Locke's *Reasonableness of Christianity* is a title fit for this age. The Gospel was being made altogether too reasonable, the servant not the master of research and scholarly discussion, little to do with the world of flesh and blood, the reality of sin and the immeasurable riches of God's grace.

For Further Study

Elliott, John H. *The Old World and the New, 1492-1650.* New York: Cambridge University Press, 1970. We may forget about developments overseas at this time but contemporaries did not. This short book is packed with insights into the effect of overseas ventures, including the conviction in some quarters that the geographical relativity of Europe accompanied religious relativity. In other words, Christianity is just the Western way of life; in India it is Hinduism, and so on.

Grimmelshausen, Hans von. *The Adventures of a Simpleton.* New York: Frederick Ungar, n.d. Classic German novel registering the impact of war, famine and disease on contemporary conduct. Told with tongue in cheek but deadly serious underneath.

Locke, John. *A Letter Concerning Toleration.* Indianapolis: Bobbs-Merrill Co., 1955. Written toward the end of the century. Implicitly, this is a milestone in the slow dissolution of the idea of absolute community.

Pascal, Blaise. *Pensées.* Translated by W. F. Trotter. New York: E. P. Dutton, 1958. Not to be read at one sitting but pondered slowly.

Rossi, Paolo. *Philosophy, Technology and the Arts in the Early Modern Era: 1470-1700.* Translated by S. Attanasio. New York: Harper & Row, 1970. Draws together these three themes to focus on the intellectual changes in the seventeenth century. A difficult book.

15

Wesley, Whitefield, and Samuel Johnson

I N 1736 JOSEPH BUTLER in his famous *Analogy of Religion* wrote: "It is come, I know not how, to be taken for granted, by many persons, that Christianity is not so much a subject of inquiry; but that it is, now at length, discovered to be fictitious. And accordingly they treat it as if, in the present age, this were an agreed point, among all people of discernment; and nothing remained, but to set it up as a principal subject of mirth and ridicule, as it were by way of reprisals, for its having so long interrupted the pleasures of the world." This situation was undoubtedly exacerbated and partly caused by laxness on the part of the church which, as someone has observed, should have been the bulwark against irreligion and ungodly conduct but often proved to be their leading exponent.

It has been said that the most popular sermon of the century was the Latitudinarian Tillotson's on the text: "His commandments are not grievous." Misunderstood in the "right" way, most ecclesiastics found themselves well able to live up to it. And Lady Mary Wortley Montagu, one of the most celebrated women of the day, could make the wry suggestion that the word "not" be removed from the Ten Commandments and inserted in the Creed. But it is when the surrounding world is barbarous and godless that such ecclesiastical irresponsibility is revealed at its most heinous. For it is a stunning fact that eighteenth-century England, that country which had enjoyed so much sound teaching and not a little sound living for so long, should have plunged so low, so quickly.

One cannot help comparing the declension with the growing

No Other Foundation

spectacle of rottenness in the former Protestant societies of northwestern Europe today where the galloping consumption of perverted sexuality and contempt for life and family is fast outstripping the diseases gripping the Catholic countries of southern Europe which have long grown used to a certain live-and-let-live attitude as regards marital fidelity and public rectitude.

There does, in fact, seem to be a universal rule in operation which is as old as the history of the Old Testament Jews: that goodness gone bad knows no bounds, for the original goodness allowed a freedom of thought and action which evil is quick to exploit. As Jesus said, the house cleansed of one demon and not filled, will soon be occupied by seven more.

Where living conditions were worsening, through the onset of industrialization, as at Manchester, one could find ten in a room, often without furniture, sleeping on wood shavings. Smallpox, typhoid, typhus and dysentery were rampant. Large common graves—"poor holes"—were left open at graveyards awaiting full occupancy: the stench was overwhelming. In the early eighteenth century, mortality for children was about one in four. In such a society, gin drinking was rife and gambling a great passion. One could gamble on anything, a writer notes, from the fertility of the archdeacon's wife to the weekly death toll of neighboring streets. Violence, riot, bestiality, looting were the order of the day.

Dickens's retrospective pictures in such novels as *Barnaby Rudge* are accurate enough. But no one depicted the situation better than the contemporary social satirist William Hogarth in his famous prints of London life. Yet no one confronted it more fully than one of the men we must soon discuss: John Wesley. Which brings us to our topic—the extraordinary outbreak of a dynamic religious revival in Great Britain that added fuel to a native movement in the American colonies. The American part of the story must have its own chapter, however. Here, first, we need to examine the antecedents of the British revival.

There was a very definite stream of High Church piety which, though most notably a seventeenth-century phenomenon and illustrated by figures of the stature of George Herbert and John Donne, was still around in the 1730s. This piety was focused in private, informal "societies" or religious circles which bear a resemblance to similar groups on the eve of the Continental Reformation 200 years earlier.

Who joined these societies? Men and women earnest in their search for God and righteousness—or even plain decency—in an age run riot. To the degree to which there was a strong introspective, pietistic tinge to them, they were ultimately abandoned by those who, like the Wesleys and Whitefield, of the Oxford "Holy Club," found an assurance of sins forgiven in justification by faith in Christ.

The "Holy Club"—to give you an exaggerated idea of the possible zeal of the societies—practiced austerities of such outrageous proportions as even to result in the death of one of the members. They denied themselves food, drink and sleep, and were known to prostrate themselves at night for hours in winter frost. They visited prisons and pest houses, seeking to follow Christ's commands to the letter. In short, however Luther may have tried to save his soul, they tried the more—but with no greater success.

One of the great antitheses of the eighteenth century—though it can be exaggerated, for Wesley was intensely reasonable and detached, as one can see from his *Journal*—was the coincidence of natural, rationalistic religion and the reaffirmation of an orthodox, supernatural, revealed Christianity, ablaze with the experience of God. Some have seen in this coincidence a natural reaction away from rationalism to Wesley's brand of religion and, certainly, on one level, one need not dispute the judgment. The desert wanderer does, after all, long for water.

But one can also see—and this is plain in Wesley's own case—the influence of the pietistic tradition of the seventeenth century which, as we have seen, was itself a reaction from the dead, rationalistic orthodoxy in the major Christian churches. The eighteenth-century revival had, then, not only positive roots in High Church piety; it had negative roots in a rejection of purely naturalistic Deism where God is essentially impersonal, the capital *N* in Nature. Charles Wesley pointed the contrast in that wonderful verse from one of his hymns:

> Long my imprison'd spirit lay,
> Fast bound in sin and nature's night;
> Thine eye diffus'd a quick'ning ray,
> I woke, the dungeon flam'd with light;
> My chains fell off, my heart was free,
> I rose, went forth, and follow'd Thee.

It is well known that John Wesley had no great sympathy for

Calvinism which had been such an important strand in Puritan life and thought, though admittedly his brother Charles and friend Whitefield were far closer to this tradition. It is also well known that the Dissenting tradition played very little part in the Methodist Evangelical revival. While an Isaac Watts continued the best elements of Nonconformity up to the eve of Wesley's conversion, the Dissenters as a whole were very slow to heed and welcome the new movement.

Probably, the impact of the older seventeenth-century Puritanism was most felt through the great Puritan classics which were read and assimilated in the eighteenth century. The influence of this literature can be traced in many conversions. There was, then, some Puritan influence.

It is, however, fair to say that the average Evangelical of the age of Wesley and thereafter was less learned, less political, less concerned with doctrinal definition and church polity than his seventeenth-century antecedent. Perhaps in a world fragmented beyond the wildest fears of a Richard Baxter, the eighteenth century preacher was necessarily concerned with evangelism on a wider front—and more exclusively to the poor and ignorant—than had been the need or the case in the seventeenth century. It, is, of course, easy to set up stereotypes or unfair comparisons. Yet a detailed comparison between, say, a Richard Baxter and a John Newton would be most instructive.

Relatively few have heard of William Law (1686-1761) and yet he exercised a great influence on Wesley at the beginning and influenced a much wider audience throughout the eighteenth century. He was, in summary, a sort of bridge between the purely intellectual defence of Christianity against rationalism and the radical experiential answer. In the careful balance in Wesley's own life between sound doctrine, devout living and obedience to the implications of loving one's neighbor, one can feel some of Law's influence. Charles Wesley later referred to Law as "our John the Baptist," and even his brother, who fell out with Law, could still see him as a parent of Methodism.

Law is of interest, I think, to Christians—or should be—in our own day. For he saw very precisely that to win debates with non-Christians, "to treat Christianity as a problem of evidence, was to play the Deist's own game." We might echo Law's conviction that we are not Christians unless our life "is a common course of humility, self-denial, renunciation of the world, poverty of the spirit, and heavenly affection.'' He says no more than the Apostle John.

Wales had been such a spiritually barren place in the seventeenth century that when, at the beginning of the Commonwealth in 1649, the government was taking seriously the spiritual state of the realm, it despatched over 150 ministers into the thirteen Welsh counties in three years and placed a schoolmaster in every market town. Thirty itinerant preachers were also appointed and a number of lay workers, including the great Vavasor Powell.

Perhaps because of the obvious need and the necessity for itinerating, one sees in Wales the first great pioneers of open-air preaching and the first fruits of it. Griffiths Jones (1683-1761) was preaching in the fields long before Wesley had been converted. Not only in message and method, but also in the opposition he aroused, Jones anticipated the Methodists. The hostility of local clergy was venomous. Jones's most striking contribution, though, was the famous Welsh Charity School movement. This developed quite naturally, like most genuine works of God, not from a fanfare of organization but from his Sunday catechism class. All ages were welcome; the curriculum stressed basics of education as a foundation for positive Biblical teaching and learning. From the start in 1731-32 till his death in 1761, nearly four thousand schools were established with about 158,000 scholars enrolled.

I am inclined to think that if from Law we learn that rational apologetic among the highly educated is insufficient, then from Jones we learn that in an age when people are, in a sense, profoundly ill-adjusted to any possible comprehension of the Gospel message, we need to combine preaching with a systematic reeducation in the facts of life.

I am not speaking here of literacy, though that itself is now becoming an area of real concern; I am talking about education in a view of reality which boldly confronts the anti-Christian flavor of public instruction. People, including some who sit in pews, must be taught to see existence as more than biologically conditioned. They must be taught to recognize the flaws in the generalized educational assumption that revealed, biblical, personal religion may be psychologically interesting or emotionally fulfilling but not fit for rational examination. We must emulate Jones and face the needs of the modern apostate world in the same spirit of faithful, objective determination. Our Christian education programs must adjust aggressively to challenge the new consensus of Christian illiteracy.

I have emphasized Jones, and yet better known to students of the revival in Wales are the trio who looked to him as spiritual father: Daniel Rowland, Howell Harris and Howell Davies. Rowland was converted when Jones preached in a neighboring church and, catching Rowland's supercilious gaze after reading the text, quickly asked God not only to save him but to make him a Welsh apostle. Rowland became possibly the greatest preacher Wales has ever known and the equal of Whitefield.

Rowland and Jones were both ordained clergymen. Harris was a layman, and it is his conversion in 1735 that is the real beginning of the Welsh Revival. Ordination was refused him. A reticent man, he did not take to preaching at once, though eventually he was reckoned not much less effective than Rowland. He was concerned not to offend the ordained clergy despite their godless treatment of him. His remarkable ministry started, like Jones's, from modest beginnings. He simply felt impelled by compassion to go and read the Bible to his neighbors and tend to the sick, going from house to house upon invitation, and finally evangelizing in halls and the open air. Incidentally, he somehow managed to hold down a job as a schoolteacher at the same time, till sacked because of his faith.

Although the American revival associated with Jonathan Edwards had an important influence and was another sign of the revival of the Spirit's sovereign working, I am not going to dwell upon it here. Edwards's published description of the revival had a strong impact upon earnest believers in England like John Wesley. And George Whitefield's personal participation in the Great Awakening was a sort of preview of his and Wesley's participation in the British revival soon to start.

What I do want to summarize, before speaking directly of Whitefield and Wesley, is the Moravian contribution. The Moravian Brethren came from the original Hussite movement. By the early eighteenth century they had left their native Moravia, which had been forcibly re-Catholicized, and had settled in Saxony, thanks to the hospitality and spiritual sympathy of Count Zinzendorf, a prominent Saxon noble.

A powerful revival experience in Saxony (at Herrnhut) led to the characteristic Moravian outreach to other parts, including England and the American colonies. And God ordained that the two Wesleys should be on the same ship as Moravians going to Georgia and should observe their missionary impact there. And God ordained that Wesley, having returned from Georgia a disappointed man, should meet again with the Moravians in London and experience his full "settlement" with God in their midst.

Though the future Methodists and Moravians would split in 1740 when a Quietist element temporarily surfaced at the Fetter Lane Moravian assembly, inducing Wesley to move on, it is important not to forget how much the Evangelical Revival owes to this spiritual impulse from the Continent.

Too much time can be spent fruitlessly comparing the two obvious giants of the Methodist Revival. John Wesley (1703-91) was a man of immense measure, gifted not only in extraordinary energy of mind, body and spirit, but also in common sense and moderation. George Whitefield (1714-69) as a preacher had greater natural gifts. He certainly kindled the imagination of the epoch more strongly than Wesley. Though Wesley was no stay-at-home, the actual range of Whitefield's ministry was broader and he crossed the Atlantic thirteen times, eventually dying in America. Furthermore, in most of the ways in which the Revival became known, Whitefield preceded Wesley: open-air preaching; deploying lay preachers; holding conferences; and even bringing the disparate elements of international revival together by his role in the American, English, Welsh, and Scottish movements.

One senses in Whitefield a freer range to the imagination and a more spontaneous warmth. There was something about the adamantine stability of Wesley's faith which commanded the respect of intelligent sceptics. But there was an extra element of the inexplicable about Whitefield which produced an awe that was quickly rationalized into suspicion by the embarrassed cynic.

Whitefield actually found spiritual release and new life before the Wesleys, at Oxford in 1735; and in 1739, a year after Wesley's Fetter Lane experience, had gone into the open air at Kingswood near Bristol, to speak to the miners after the bishop had forbidden him to preach in the diocese. It was Whitefield who encouraged Wesley to do the same.

No Other Foundation

Given to exaggeration, sometimes, in describing his own experiences—and certainly given also to unintentional lapses of responsibility which brought criticism upon his head with respect, for example, to money matters—Whitefield was, in his very being, something of an exaggeration. Preaching an average of forty to sixty hours a week, on one occasion he collapsed into sleep after Sunday service and didn't wake up till Tuesday. He was gifted with a beautiful voice that he could play like a delicate instrument. As a boy, he had shown marked theatrical talents and undoubtedly God used them in his ministry.

Certainly, not all those who were initially affected by his preaching proved to be converts. The urbane Lord Chesterfield and the sceptical Ben Franklin were alike reduced to tears on hearing Whitefield speak—but without showing any fruits worthy of repentance. For thousands of others, however, the result was otherwise. The beneficial impact of this man of God is beyond any normal accounting. He survives his critics for the same reason that the Church will survive the world.

In coming to Wesley, it is worth adding, as regards comparisons between him and Whitefield, that there are no valid comparisons in God's work. The harvest is the Lord's. *He* selects his workers and empowers them; if blessing comes, it is because *his* strength is made perfect in our weakness. Finally, as Jesus said, we must remind ourselves that, after doing everything, we have still to confess that we are unfaithful servants.

Very often, God's servants mislead us by insisting on the primacy of their experience, the method which was blessed. They think to help by itemizing the apparent ingredients of success. But they forget—and we forget, also, if we heed them too readily— that "experience" and "method" are only the vehicles of a grace which is mediated differently, for complementary purposes, to each of us, so that, as Paul knew, the Body would be able to function as a balanced unit.

What is staggering is how God works through personalities as different as night from day. Not only that, he takes men with characters and gifts as strongly defined and diverse as Wesley's and Whitefield's, and makes them work together harmoniously, despite disagreements over doctrine and strategy.

The story of Wesley—or should we say the two Wesleys, for Charles and John were so close?—is so familiar as to require no more than a summary. The family tradition of Christian seriousness and vocation going back to the mid-seventeenth century; the strong personality of both parents, the father being the more passionate, the mother the more iron-willed; the remarkable mothering by Susannah, as she gave her all to ensure that her large brood, such of it as survived infancy, would serve Christ. Then, the successful academic careers at Oxford; the "Holy Club" experience; the trip to Georgia to save the Indians, even without their having any real assurance of salvation themselves. Finally, in May 1738, for both brothers, the wonderful experience of the personal meaning and reality of justification by faith, mediated through the Moravians, whereby from having been, as John expressed it later, " 'servants' of God, we now knew ourselves to be 'sons.' " As already indicated, John quickly followed Whitefield's lead, as did Charles, too, till marriage caused him to alter his work and adopt a different strategy.

Something more has to be added about the Fetter Lane experience, however, to point up an important historical parallel. What precisely Wesley heard in 1738 was the reading of Luther's preface to his commentary on *Romans,* in which the great reformer deals with justification by faith. In other words, what had opened the eyes of the earnest Luther, trying to save himself by works in the sixteenth century, opened the eyes of an equally earnest, equally "works ridden" Wesley two hundred years later. The wheel had come full circle. Man drives resolutely away from acknowledging his utter dependence upon God. The revelation which had burst like the sun upon Luther was already hidden again to Wesley seven generations later.

Rather than elaborate upon John Wesley's ministry, I want briefly to explain his peculiar contribution and then illustrate what it meant in practical sacrifice from his *Journal.*

If Whitefield was the gatherer of souls, par excellence, Wesley was also a shepherd of souls with a genius, harnessed by God, for keeping people together and organizing them without destroying the delicate filigree of mutual love and individual diversity. If Whitefield's task did not place upon him in the same degree the "burden of all the churches" to which Paul refers, Wesley's task did. And if Wesley is often especially honored, it is not because he was the greater evangelist (he wasn't); nor the one peak in the movement (rather, as someone has said, he was simply the high-

No Other Foundation

est point in a great mountain range); but instead because, as the last statement suggests, he brought to a steady and certain coordinated conclusion not only his own work but also that of others. His was the genius for careful planning, for systematic methodical catechising, and visiting of the "circuits" year in and year out, from decade to decade, during half a century. Furthermore, in essential counterpoint to his gift for organization went a totally childlike faith, such that he was never counting the pennies, cutting the corners. He knew well that what God starts God sustains. He was afraid of no man; he was indebted to no man. He was entirely indebted to the Lord who has given believers the privilege of laboring together with him to bring in the harvest. Woe betide anyone who might think that his labors and finance bought him position or authority.

Note that this was not a young man to whom God entrusted such a mission. At Fetter Lane in 1738 he was turning thirty-six. A bit old to start? God knew he had fifty years of maturity left and he lived them unstintingly. For the rest of his life he averaged fifteen sermons a week. He rode on horseback about a quarter of a million miles. At eighty-eight, he could attribute his health and strength to rising always at 4:00 A.M.; preaching his first sermon to early morning workers at 5:00 A.M.; riding on horseback; eating sparingly; and retiring at 9:00 P.M.

For all that Wesley was a man of pronounced opinions and indomitable will, one thing that is very clear from his reluctance to break with the Church of England (in which he was ordained) is a refusal to seek a name or organization of his own. He sought the reviving of the church, and his "methodist" societies were leaven in the lump of the local churches. They were never encouraged to be anything but this, and Wesley had stern words for members who neglected attendance at church, however hostile the local incumbent.

What might have been his stance toward the confessionally compromised churches of our own day is another question. Perhaps a clue is given in his decision of 1784 when he felt forced by the intransigence of the church authorities to act as a bishop and ordain men to preach in America. In other words, when the proclamation of the Gospel brought a choice between proceeding scripturally and supinely accepting the obtuseness of the church hierarchy, there could be no doubt as to where the priority lay.

Wesley proceeded scripturally and defied the hierarchy.

In Great Britain, Wesley never had to make this choice but after his death a break with the Church of England proved inevitable. As a distinguished historian has written: "With the slightest amount of goodwill Methodism would never have become a separatist movement, but the implacable hostility of the Anglican hierarchy" drove first Wesley, and then his followers, to the brink.

Wesley's last words were "I'll praise, I'll praise." They are a fitting introduction to a life of praise which is described in all its facets in his *Journal*. The full journal occupies no less than twenty-six volumes but Wesley himself, towards the end of his life, carefully selected portions of it for a four-volume edition. This has been further reduced to one volume in our own day, and no Christian with the ability and opportunity should fail to peruse it. Some of the flavor is conveyed in these few extracts. (I am citing *The Heart of John Wesley's Journal*, ed. Percy Livingstone Parker [New York: Fleming H. Revell Co., 1903].)

October 17, 1735 [en route to Georgia]: I began to learn German, in order to converse with the Germans, six-and-twenty of whom we had on board [p. 3].

April 4, 1737 [in Georgia]: I began learning Spanish, in order to converse with my Jewish parishioners; some of whom seem nearer the mind that was in Christ than many of those who call him Lord [p. 16].

June 11, 1739 [quotes a letter he wrote defending his freelance preaching]: God in Scripture commands me, according to my power, to instruct the ignorant, reform the wicked, confirm the virtuous. Man forbids me to do this in another's parish; that is, in effect, to do it at all; seeing I have now no parish of my own, nor probably ever shall. Whom then shall I hear, God or men?

I look upon all the world as my parish; thus far I mean, that, in whatever part of it I am, I judge it meet, right, and my bounden duty, to declare unto all that are willing to hear, the glad tidings of salvation [pp. 55-57].

Jan. 21, 1740 [near Bristol, England]: In the evening I made a collection in our congregation for the relief of the poor, . . . who, having no work (because of the severe frost), and no assistance from the parish wherein they lived, were reduced to the last extremity. . . . we were enabled to feed a hundred, sometimes a hundred and fifty, a day, of those whom we found to need it most [p. 70].

April 2, 1740 [Newgate Prison, London]: Calling at Newgate in the afternoon, I was informed that the poor wretches under sentence of death were earnestly desirous to speak with me; but that it could not be; Alderman Beecher having just then sent an express order that they should not. I cite Alderman Beecher to answer for these souls at the judgment-seat of Christ [p. 71].

November 25, 1740 [helping the unemployed in London]: Our aim was, with as little expense as possible, to keep them at once from want and from idleness, in order to which, we took twelve of the poorest, and a teacher, into the society-room, where they were employed for four months, till spring came on, in carding and spinning of cotton. And the design answered: they were employed and maintained with very little more than the produce of their own labour [p. 72].

June 12, 1742: [near Epworth, Lincolnshire]: I preached on the right-eousness of the law and the righteousness of faith. While I was speaking, several dropped down as dead; and among the rest, such a cry was heard, of sinners groaning for the righteousness of faith, as almost drowned my voice [pp. 87-88].

April 1, 1743 [visits the poor colliers of Placey, near Newcastle]: Between seven and eight I set out with John Heally, my guide. The north wind, being unusually high, drove the sleet in our face, which froze as it fell, and cased us over presently. When we came to Placey, we could very hardly stand. As soon as we were a little recovered I went into the square, and declared Him who "was wounded for our transgressions" and "bruised for our iniquities." The poor sinners were quickly gathered together and gave earnest heed to the things which were spoken [pp. 105-06].

September 21, 1743 [Cornwall]: I was waked between three and four A.M. by a large company of tinners, who, fearing they should be too late, had gathered round the house, and were singing and praising God. At five I preached once more, on, "Believe on the Lord Jesus Christ, and thou shalt be saved." They all devoured the word. O may it be health to their soul, and marrow unto their bones [p. 114]!

June 26, 1744 [a "Methodist" conference in London]: The next day we endeavoured to purge the society of all that did not walk according to the Gospel. By this means we reduced the number of members to less than nineteen hundred. But number is an inconsiderable circumstance. May God increase them in faith and love [p. 124]!

January 5, 1745: I had often wondered at myself (and sometimes mentioned it to others), that ten thousand cares, of various kinds, were no more weight and burden to my mind, than ten thousand hairs were to my head. Perhaps I began to ascribe something of this to my own strength. And thence it might be, that on Sunday, 13, that strength was withheld, and I felt what it was to be troubled about many things. One, and another, hurrying me continually, it seized upon my spirit more and more, till I found it absolutely necessary to fly for my life; and that without delay. So the next day, Monday, 14, I took horse, and rode away for Bristol.

Wesley, Whitefield, and Samuel Johnson

Between Bath and Bristol I was earnestly desired to turn aside, and call at the house of a poor man, William Shalwood. I found him and his wife sick in one bed, and with small hopes of the recovery of either. Yet (after prayer) I believed they would "not die, but live, and declare the loving-kindness of the Lord." The next time I called he was sitting below stairs, and his wife able to go abroad.

As soon as we came into the house at Bristol, my soul was lightened of her load, of that insufferable weight which had lain upon my mind, more or less, for several days [pp. 125-26].

July 4, 1745 [Falmouth, Cornwall; a mob has just smashed down the door of the house and is howling for his blood]: I stepped forward at once into the midst of them, and said, "Here I am. Which of you has anything to say to me. To which of you have I done any wrong? To you? Or you? Or you?" I continued speaking till I came, bare-headed as I was (for I purposely left my hat that they might all see my face), into the middle of the street, and then raising my voice, said, "Neighbors, countrymen! Do you desire to hear me speak?" They cried vehemently, "Yes, Yes. He shall speak. He shall. Nobody shall hinder him." But having nothing to stand on, and no advantage of ground, I could be heard by few only. However, I spoke without intermission, and, as far as the sound reached, the people were still; till one or two of their captains turned about and swore, not a man should touch him [p. 134].

August 28, 1748: I wonder at those who still talk so loud of the indecency of field-preaching. The highest indecency is in St. Paul's Church [Cathedral], when a considerable part of the congregation are asleep, or talking, or looking about, not minding a word the preacher says.

August 28, 1748 [opposition to preaching at Bolton, Lancashire]: Then they began to throw stones; at the same time some got upon the Cross behind me to push me down; on which I could not but observe, how God overrules the minutest circumstances. One man was bawling just at my ear, when a stone struck him on the cheek, and he was still. A second was forcing his way down to me, till another stone struck him on the forehead: it bounded back, the blood ran down, and he came no farther. The third being got close to me, stretched out his hand, and in the instant a sharp stone came upon the joints of his fingers. He shook his hand, and was very quiet till I concluded my discourse and went away [p. 165].

September 24-October 15, 1750 [at the "Methodist" school at Kingswood, testing the children and preparing text-books for them]: . . . selected passages of Milton . . . selected passages of the "Moral and Sacred Poems" . . . spent most of the day in revising Kennet's "Antiquities," . . . I revised, for the use of the children, Archbishop Potter's "Grecian Antiquities"; a dry, dull, heavy book. . . . I revised Mr. Lewis's "Hebrew Antiquities" . . . I nearly finished the abridgement of Dr. Cave's "Primitive Christianity"; a book wrote with as much learning, and as little judgement, as any I remember to have read in my whole life . . . I prepared a short "History of England" for the use of the

No Other Foundation

children; and on Friday and Saturday a short "Roman History," as an introduction to the Latin historians. . . . I read over Mr. Holmes's "Latin Grammar"; and extracted from it what was needful to perfect our own [pp. 191-92].

March 31, 1753 [persecution of a gardener]: Is it possible the earl should turn off an honest, diligent, well-tried servant, who had been in the family above fifty years, for no other fault than hearing the Methodists [p. 206]?

October 15, 1759 [in the Seven Years War, the Gospel opposes chauvinism]: I walked up to Knowle, a mile from Bristol, to see the French prisoners. About eleven hundred of them, we are informed, were confined in that little place, without anything to lie on but a little dirty straw, or anything to cover but a few foul thin rags, either by day or night, so that they died like rotten sheep. I was much affected, and preached in the evening on (Exodus xxiii. 9), "Thou shalt not oppress a stranger: for ye know the heart of a stranger, seeing ye were strangers in the land of Egypt." Eighteen pounds were contributed immediately, which were made up four-and-twenty the next day. With this we bought linen and woollen cloth, which were made up into shirts, waistcoats and breeches. Some dozens of stockings were added: all which were carefully distributed, where there was the greatest want [pp. 262-63].

January 31, 1766: Mr. Whitefield called upon me. He breathes nothing but peace and love. Bigotry cannot stand before him, but hides its head wherever he comes [p. 322].

September 19, 1769 [opposition surprised]: They then lifted up their voice, especially one, called a gentleman, who had filled his pocket with rotten eggs: but, a young man coming unawares, clapped his hands on each side, and mashed them all at once. In an instant he was perfume all over; though it was not so sweet as balsam [pp. 349-50].

January 1, 1790. I am now an old man, decayed from head to foot. My eyes are dim; my right hand shakes much; my mouth is hot and dry every morning; I have a lingering fever almost every day; my motion is weak and slow. However, blessed be God, I do not slack my labour: I can preach and write still [p. 481].

October 11, 1790: I went (from London) to Colchester, and still found matter of humiliation. The society was lessened, and cold enough; preaching again was discontinued, and the spirit of Methodism quite gone, both from the preachers and the people: yet we had a wonderful congregation in the evening, rich and poor, clergy and laity [p. 483].

October 24, 1790 [last journal entry]: St. Paul's, Shadwell, was still more crowded in the afternoon, while I enforced that important truth, "One thing is needful"; and I hope many, even then, resolved to choose the better part [p. 485].

I am deliberately ending this chapter not with John Wesley but

Wesley, Whitefield, and Samuel Johnson

with Samuel Johnson (1709-84) because Johnson rather than John Wesley typifies the usual state of Christians. Johnson and Wesley were, incidentally, good friends. This was a union of the totally committed, totally confident, spiritual engine, and the self-doubting, spiritually fearful, literary giant.

Having quoted at length from Wesley's daily jottings, it is not inappropriate to do the same with Johnson—but for a different effect. (The following quotations from Johnson's *Prayers and Meditations* are adapted from Walter Jackson Bate, *The Achievement of Samuel Johnson,* 1961, pp. 9-10).

1738: O Lord, enable me to redeem the time which I have spent in sloth.

1757: Almighty God . . . enable me to shake off sloth, and redeem the time misspent in idleness and sin by a diligent application of the days yet remaining.

1759: Enable me to shake off idleness and sloth.

1761: I have resolved . . . till I am afraid to resolve again.

1764: My indolence, since my last reception of the Sacrament, has sunk into grosser sluggishness. . . . My purpose is from this time . . . to avoid idleness. To rise early.

1764 [five months later]: [Resolves] to rise early. Not later than six if I can.

1765: I purpose to rise at eight because though I shall not rise early it will be much earlier than I now rise, for I often lye till two.

1769: I am not yet in a state to form many resolutions; I purpose and hope to rise early in the morning, at eight, and by degrees at six.

1775: When I look back upon resolutions of improvement and amendments, which have year after year been made and broken . . . why do I yet try to resolve again? I try because Reformation is necessary and despair is criminal. [He resolves again to rise at eight.]

1781: I will not despair. Help me, help me, O my God. [He resolves] To rise at eight or sooner . . . To avoid Idleness.

Need more be said? Is not this very much the portrait of you and me—even if exaggerated, if it *is* exaggerated? Perhaps most believers, indeed, unlike Johnson, cease to berate themselves and therefore "despair" which, as Johnson says, is "criminal."

What is the secret? What differentiated Wesley and Johnson? Or rather, because Johnson had well-known and deep personal problems, what differentiates Wesley and the *irresolution* we see in Johnson? I think it is partly the distinction Wesley had seen in

No Other Foundation

his own life between being a "servant" of God and knowing himself to be a "son." This spells spiritual confidence in the Father who gives bread when we ask for it, and not a stone. It spells the full realization that Jesus died for me and therefore also lives for me. He was raised for me!

It is the real and full appropriation of these facts, with the reality of Christ's power in us to enable, that made the generation of revival in the eighteenth century. It can make it in our day, too, if we will only believe it again and "count all things loss" for the privilege of knowing him and the power of his resurrection, becoming like him in his death.

For Further Study

Gibbon, Edward. *Gibbon's Autobiography.* Edited by M. M. Reese. Boston: Routledge & Kegan Paul, 1970. The story of a self-satisfied man in a world without God before the flood came. The best way to appreciate what "reason" meant.

Hogarth, William. *Engravings by Hogarth.* Edited by Sean Shesgreen. New York: Dover, 1973. The other side of English life: gin, poverty and riot. These engravings are a sophisticated equivalent of the modern newspaper cartoon. In the French Revolution such engravings were very effectively used for popular propaganda.

Wesley, John. *The Journal of John Wesley.* Edited by Percy L. Parker. Chicago: Moody Press, 1974. No further advertising needed. However, if this new edition still has the strange introductory remarks of Birrel and Hughes, don't read them till the end—then you will see how odd they are.

Wesley, John. *Primitive Remedies.* Santa Barbara, CA: Woodbridge Press, 1973. Gives special insight into Wesley's methodical approach and concern for evidence. Many of his cures have been rediscovered in recent years, disguised in the terminology of vitamin therapy. This book was a standard medical guide for laymen for a century.

The standard, recent biography of Whitefield in two volumes by Arnold Dallimore is soon to be issued by Cornerstone Books.

16

The Revival Tradition in America: From Coast to Frontier

THE MODERN MIND dislikes conversion because it is an absolute and uncompromising indictment of man's natural state.* This was also true, of course, in the Roman Empire. "Natural" man is doomed, and our evangel must not shirk the responsibility for saying so. If Wesley had sometimes to recommend preachers to stress the love and mercy of God, along with his justice, nowadays he would find himself giving the opposite advice in most of our churches.

The early church refused to compromise with its own day over the necessity of conversion. It is, however, worth pondering the threefold understanding of spiritual rebirth presented in the New Testament, in order to gain perspective for our consideration of eighteenth- and nineteenth-century revival in America. The church of reborn believers was seen as an extension of Israel (baptism being the New Covenant version of circumcision); a fellowship of believers (repentance and faith being the conditions of belonging); and a community of the Spirit (Christ's Spirit having access to our hearts).

All three aspects are treated as valid descriptions of the church. Any one aspect taken in isolation leads to a lopsided view of the church. The early church kept all three in balance, but the church has not found that easy to do since. Historically, Roman Catholics have stressed the first aspect—this has led to the idea of baptismal regeneration. Protestants have stressed the second—

*I am indebted for this thought and the following analysis of conversion in the early church to Michael Green's *Evangelism in the Early Church* (Grand Rapids, MI: Wm. B. Eerdmans Publishing Co., 1970), ch. 6.

No Other Foundation

this has often led to a deficient understanding of the Spirit's continuing work. Pentecostals and many "charismatics" have stressed the third—this has led to a sense of rootlessness in some quarters.

Apostolic preaching, which expressed this threefold view of salvation, may have been more, or less, emotional, but it was always decisive, demanding a verdict upon an objective, historical event. Retold no less than three times in Acts, Paul's conversion would appear to be, if not in circumstance, then certainly in its personal elements, normative. Paul's mind was convinced; his conscience was struck; his heart was humbled; his will was yielded; and his life was changed (Green, pp. 164-65). Conversion, then, is mandatory, whichever aspect may be stressed; and the Pauline marks of conversion should all be evident in some form, bearing in mind that the New Testament always underlines the continuing nature of a salvation which is absolutely begun in our justification but is not complete till our glorification.

Only against this background is it safe to embark on the troubled waters of American revivalism.

It is important to emphasize how unique the British colonies in America were. Although we are now aware that the Crown made a determined effort to control the colonies from the late-seventeenth century, there is still quite a contrast between the tightly administered possessions overseas of the French, Portuguese and Spanish, and the far more loosely organized British settlements. As a result, there was the freedom, as well as an adequate reservoir of population fed by a liberal settlement policy, to develop a truly indigenous society.

Indeed, though Americans themselves became only slowly aware of being anything but British, foreign travellers by the mid-1700s were noticing that a brand-new country was in process of formation. In other words, the particular circumstances of the Revolution simply brought to a formal (and possibly inevitable) conclusion a long-term development. If there had not been a revolution, there would, presumably, have been the equivalent of the mid-nineteenth century Canadian arrangement whereby a measure of self-government, within the context of official Crown sovereignty, was granted. It is interesting that the later revolutions in the Latin American colonies of Spain and Portugal required the ignition spark of the American and French upheavals, not having achieved the natural internal dynamic that the thirteen colonies had generated indigenously.

Though we cannot explore all the ways in which the thirteen colonies became consciously American, we can, appropriate to our overall concerns, look at those things which were of religious importance.

Political historians have long been aware that there is no real comparison between political options in Western Europe and the Republican-Democratic spectrum in the United States. On one level, this is just a matter of gradations. But it is more complicated than that. One can see how complicated by taking a look at religious "politics" which reflect a similar divergence.

The religious history of America is marked by a great paradox. Many of the colonists came, or fled, to America to enjoy the freedom to practice forms of Christianity considered too radical or experimental back home. Once cut off from the European tradition, however, and once established in close-knit communities with the chance to realize in detail one's ideals, ideas which had represented a radical option were transformed through ironclad practice into a reactionary front. If the Massachusetts Puritans had, for example, fled an Anglican episcopal system which restrained them, they soon established a system which was far more restraining. In the meantime, they lagged behind the positive developments in the mother country.

In other words, the urge to perfect and preserve a form of belief and life (admirable enough, in itself), led in time to fossilization. Not that the fossilization was ever complete. It is a bit like the contrast between the United States' and the British constitutions.

The British constitution, like the Anglican church, is essentially organic and *ad hoc*—it develops through precedent, which is its strength and its weakness. The United States Constitution (with a capital *C* because you can pick it up and look at it), like many aspects of American church development, is essentially stated, nailed down from the start. As a result, it tends to change by explosion and division, more than by slow evolution. It is easy to exaggerate here and pretend that the Civil War is a typical way of solving problems in America. Let us say only that all change must, at the very least, be far more formal and self-conscious than in Britain. In church terms, then, America undergoes a violent bloodletting for every case of spiritual poisoning.

Geography adds another crucial dimension to the discussion

No Other Foundation

here. Radical ideas could last longer on the American continent than in Europe, where the relative intensity of settlement and more direct control by government permitted the bizarre to be quickly bottled up. In effect, until 1776 in a formal way, and informally thereafter, Britain had an American frontier where it could get rid of its odd fellows. On that frontier, with a certain amount of lip service, almost anything went. When the revolution occurred, Britain lost her private safety valve—but was fortunate to have invested in new ones in India and elsewhere. As for the new American nation, it continued to exploit its own ready-made frontier—a moving frontier.

The originally experimental nature of American colonial society and the proximity of a virgin frontier fostered the double heritage of the wild and the conformist—the paradox I referred to before. This is nowhere better illustrated than in twentieth-century California where the frontier stops (unless it be the Moon). California is America writ large. It is both more radical and more conservative than the rest of the United States put together. But because California is the end, the frontier mentality has to wash back again, over the mountains and across the plains. Hence the observation by American writers and cultural historians, that California today is America tomorrow. Campus riots, the drug culture, Jesus freaks, the divorce rate: yesterday in California, today in the Midwest.

But how does all this apply to the revival tradition in America? Listen to Charles Finney's friend, Lyman Beecher:

The religious and political destiny of our nation is to be decided in the West. The capacity of the West for self-destruction, without religious and moral culture, will be as terrific as her capacity for self-preservation with it will be glorious.

This helps to elucidate the subtitle of this chapter: "From Coast to Frontier." It also helps to underline the context of American religious life and thought which was always more raw, closer to the bone, than anything in Europe. Just as America to the immigrant was a challenge to survival, a similar knife-edge option was presented to the church. The church had to launch out into the wilderness and struggle with the pioneers. If this could mean a refreshing openness and depth of commitment, it could also mean a certain lack of that balance which the early church maintained.

The Revival Tradition in America

In accordance with our title, "The Revival Tradition," I am not going to attempt a rundown on the history of American revivalism with which, in some ways, you are probably quite familiar—from Jonathan Edwards, Frelinghuysen and Whitefield, through Finney, the Camp meetings and Moody, to Billy Sunday, Amy Semple Macpherson, the young Billy Graham, and the weekly "revivals" advertised at various churches in various places in this strange land.

It is, I think, far more useful for our purpose to examine revivalism as a sort of religious tradition and see what it tells us. It might be entertaining to talk about snake handling, sawdust trails and colorful con artists. But this would be to emphasize the accidental at the expense of the substantial, the peculiar instead of the normal: to descend, in fact, to the fraudulent level of *Elmer Gantry* and *Marjoe*.

I do, in fact, take my cue from an impeccable source—Jonathan Edwards himself, whose famous and influential *Faithful Narrative of the Surprising Work of God in the Conversion of Many Hundred Souls in Northampton, and the Neighboring Towns and Villages* (1736) concentrated on the meaning and the principles of God's working in his own congregation.

Edwards fastened on to a striking characteristic of the Northampton revival and others since: its rise and fall in time; the fact that it was localized in time as well as in space. But this is something which we can only note, without being able to do more than admit that the work of God's Spirit, who blows where he lists, is far more down-to-earth and specific than the spiritual sophisticate would prefer. The Spirit's aesthetic is not cultivated humanity's aesthetic. Their tastes are different. "For my thoughts are not your thoughts, neither are my ways your ways, saith the Lord of Hosts." True spirituality is always more practical and physical than we like to imagine. This is because we prefer to keep God out of our daily business.

There are other facets of revival which admit of more sustained comment. I am here thinking of American revivalism, of course, well aware that peculiar circumstances, already described, help to give it a special, incidental character. Not all the things observable in American revivalism are present at all or in the same degree in revivals elsewhere, whether in Wales, East Africa, or India.

No Other Foundation

Sudden conversion as the normal method of entrance into the Kingdom of God is a predictable emphasis when thousands are observed to so enter. Sudden conversion is a classic hallmark of redemption but not, as we have seen, the only one. Taken in isolation it leads to distortion and spiritual shallowness. It tempts men to think they know exactly how God works and therefore give his work a judicious assist by setting up certain conditions in which people may, in fact, be suddenly "converted"—the "right" music, the "right" cadence of voice, the "right" combination of hard and soft sell. One of the "converts" is the sociologist, who is convinced that he can describe and explain revival—and therefore Christianity—in terms of these and other factors.

The very appearance, overnight, of large numbers of converts—without the constraining influence of the Judaic assembly which lent essential form to the fledgling New Testament church—naturally fed into the typical Baptist emphasis upon the church as a company of experiential, Christian individuals (rather than covenant families) and the congregationalist emphasis upon the virtual autonomy of the local congregation (to that degree unrestrained by synodical discipline). Not that Baptist and Congregationalist church polity can be so baldly described, but I am talking about the direction of emphasis.

The emphasis on conversion as the total experience, forgetting or minimizing the biblical insistence that salvation is a process completed by Christ's return, weakens the interest in, and the quality of, regular biblical instruction. Christian education tends to become synonymous with evangelization. Once converted, the sermon or Sunday school lesson may be used to maintain a level of interest or concern, instead of to help believers to "study to show themselves approved unto God," workmen "needing not to be ashamed, rightly dividing the word of truth." Such workmen will have answers for those who ask them about their faith, not in terms of a stereotyped evangelistic "package" but from a personally appropriated grasp of scriptural truth which, by the Spirit's ministrations, is coordinated to their own mind and tongue.

An emphasis on certain strict forms of Christian living is also prominent. The explanation for this paradoxically doctrinaire attitude to conduct, side by side with a highly undoctrinaire attitude to teaching, lies in the emphasis on the local congregation. Local standards take precedence over biblical principles. Paul's "weaker brother" teaching, which anticipates the strengthening of the faith and conscience of the weak, is distorted, so that the weaker brother becomes the norm rather than the exception. In this way, much of the attractive freedom and freshness of the Gospel in the lives of individuals, families and churches is lost. What replaces it is a sub-Christian culture, like a glob of unmelted cheese in a stew, instead of salt to spice the world.

A corollary of the emphasis on local standards of conduct is a parallel insistence on the importance of local preferences with respect to minor points of doctrine. These minor points of doctrine, like minor points of conduct, become defining characteristics of the church. As a result, a splintering process takes place—so many "beams" escaping an equivalent number of "specks." This is not to minimize honest differences of opinion. If, however, assuming a shared base in the central Christian doctrines discussed in the first chapters, these honest disagreements produce barriers, then the tail is wagging the dog. Definitions of faith become more important than its substantial outworking. The details of our hope in Christ's return begin to cloud the admonitions to spiritual readiness for this great event. And both faith and hope become greater than love.

Finally, the encouragement given to Christians by the great expansion of church membership in a revival often fosters a biblically unrealistic view of the possible inroads to be made by the Gospel before Christ's return. Of course, there is a thin line between a faithful confidence in God's power and an assumption that the present spiritual climate is going to prevail indefinitely. As Edwards noted, and as we have had the leisure to observe since the mid-nineteenth century, there is an ebb and flow to the tide of revival. Furthermore, if the expansion of Christian testimony through ever more effective tools of communication—the book, the newspaper, radio, television, satellite—is impressive, it is easy to forget that the same tools are in the hands of the Prince of this world. It would be fair to say that in a fallen world, evil increases geometrically. The Gospel spreads mathematically, save in times of revival. Bearing in mind the prevailing secular climate which provided the context for the nineteenth-century American revivals, it is tempting to see in the taste for postmillennialism a Christian counterpart to the growing belief in human progress. Finney could write, in words more expressive of literal

No Other Foundation

truth than providential likelihood: "If the church will do her duty, the millennium may come in this country in three years."

About the same time, in 1831, the Frenchman de Tocqueville in his great book *Democracy in America,* wrote: "I have seen no country where Christianity presents more distinct, more simple, or more general notions to the mind." Noting that "by respecting all democratic tendencies not absolutely contrary to herself" Christianity became an ally of the "spirit of individual independence," he warned that the clergy might therefore "readily adopt the general opinion of their country and their age." The children of this world are wiser in their own generation than the sons of light.

So far, our approach has been overly critical. Each of the characteristics of the American revival tradition may be matched by others which balance or oppose them. After all, the very ingathering of so many to the church represented a material addition to that Kingdom whose completion is the essential prelude to Christ's return. From the revivals came significant contributions to human well-being as men and women strove to obey the Gospel in daily life. The abolitionist movement, for example, owes much to the revival of nineteenth-century American Christianity. And Oberlin College is only a better-known example of the many contributions to American education. American educational institutions, indeed, reflect in miniature the ebb and flow of the spiritual life of the country: almost all the old, great colleges and universities, and seminaries, were founded in faith. And almost all have departed that faith.

It is this theme of ebb and flow to which we must again return in closing. As professor of theology at Oberlin, that man greatly used of God and possessed of extraordinary gifts of mind and imagination, Charles Finney, declared in his famous 1835 *Lectures on Revivals in Religion:* "The connection between the right use of means for a revival, and a revival, is as philosophically sure as between the right use of means to raise grain, and a crop of wheat."

At first sight this might seem an unexceptionable statement. Closer inspection reveals that it is folklore. For one thing, it betrays a mechanistic naturalism which tells you more about currently accepted methods of knowledge or epistemology than it does about the workings of God's Spirit. For another thing, the similarity between revivals is more apparent than real. What is absolutely similar is precisely what cannot be plotted or simulated. It is the sovereign movement of God which always surprises his presumptuous well-wishers. The anticipated channels never turn out to be the main ones. The chosen son is invariably the eighth, who happens to be in the fields, not the first two or three, expectantly lined up.

Finney was surely right to stress genuine repentance as a prelude to revival. But God holds the watch. To preach repentance to get revival would be a barren procedure. The real preaching of repentance issues from repentance, just as the real preaching of joy and victory only carries conviction when it results from joy and victory.

In other words, revival is not an end to seek. Revival is a result, sovereignly bestowed, of genuine turning to God in humility and regular obedience to his stated commands. Where the American revival tradition turned sour—as in the spiritually scarred "burned-over" district of upstate New York, a scene of Finney's early preaching—it followed a thirsting after revival for the sake of spiritual "accreditation."

The mark of a godly life, of a godly congregation, is not revival—it is godliness itself. If God further visits his children with revival power, then all praise to him whose desire is that none should perish and who thus allows us a foretaste of the communion which will be our normal state when Christ completes our salvation.

The Christian's safest preoccupation—it will occupy him enough!—is doing the truth. "Feed my sheep," Jesus said to Peter. And "What is that to thee?" he countered, when Peter expressed curiosity about John.

For Further Study

Finney on Revival, ed. E. E. Shelhamer (1974). A good way to sense the freshness and clarity of Finney.

Edwards, Jonathan. "A Narrative of Surprising Conversions." In *Select Works.* London: Banner of Truth Trust, 1965.

The Great American Gentleman: The Secret Diary of William Byrd of Westover in Va. Edited by Louis B. Wright and Marion Tinling. New York: G. P. Putnam's Sons, 1963. Fascinating glimpse of a different world in the very same colonies. Byrd's ability to read Hebrew and

No Other Foundation

Greek and his regular schedule of prayer and Bible reading puts our relative lassitude into perspective. He was, of course, a "mere" landowner, not a scholar or a pastor.

Tocqueville, Alexis de. *Democracy in America.* Edited and abridged by Richard D. Heffner. New York: New American Library, n.d. Indispensable for American self-knowledge.

West, Nathanael. *The Day of the Locust.* New York: Bantam, 1975. This is what I meant by some of the remarks about California. A novel.

17

The Enlightenment, the French Revolution, and Non-Christian Society

A S WE MOVE into modern times, it is necessary to pause in order to scrutinize the secular context of church history rather deliberately. With the size and influence of the church in the West shrinking, it is strategically important to understand precisely the nature of the world around it. Though European society was often more Christian in name than in fact before the eighteenth century, yet the formal acceptance of Christianity as the basic structure of life and thought forced even what was not Christian into a recognizable Christian mold. From the eighteenth century, this has been less and less the case, until in our own day social and political reflexes and the presuppositions of much of our education are not merely non-Christian but increasingly anti-Christian.

This being the case, it is apparent that the place and role of the church in the modern world is essentially the same as that of Abraham and the Jews in Old Testament times, and that of the fledgling Christian church in the Roman Empire. The church is the more obviously a light when the surrounding darkness is thicker. The classic trial for the church in this setting is that it must learn to walk in God's darkness, rejecting the world's artificial light.

The biblical image here, drawn from Isaiah 50:10-11, is not an idle one. Wherever culture is deliberately apart from God, who gives true light, it manufactures its own light. Wherever culture is in fact foolish (because "The fool hath said in his heart, 'There is

no God' ''), it generates its own wisdom to replace the wisdom of
the Creator. As Paul put it, echoing the sentiments of Psalm 14,
men exchanged the truth about God for a lie and worshipped and
served the creature rather than the Creator.

I find it most striking that in the epoch—namely the eighteenth
century—in which modern Western humanism came of age, became self-confident, strong enough to deny that true wisdom lies
in obeying an infinite, personal God—in this of all epochs, such
convictions were described as ''enlightened,'' suffused with true
light. Exactly how far contemporaries were aware of the obvious
mimicking of the biblical claims is impossible to say. I suspect
that in an age still well schooled in biblical knowledge and im-
agery, the juxtaposition of the light (or Light) described in the
Bible with the light shed by human reason must have been self-
conscious. Indeed, Alexander Pope's famous lines testify to this:

> Nature and Nature's Laws Lay Hid in Night
> God said, Let Newton be, and there was Light!

The contrary hypothesis is powerfully and, I think, just as
self-consciously expressed by Charles Wesley in that hymn
stanza cited in a previous chapter:

> Long my imprison'd Spirit lay
> Fast bound in sin and Nature's night;
> Thine eye diffus'd a quick'ning ray,
> I woke; the dungeon flam'd with light.
> My chains fell off, my heart was free;
> I rose, went forth and follow'd Thee.

It took considerable boldness and perception, spiritually and intellectually, to cast nature in the role of night in an age whose
central conviction was that nature was the source of light. It takes
even more perception and boldness now because we are so unaware of the currents of thought around us, being subtly influenced
by them, that we do not realize that a contrary affirmation is
called for. The chief value in studying the Enlightenment and the
French Revolution is that it acclimatizes us to our own day.
Knowing the enemy is half the battle.

Nature abhors a vacuum, they say. In any consideration of the
Enlightenment, as also in any consideration of the contem-
poraneous spiritual awakening, one must draw attention to the

weakness of the church. This weakness was in the two cardinal areas of idea and practice, truth and experience.

The impoverishment of Christian experience, the lukewarmness of much of the church, quite naturally caused some people to seek elsewhere for solutions to society's ills. Take Geneva. In the sixteenth century, Sicilian peasants could look there for a model of a just society, where the leading pastors even refused money for better clothes on the grounds that the poverty of a few precluded their accepting such a gift. By the eighteenth century, Geneva was very much part of the elitist social structure of contemporary Europe. Its pastorate obeyed the sumptuary laws of the day. The tragedy here is that such false conduct was associated by the skeptic, as effect follows cause, with the Gospel which these ministers supposedly embodied. If society needed change, how could it come from the Gospel? The Gospel was apparently found wanting.

If Christian experience, or conduct, was often treasonous, we can expect that the Christian's statement of truth betrayed the one who identified himself as the Truth. Creeping into statements of Christian doctrine were elements far more human than divine. Good works and the good will of men (ironically, in view of the behavioral apostasy), were being emphasized over against the free grace and forgiveness of God. One cannot preach need and repentance when one believes in self-sufficiency and self-righteousness.

The result of this slow defection from biblical religion was the caricaturing of the truth. Jesus, for instance, far from being presented as *the* Truth, was reduced to an *example* of truth—a good man, a Jewish Socrates, a Christian Moses. Voltaire unwittingly levelled a telling indictment against the clergy when he praised the "crowd of theologians" who had "already embraced Socinianism [roughly equivalent to present-day Unitarian-Universalism] which closely approaches the worship of a single God, free from superstition" (from his "Sermon of the Fifty," reprinted in *Deism: An Anthology,* ed. Peter Gay [New York: Van Nostrand Reinhold Co., 1968], pp. 156-57). This brings us to a second point.

Certainly, the weakness of the church was a great help to the Enlightenment. Voltaire's gibe at monks, though unfair as a wholesale judgment, had its point: "A monk—what does he do for a living? Nothing, except to bind himself by an inviolable oath to be a slave and a fool and to live at the expense of other people." But when such corruption was joined to an outright acceptance of "enlightened" ideas, the defection was total.

It might be noted in passing that Voltaire was more ready to criticize the gluttony of the church than the corruption of his own semireligious movement. In the same way, Diderot could complain about censorship and yet work hard when he had a foot in the door to censor works critical of the Enlightenment. Hedonism and hypocrisy are more excusable when lip service is paid to one's own doctrines.

There is a good example of moral irresponsibility and defection from the truth in the famous Archbishop of Toulouse, Brienne, whom Louis XVI of France appointed to straighten out financial affairs just as the revolution was about to explode. He has been described as "a luxurious unbeliever who called on his countrymen for financial sacrifices, and awarded himself huge compensations in promotions and benefices when he left office a few months later. This archbishop . . . spent more time leaning on his billiard cue than in saying masses . . . As a churchman, he had risen to high responsibilities solely because of noble birth; intellectually, he belonged to the party of the *philosophes; . . .*" His basic demeanor is underlined by Louis XVI's reaction to the suggestion that he be a candidate for the archbishopric of Paris: "At the very least, the Archbishop of Paris must believe in God!" (John McManners, *The French Revolution and the Church* [London: S.P.C.K., 1970], pp. 2, 16).

Brienne is, of course, a technicolor example of an "enlightened" Christian. He is not, therefore, typical. On the other hand, the combination of the church seen as a path to power or a way of earning a living, and the adoption of the secular ideas of the world whose mentality was thus aped—this *is* typical. Diderot's multi-volume *Encyclopedia,* the greatest single monument to the Enlightenment, was not without its clerical contributors, drawn from the ranks of Roman Catholic priests and Reformed pastors alike. To indulge in the old cliche, with such friends, the church had no need of an enemy. But it had one anyway.

In view of the remarks made earlier about human light, it will make sense to discover that basic to Enlightenment thought is a set of postulates and a method of reasoning that provides a foundation for a program of enlightenment purely human. In other words, we shall expect to find an emphasis upon the power of the unaided human mind and a rejection of any questioning of this. To summarize such an ideology is not easy, but we must try.

It drew heavily on the method of reasoning, or the approach to knowledge, called induction, along with the complementary insistence upon experimentation. Much of the impetus here came from the first of a trinity of Englishmen who had a great influence upon the Enlightenment: Francis Bacon (1561-1626). This was not a novel approach. It was implicit in the Florentine Renaissance and received precocious, though private, articulation in the work of Leonardo da Vinci. But it was Bacon above all who, in his printed works, popularized for a select audience the inductive method.

Bacon, a Christian, rightly saw induction as a child of Christian belief. The Enlightenment would, however, seek to use it as a tool of skepticism as well as a tool of discovery. Enlightenment writers were fond of exposing the ignorance which accrued from a culture which honored verbal logic and argumentative subtlety, contrasting it to the illumination that came from honest, open investigation. To hear Voltaire on this theme is to hear the echoes of Erasmus. The ends to which Voltaire bent his endeavors describe in a nutshell the evolution of European thought between 1500 and 1750.

Induction is all very well, but logic and reasoning have to come in somewhere, if one is to arrange and understand the results of one's research and experiment. This is where the legacy of the French philosopher and mathematician Descartes (1596-1650) comes in. This is the Descartes who wrote: "I think, therefore I am" and who described a way of arriving logically at "clear and distinct ideas." Note the emphasis upon "I think" as the basis of being "I am." In other words, mind, reason, the intellect, is primary. Though Descartes claimed, no doubt sincerely, that all thought processes depend upon God, his intellectual children can hardly be blamed for quietly forgetting God and depending solely upon mind.

I referred to Bacon as the first of a trinity of influential Englishmen. The other two were Isaac Newton (1642-1727) and John Locke (1632-1704).

No Other Foundation

Newton, proceeding according to clear, Baconian methods, so it seemed (the reality was a little different), examined all the available evidence and was able to reduce the workings of the physical universe to a few general laws. The significance of this achievement for the eighteenth century was colossal. If the application of the human mind, unencumbered by prejudice, could uncover the mystery of planetary motion, could not the same mind, applied to other tasks, work out the laws of politics, society, education and morals? This was in fact the overwhelming hope and expectation of the Enlightenment.

The mention of education brings us to Locke whose *Essay on Human Understanding* (1690) argued that the newborn infant's mind is like a blank slate upon which experience starts to write. If so, then education is crucial. One can entirely enlighten mankind by subjecting people to the right ideological conditioning. This proved to be one of the deepest impulses to educational endeavor in the eighteenth and nineteenth centuries. Rousseau's *Emile* is an early treatise on the sort of educational program likely to yield the best results. B. F. Skinner's *Walden Two* is a more recent one, illustrating an evolution between him and Rousseau almost as great as that between Voltaire and Erasmus.

While the evidence is now overwhelming that pure behaviorism (which is what we are talking about) contradicts known facts, there is still a very powerful body of social psychologists and educationalists in our own day who accept the Lockeian conviction. They wish to indoctrinate our children and ourselves in a program that bears little relation to any utopia that we should ever wish to inhabit. The persistence of the behaviorist impulse is, incidentally, due to the fact that it represents the ultimate logic of the rejection of a creating God.

This entire way of looking at things, coupled to a still strong memory of biblical values which gave shape and direction to many Enlightenment aims, resulted in a cluster of convictions which roughly summarize Enlightenment opinion. They may be itemized thus: a government responsible to its citizens, operating according to a constitution; toleration of civil and religious minorities; enjoyment of private pleasure balanced by public duty; a devotion to the spirit of criticism, viewing all positions as tentative; the belief that everything can be physically or biologically explained; the belief, therefore, that the supernatural is only a subtle aspect of the natural.

Accompanying—indeed inspiring—all these opinions, was the twin conviction that man is alone responsible for his destiny and that original sin is a myth to cover up man's failure to act decisively. Redemption, therefore, is the self-achieved redemption of being true to oneself and one's species. Listen to Voltaire's description of true, human natural religion. It is the heart of Deism.

We must have the courage to go a few steps farther; the common people is not as idiotic as many think; it will accept without difficulty a wise and simple creed of a single God, such as (they tell us) Abraham and Noah worshipped, such as is accepted in China by all literate men. We do not claim to deprive the priests of that which the liberality of the nations has bestowed on them; but we want these priests, who nearly all secretly ridicule the lies they retail, to join us in preaching the truth. Let them watch out; they offend the Divinity and dishonor it, and instead should glorify it. What inestimable good would be produced by such a happy change! Princes and magistrates would be obeyed more readily, people would be more peaceful, the spirit of division and hatred would be dissipated. One would offer God, in peace, the first-fruits of one's labor; there would certainly be more honesty in the world, for a large number of weak-minded persons who hear contemptuous talk every day about this Christian superstition, who know that it is ridiculed by the very priests themselves, imagine, without thinking, that actually there is no true religion—and they surrender themselves to a life of excess. But when they will know that the Christian sect is actually nothing more than the perversion of natural religion; when reason, freed from its chains, will teach the people that there is only one God, that this God is the universal father of all men, who are brothers; that these brothers must be good and just to one another, and that they must practice all the virtues; that God, being good and just, must reward virtue and punish crimes; surely, my brethren, men will be better for it, and less superstitious.

We are making a beginning by giving this example in secret, and we dare to hope that it will be followed in public.

May this great God who listens to me; this God who surely cannot have been born of a girl, nor died on the gibbet, nor be eaten in a piece of dough, nor have inspired these books filled with contradictions, madness, and horror; may this God, creator of all the worlds, have pity on that sect of Christians that blasphemes him! May he lead them back to the holy and natural religion, and spread his blessings over our efforts to have him truly worshipped. Amen. (from the "Sermon of the Fifty" in Gay, *Deism*, pp. 157-8)

I hardly need comment on this. It represents a brilliant indictment of all so-called Christianity which has wandered from the truth in word and deed. The line about people doubting the faith because of the apostasy of the priests could have been written yesterday. Intriguingly, the hope that by the example of a few who start in secret there will eventually be a public acceptance is like nothing so much as the recent sentiments of a latter-day Voltairean humanist, Arthur Koestler.

At the end of his *The Ghost in the Machine* (New York: Macmillan Co., 1968), which is an incisive attack upon modern behaviorism, he makes an appeal in favor of the acceptance of some sort of miracle pill to eradicate man's violent, anti-social tendencies. He speculates that once such a pill is found beneficial by a small segment of the population, it will then be accepted by governments and be introduced to the masses.

What is interesting, further, is that whereas Koestler's faith in man is similar to Voltaire's—he speaks of man taking his fate into his own hands to avoid disaster—he has had to recognize the total failure of the Enlightenment program and propose a drastic change in men's chemistry to achieve a good society. Ultimately, therefore, the Enlightenment's desire to command fate proves to require an artificial adulteration of man himself (see Koestler, pp. 337-39). The only worthwhile deposits in the Bank of Enlightenment prove to have been the vestiges of Christian values. With these withdrawn, the bank is broken. The expensive programs are discontinued. And the managers propose to appease the depositors with tranquilizers.

The title of this chapter included the French Revolution; one of the big questions that historians have debated periodically is the possible connection between it and the Enlightenment. The Enlightenment, of course, was much more than a French movement, though the French were the leading enthusiasts and propagandists. But in considering its relation to the French Revolution I am thinking above all of its manifestations in France.

Two things may safely be said about the question at issue. First, the causes of the French Revolution are far too complex and various to be tied down to a rather elitist philosophical movement. The obvious social, economic and political causes are very direct and demonstrable, as also the element of misadventure. Second, although the French Revolution cannot then be seen as a direct result of the Enlightenment, the Enlightenment had dreamed of significant changes in society and had provided an informal arsenal of suggestions for the renewal or transformation of society. The fact that the men who led the revolution were articulate and literate men who had absorbed the ideas of their century makes it safe to affirm that, however much in some ways the revolution betrayed aspects of Enlightenment belief, it certainly provided the matrix for thoroughgoing changes in France and, by influence and force of arms, elsewhere. The revolution did, indeed, illustrate the central Enlightenment conviction that man is responsible for his own destiny and must be given a chance to achieve it.

I want to look at the French Revolution, however, as more than just a reflection of certain humanistic values. Furthermore, I want to examine it not as one might at school, detailing the stirring events and the inexorable breakdown leading to the dictatorship of Napoleon. Rather, I wish to outline the cultural dynamic of the revolutionary years.

While proceeding in a fashion that would have appalled Voltaire (although not, perhaps, Rousseau), the revolution did reflect the Enlightenment's desire to change society. The revolution did, as it were, live out the inner implications of the Enlightenment. These implications were, quite simply, that the problem of culture is a matter of structure, not of mere function; of principle, not detail. Therefore, structural change is required. But structures do not change peacefully. A structure may be reformed. To replace it, revolution is called for.

Though a Voltaire would have shied away from the blood and treachery, the revolution in its basic cultural implication was far more Voltairean than Voltaire would have cared to admit. By the 1790s, of course, Voltaire was safely dead, and no one could see him turn over in the coffin that the revolutionaries reverently bore to the Pantheon.

Installing Voltaire—and Rousseau, too—in the Pantheon in Paris may seem a little absurd at this distance. The cult of the Goddess of Reason seems even more so, being saved from entire ridicule by the fact of having only a very short run. The switch to a brand-new calendar and a ten-day week, with new names for the months, merits closer attention. It marks a serious articulation of a mentality which the cult of reason had merely baptized. If the cult of reason stood for the purely human ordering of human affairs, the new calendar was a forthright effort to alter one of the deepest of all facts of existence—time itself—to accord with a rational, a "natural" way of looking at things. The pope who agreed to grace the coronation of Napoleon as Emperor in 1804, partly in exchange for the abolition of this revolutionary calendar, knew what he was doing. He deserves our applause.

In another crucial way the French Revolution marked the new humanistic world. Far more so than the American Revolution, it posited the great break between individual beliefs and values, and the practice of government. Hitherto, government was a reflection of values and it was axiomatic that no society could last long or function humanely without most people subscribing to these values. The French Revolution, especially as interpreted by Napoleon, gave notice that government is a question of pure efficiency. Values are not, therefore, positive ideas undergirding government, but potential obstacles in the way of government. The government can either crudely eradicate such ideas or condition society so as to tame them.

Just as developments in Renaissance Florence were a precocious indication of what Europe as a whole would eventually experience, likewise the history of France between 1789 and 1815 pointed forward to the alternatives facing the West in the next 200 years.

Anyone who knows anything about the Enlightenment will be aware that I have said nothing about the important influence of Classical Greece and Rome and the sense that many *philosophes* had of clearing the clouds obscuring the bright, clear sky of Athens and Rome. It is not for nothing that the revolutionary epoch is strewn with classical titles: senators, consuls, censors—and an emperor. The fact is that all movements have a strong sense of ancestry and can trace their own genealogies lovingly across the ages.

This is certainly true of biblical, Christian religion. With deep affection, we look back to an Abel, a Noah, an Abraham; a Moses, David or Ezra; not to mention the Apostles and the witnesses since. We see in them, in their trials, their weaknesses and their faith—as did the author of Hebrews—the same loving hand of God which deals mercifully and chasteningly with his children. Without a strong sense of this living heritage, our faith is the weaker. God works in history; and the history of the faithful is a reminder of this fact.

But, equally, the Enlightenment had its genealogy. One of the important histories of the Enlightenment written in the last two decades is subtitled: *The Rise of Modern Paganism.** The author is quite right to emphasize this. The Enlightenment does represent the return to pre-Christian paganism. The genealogy has a yet wider reference. Earlier we spoke of the significance of the very term "enlightenment" in view of the biblical stress on light. Have you pondered such modern groups as the Divine Light Mission? Have you argued recently with someone enamoured of Eastern religions who told you that he also worshipped the "Light" and that there is no difference between this "Light" and Jesus' claim to be the Light?

What I am suggesting is that this is a worldwide phenomenon which is entirely to be expected if there is a family likeness to all beings made by the same Creator. In other words, rebellion against God is as uniform as is the faith that binds men together in their worship of him.

"Divine Light," "Inner Light," "Enlightenment"—all are, whatever their different histories, related. And all are, whatever their incidental insights, counterfeit hopes. They are the rebuilding of Babel. They are total dependence upon self-achieved salvation. They are the hallmark of the society in which we now live.

This chapter, which has been solely devoted to the shape of the world around us as it began to form 200 years ago, will have performed a service if it opens our eyes to a sober fact: that the basic structure of Western society, which was once Christian, is now pagan. Thus, if Christian reviving once called for a reform of the structure, now it calls for a change of the structure. But a change not by blood; rather through *the* Blood. As an old hymn puts it, even if a little tritely:

> Conquering kings their titles take
> From the foes they captive make;
> Jesus, by a nobler deed,
> From the thousands he hath freed.

*Peter Gay, *The Enlightenment: An Interpretation—The Rise of Modern Paganism,* Vol. 1 (New York: W. W. Norton, 1977).

No Other Foundation

For Further Study

Becker, Carl. *The Heavenly City of the Eighteenth-Century Philosophers.* New Haven, CT: Yale University Press, 1932. Classic; argues the "faith" underlying humanism. Overstated but accurate enough to earn a whole book of angry responses from devotees of the Enlightenment!

Diderot, Denis. *Rameau's Nephew and D'Alembert's Dream.* Translated by L. Tancock. Harmondsworth, Eng.: Penguin Books, 1976. Two basic works precociously anticipating modern alienation and modern psychology.

Palmer, Robert R. *Catholics and Unbelievers in 18th Century France.* Princeton, NJ: Princeton University Press, 1939. Detailed study, modifying generalities.

Voltaire on Religion: Selected Writings. Edited and translated by Kenneth W. Applegate.

Pope, Alexander. *Essay on Man.* Edited by Frank Brady. Indianapolis: Bobbs-Merrill, 1965. Foretells much of 18th century preoccupation. Better poet but more embittered man than Voltaire.

18

The Church Under Attack: Apes and Theologians

THE BIBLE IS EMPHATIC that we are not disembodied souls and minds, or mere bodies, but unified beings. Therefore, what is true of our soul and mind will be true of our body—that is to say, of ourselves as a totality. Beliefs, in other words, are present in our actions.

If this is true on the individual level, it is equally true socially. When certain ideas gain currency in a society, there are practical results. And the practical application of ideas, loosens up society to accept more radical views along the lines of those already entertained. For any standing against such a stream, the adverse current pulls ever more strongly.

All of this is clearly illustrated in nineteenth century church history. On the one hand, nineteenth century natural religion—religion cut down to human size—gushes forth into the post-Napoleonic world, often in sophisticated guises, but "natural" nonetheless. Being a religion made to human order, it is always the flexible matrix for current fashions in scholarship and philosophy. Indeed, marking the growing secularization of society, rather than the crucible in which men's ideas were formed, this natural religion was becoming a mere repository of ill-sorted, ill-defined problems within the crucible of contemporary thought. The day would come when, most of these problems having been catalogued under different headings, religion could be thrown aside as excess baggage. This is illustrated by the demise of non-supernatural religion in the face of biological determinism, come of age in Darwin's *Origin of Species* (1859).

On the other hand, because these things cannot be separated from everyday life, there was being explored at the same time the

No Other Foundation

heritage of a new, implicitly pagan world; of a society without values, save the value of its own survival. Thus, cheek-by-jowl with fierce debates over orthodoxy, reason and faith, science and religion, went a striking battle in several countries over the relation between church and state. Although one might not always wish to support the church in each of these battles, one cannot help reflecting upon the parallels between the Christian religion being forced out of the citadels of learning, and the Christian church being evicted from the halls of power. Willy-nilly, whatever the specific rights and wrongs in each case, the situation had a moral: "My kingdom," said Jesus, "is not of this world."

Let us first examine the intellectual currents swirling around and through the church. Then we shall look at a few of the public conflicts, visible to the rank-and-file layman as well as to the educated elite.

Pilate asked, "What is truth?" But we know that he was not seeking it. It would, in many cases, be unfair to suggest that theologians in the 19th century were asking this question in the same fashion. But there is something to the observation (Alec R. Vidler, *The Church in an Age of Revolution: 1789 to the Present Day* [Harmondsworth, Eng.: Penguin Books, 1972], p. 113) that the Victorian epoch—on the Continent, too—was not so much an age of faith as one of "religious seriousness."

Men were seriously interested in religion as a phenomenon to be explained and to be reconciled to other things. The fact that religion existed, as it were, earned it the right to be taken seriously. The fact that Jesus was, legally, the legitimate object of Pilate's attention, forced Pilate to address questions to him. But no commitment was implied. Indeed, Pilate mocked the idea of any absolute truth when confronted directly with Jesus' claim to be a witness to the truth. Much the same sort of thing seems to have been true of certain quests for theological truth in the nineteenth century.

Several chapters ago, we noted Erasmus's surprise when his Greek New Testament received such a hostile reception in Rome. I pointed out that he was a bit naive not to expect alarm at the principle of uncontrolled scholarly examination of sacred texts. Two things were taken seriously at Rome: the possibility of the ignorant being led astray by apparent challenges to religious authority; and the possibility that what might be a positive instrument in the hands of a believer like Erasmus could be a weapon of war in the hands of a hostile critic.

In the spirit of Paul on the Areopagus and Nicodemus in the Sanhedrin, we should always opt for open, fair discussion, despite the obvious potential for misconstruction and perversity. At the same time, we would be simple-minded not to recognize that the mind is a tool of the will, and an ill-will blows nobody good. An essentially destructive biblical criticism, for example, was the subject of more than 50 percent of all clandestine, "enlightened" manuscripts circulating in France between 1700 and 1750 and since catalogued by scholars. What would later be called "Higher Criticism," was, then, finding its feet during the Enlightenment. So pugnaciously, in fact, did eighteenth century intellectuals take off in pursuit of supposed errors in the Bible, that by the early nineteenth century theologians and philosophers were rushing forward with human plans to save the tottering "ark" of religion. Most of these plans owed an incalculable debt to three seminal figures: Kant, Schleiermacher and Hegel.

Immanuel Kant (1724-1804) had denied that by reason one could know God or that, indeed, one could know anything in the abstract. Knowledge comes through the senses, he maintained, thereby fueling the prophetic alarm of his younger contemporary Goethe who foresaw the disastrous separation of the scientific and religious realms. If Kant's assertion seemed negative, if the function of religious belief was, in effect, to inject an imperative note into otherwise voluntary moral notions, then it could also be twisted into a positive argument for religion. That is, religion is secure from rational attack if it deals with matters beyond the reach of reason. In other words, if Christianity cannot be proved, then it cannot be disproved, either. Two men reacted from Kant in their own distinctive ways. Both were professors in Berlin and, like Kant, Germans.

Schleiermacher (1763-1834), both in his wonderfully entitled *Religion: Speeches to its Cultured Despisers* (1799) and in his fuller *The Christian Faith* (1821-22) labored to recover for Christianity its place in intellectual life. Wary of what, in the footsteps of Kant, he saw as mere logic, a presumptuous intrusion of reason onto holy ground, he stressed man's basic consciousness of God as the most profound evidence of his existence. But, in so doing, he tended to de-emphasize the sense in which one's redemption marks any sort of break. Redemption is seen more as a gradual and natural awakening of an underlying consciousness of God. What Schleiermacher saw as a process on the personal level had its counterpart on the social and historical level. Thus, any talk of such a dramatic break as the Fall dies on the lips. And when the Fall goes, true Christian redemption goes. He was said to evince a warm personal devotion to Christ. He certainly thought that he was restoring a lost emphasis on personal experience and commitment. But to remove the signposts that brought you to faith is disastrous for those following behind.

Hegel (1770-1831), a far more systematic and more generally influential thinker, was also a far less attractive personality. He elaborated much more carefully this theology of process or consciousness. He denied Kant's assertion that the metaphysical and the abstract cannot be known, insisting that they are embedded in our self-consciousness. The fact that we have a sense of there being a divinity, for example, is clear evidence for it. A response to Hegel, here, could be to ask why people have conflicting ideas about God. But Hegel was ready with a brilliantly original answer. He articulated his characteristic theme of a cosmic process in nature and history whereby, through a running battle between opposing tendencies which spark each other along, the universe is reaching towards a final summing up or synthesis.

Hegel would say that there is such a thing as truth, but it is highly abstract and impersonal, and sin is simply a matter of degrees of distance from it. He described all religions as figures of speech, popular caricatures of reality, shadows cast upon the wall of human experience. Christianity, of all these religions, happens to be the only one that depicts the truth accurately—but, again, only in picture form. The distinctive "stories" of Christianity are only incidental to the real truth. As one might expect, therefore, Hegel had little time for the idea that God actually expressed and expresses himself in literal, historical events. This was crudity at its worst. He wished to liberate Christians from such a dangerous dependence on the transient.

Unfortunately, and inescapably, his theology became pure philosophy of the most abstract variety, full of powerful images which dissolve into the mist as soon as you try to grasp them. Yet, Hegel's work, as also that of Schleiermacher, made strong headway among the intelligentsia precisely because it dealt with faith without causing embarrassment. For the mind which delighted in dotting every *i* and crossing every *t* Hegel and Schleiermacher's theology performed the service of making Christianity a moving target, proof against rationalistic marksmanship.

It should be noted in passing that if the men of greatest influence were German, this direction of thought was not just Teutonic. Coleridge, the poet (1772-1834), a man of powerful but erratic genius, was also testing the weather and sought, in a glancing, nonsystematic way, to protect faith from the onslaught of reason. He prepared Englishmen for Higher Criticism by drawing attention to Scripture's power to evoke faith. Its infallibility in terms of historical accuracy and the like he declared to be unimportant in the light of its proven worth in spiritual experience.

An objective post mortem of much of the theological scholarship coming out of Germany in the first half of the nineteenth century, particularly from the famous Tübingen school, must conclude that whatever its benefits in terms of the collation of facts it was mainly at the service of a set of sub-Christian presuppositions.

The famous Strauss (1808-1874), pupil of Hegel and Schleiermacher, whose *Life of Jesus* (1835) created a storm, was guilty of a transparent antihistorical bias towards the New Testament documents. Having decided in advance that though Jesus had existed he had nevertheless been enshrouded by his followers in mythical clothes, he succeeded in writing the biography of such a figure. Faithful to his mentors, his Jesus was an idea which had benefited men in the developing process of reaching towards full human self-realization. He was innocent of any careful appraisal of his conjectures in the light of the documents he purported to criticize.

Though Baur (1792-1860) was a much better historian than Strauss, and saw Strauss's weak points, he was just as much enmeshed in the Hegelian net. Thus, true to the Hegelian dialectical process, the New Testament in Baur's hands was made to fit the pattern of thesis, antithesis and synthesis. Judaic, legalistic Christianity, was set off against Pauline, liberated, universal Christianity. They would both be synthesized in Catholic Christianity, with its joining of both elements: all-embracing yet priestly; worldly yet ascetic; loosely articulated yet tightly sacramental. Baur, the real head of the Tübingen school, arrived unerringly at the conclusions with which he had started.

I spend time on Strauss and Baur because they provide a frame of reference for myriads of theological higher critics following them. When we think of Higher Criticism, we think of different theories of Pentateuchal authorship, and so on. But, fundamentally, these are simply the details. The principle lies in the controlling idea which, to be candid, was a view of life which spawned a cavalier attitude to the very standard of objective enquiry to which the critics were ostensibly dedicated.

So tenacious was this world view, rooted as we have seen in the thought of Kant and his followers, who were exploring the results of the Enlightenment, that no amount of evidence to the contrary has proved capable of shaking it. At least, if shaken, the impulse to examine afresh the biblical documents on the basis of a nonabsolutist epistemology has been notably lacking. Already, in the second half of the century, the British scholar Lightfoot, in his commentary on Galatians, would demolish Baur's elegant contentions on the anvil of painstaking study. But the stream was not checked; merely diverted slightly.

And when, in the next generation, reflecting on the work of men like Lightfoot, Albert Schweitzer (1875-1965) condemned the entire critical enterprise as hitherto conceived, he did not condemn the ideas upon which it was based. Rather, he redirected attention to them. He urged the need to explore the meaning of dialectical process and a faith beyond reason, thereby preparing the soil for the acceptance of the ideas of the Dane who had found little support in his own day: Kierkegaard. But, Kierkegaard's influence being felt only in our own day, we shall deal with him in the twentieth century context.

In turning, as now we must, to what was going on outside the church and the seminary, it is worth pondering briefly the overall meaning of what we have just been discussing. In a nutshell, those theologians whose work would prove most influential were endeavoring to reconcile Christianity to the Enlightenment, much as certain thinkers in past epochs had tried to reconcile the Gospel with Greek thought. But Enlightenment humanism was much more virulently antisupernatural than anything that had preceded it. It reckoned, for reasons we shall soon explore, that it had reality by the tail. Its injection into Christianity was, consequently, far more dangerous. There had been heterodoxy in the church before; but it had never been paraded and increasingly accepted as orthodoxy in quite the same way prior to the nineteenth century.

Nineteenth-century theology is yet more comprehensible when we know a little about contemporary intellectual currents. In particular, the idea of evolution—identified with the name of Charles Darwin—has to be reckoned with.

Evolution, properly understood, belongs to a broad philosophic movement already well defined in the Enlightenment. Darwin's contribution was to provide what seemed to be the necessary scholarly vindication, much as Newton's work had, in the hands of humanists, seemed to bolster faith in the powers of the human mind. Before 1800, it was becoming common in advanced circles to claim that what distinguished man from the animals was greater biological complexity. In this, one was reviving a view held by Epicureans before Christ. Now Darwin's researches provided the apparent proof. What might be dismissed earlier as an interesting theory or atheistical rubbish, had to be confronted as a serious challenge.

It is possible that the degree to which the reaction of some theologians and churchmen was initially rather frenetic was the degree to which the Hegelian de-emphasis upon a reasoned faith had lulled the church into intellectual sluggishness. A certain acuity in arguing cases was missing through lack of practice. Surely, no one had expected to have to fight Voltaire again. Indeed, the forcefulness of the Darwinian challenge had the effect of pushing theologians yet closer to the Hegelian option of brushing aside such issues as essentially transient and irrelevant. After all, Darwinian evolution—for those prepared to look it in the face—rang the death knell on the doctrine of an historic Fall. And had not Hegel and Schleiermacher already dealt with this issue?

It is interesting that from the beginning of the evolution debate, the three options which mark similar discussion now were expressed. The first was to accept Darwin and, therefore, with total consistency either reject Christianity altogether or else place it in a watertight Hegelian compartment—which is close to the same thing. The second was to treat evolution as an unproved hypothesis which, furthermore, through its anti-Christian implications,

No Other Foundation

contradicted the living experience of the church. Even from a secular point of view, this option can now be seen, a century later, to have been the most responsible—it was most true to the method of science. The third was an impossible mixture: to accept Darwinian evolution as mere biological dogma, without further implications, and to sit loose to the particular parts of Scripture bearing in an overt way upon the process of creation. Evolution becomes, in this option, an undigested lump around which the juices continue to flow. Unfortunately, digestion takes place anyway. The mentality which can qualify Scriptural exegesis to accommodate one sort of lump will develop a suitable reflex to accommodate others.

To return to 1859, however, the year Darwin published his *Origin of Species*. You are perhaps familiar with the famous confrontation at the British Association meeting of 1860 between Bishop Samuel Wilberforce and Darwin's self-appointed champion, Thomas Huxley. Huxley made the statement which has been quoted ever since: "If I had to choose, I would prefer to be a descendant of a humble monkey, than of a man who employs his knowledge and eloquence in misrepresenting those who are wearing out their lives in the search for truth." The tension of the occasion is further evoked by the riposte of an anti-Darwinian: "Leave me my ancestors in Paradise, and I will allow you yours in the Zoological Gardens."

The actual position defended by Huxley in 1860 has long since been abandoned. Evolutionary biology considered as a form of religion has, in fact, now entered what may best be described as the mystical phase. General dogmas are maintained for the sake of the faithful but the devotee has long since embraced positions which demand spiritual exercises beyond the ability of the man in the street.

One must not be lost in the details of the argument, however. As in the Scopes trial of the 1920s, we must grasp the overall setting to discover the full significance of what was going on. Historians of nineteenth century culture have seen Darwinism as a self-fulfilling prophecy. Most people are vaguely familiar with the phrase "Social Darwinism." This is the idea that just as in the biological realm there is a natural selection of the fittest, so in the social, cultural, ethnological, and national realms there is a weeding-out process.

The Church Under Attack

In Darwin's England, it was very easy for the highly successful Victorian Englishman, master of an empire upon which the sun never set, to feel that he had "arrived," that he had been "selected" because of his peculiar fittedness. Accompanying this feeling, went a characteristic sense of responsibility for educating the less fortunate tribes and nations until they, too, should arrive at the Englishman's high estate. While this sense of responsibility was by no means always condescending and was not without important benefits, the root idea of superiority—buttressed by Darwin's findings—more and more pervaded Britain's administration of her overseas possessions.

In other words, people were prepared to accept—hook, line and sinker—a body of biological theories as if they represented hard fact, because they offered a convenient scientific explanation for one's own success. It is reassuring to go on with what one is already enjoying doing, firm in the knowledge that one is in the vanguard of mankind's emerging destiny. No wonder that Wallace, the codeveloper of Evolutionary theory, was treated harshly when he spoke favorably of the culture of certain Pacific islanders. How could these backward, almost-apes, produce cultural forms and artifacts worth serious consideration? They were not at the right stage of evolution to have reached the level of sophistication that Wallace claimed. What was at stake, of course, was more than a mere scientific theory—it was a whole mentality. Wallace had to be hooted out of court because his claims could not be rationally discussed.

We are now in a better position to see how Darwinian evolution complemented the evolutionary theology of Hegel and Schleiermacher and the evolutionary exegesis of Strauss and Baur. Not only did it complement it; it justified it. The hunches of the metaphysicians were "proved" correct by the researches of the scientists.

It is worth noting, in addition, to gain an overview of the contemporary setting, the general political situation in Europe. From 1789, the start of the French Revolution, till the final defeat of Napoleon in 1815, Europe had been riven by wars and rumors of wars, revolutions and fears of revolutions. After 1815, reaction set in. The world was made safe for conservatism, and Europe enjoyed an unprecedented if uneasy peace for decades thereafter.

If the terms of this peace enjoined the silencing of any outspo-

No Other Foundation

ken versions of political liberalism, the climate of peace and prosperity was ideal for the expression of ideas of evolutionary progress. It did seem, indeed, that enlightened men were beating their swords into plowshares. If the revolutions of 1848 caused misgiving, it was momentary. If the conflict with Russia in the Crimea in the 1850s cast aspersions on the Holy Alliance engineered by Russia a generation before, then at least it was not a war on European soil. And if the achievement of Italian and German nationhood in the next two decades involved rather more serious national and international tensions, then one could say that the greater good of the evolving identity of two great peoples was served. To make an omelette you have to break a few eggs, after all.

And thinking people were not hopelessly naive. Obviously, the millennium had not arrived yet. There was important business to deal with first. But things were improving; and the more people were prepared to talk over their differences, the more likely that reason would prevail. Not for nothing was the nineteenth century a century, par excellence, of furious endeavor. It was the more difficult in this situation for orthodox Christians to buck the prevailing theological trends. It seemed as if they were trying to hold mankind back by insisting on ideas and dogmas which had been perfectly appropriate at a certain stage in man's development but clearly were now redundant.

The one difference between this situation and that prevailing in the late twentieth century is that the Christian is now accused not so much of impeding man's glorious destiny as of hindering his efforts to survive. In other words—and this summarizes the cultural history of one century in a nutshell—whereas man in the nineteenth century saw himself on the crest of the wave of evolution, now he is afraid that he is unable to swim. He must therefore change himself, and the stubborn Christian says: No! Your problem is not in your being, it is in your choices.

We have, however, wandered away from the immediate nineteenth century reality. Let us remind ourselves of the acceptance of Darwin by a few sentences from a sermon by the English theologian Headlam, preached in 1879: (quoted in Vidler, *op. cit.*, p. 119)

Thank God that the scientific men have . . . shattered the idol of an infallible book, broken the fetters of a supposed divine code of rules; for so they have helped to reveal Jesus Christ in his majesty. . . . He, we say, is the Word of God: he is inspiring you, encouraging you, strengthening you in your scientific studies: he is the *wisdom* in Lyell or in Darwin. . . .

It gives us far grander notions of God to think of him making the world by his Spirit through the ages, than to think of him making it in a few days.

This sounds like the progressive parent commending his delinquent child.

There were replies, certainly. At just the time when Englishmen were being brought up to date with German critical scholarship by the 1860 publication *Essays and Reviews*, a powerful German theologian was beginning to question this scholarship and expose the methodological deficiencies of contemporary natural science. This was Ritschl (1822-1889).

In brilliant fashion, he demonstrated the necessarily finite, tentative nature of all scholarly procedure. He insisted on the primacy of the will over the intellect. Faith, he said, is a response between two persons. He defended the dependability of the New Testament documents. He did understress the objective, intellectual apprehension of the historical facts about Jesus and their role in faith. But I think that because Karl Barth was impressed by Ritschl, in whom he recognized some kinship, scholars have tended to see him through Barthian spectacles, instead of through the circumstances of his own day, thereby artificially isolating his "Barthianism."

It cannot be gainsaid, that although precious few were prepared to digest what he was saying, Ritschl warned his optimistic contemporaries that the human mind is not a reliable instrument by itself and that any quest for truth without humble submission to God's illumination will only ever yield self-flattering theories and self-destroying fantasies. There was a basic balance to Ritschl which was lacking in the prophet chiefly beloved of Barth: Soren Kierkegaard.

On the intellectual front, the tension between Christianity and non-Christian ideas produces open conflict in which a minority are prepared, as Christians, to be left out in the cold, whereas most compromise—some gladly. It is the same in the general affairs of the world. There is a tension between the church and society at large. As society becomes secular in its basic orienta-

No Other Foundation

tion, does one embrace secularism as a new form of worship? Does one mutely tag along? Or do you strongly resist? I wish, in closing, to examine three cases: two Catholic, and one Protestant.

Among certain so-called "High Churchmen" in England in the 1830's and 1840's, a strong sense that the Church of England was being gobbled alive by society provoked an aggressive and outspoken literary assault. Directed to an educated elite, the Tractarians as they came to be known (from the Tracts in which they expressed their thoughts), defended the ideal of a church established and ruled by God, not men. They held up the vision of a church not subject to the foibles of history but protected by God's Spirit through an apostolic succession; not dominated by timeservers but by holy ministers committed to Christ's teachings.

In many ways, despite a certain academic flavor and isolation from the everyday world, the Oxford Movement through the Newmans, Kebles, Puseys, and Froudes (all Oxford men, hence the appellation), was a valuable reminder that the church is not a mere human institution to be manipulated at will. At the same time, it played into the hands of the very intellectual movements we have been discussing, by so emphasizing holy living and time-honored ceremonial forms that it lost doctrinal clarity.

This was not the first time in the history of the church that formal rectitude and an insistence upon absolute independence of human institutions accompanied tolerance of theological deviation. We saw that in the eleventh and twelfth centuries, the pugnacious stance of the church towards kings and rulers went hand in hand with an evolution in theological thought and practice which was far from orthodox. It is almost as if secular interference is permissible as long as it is not seen to be such. Thus, the Oxford Movement would make its own peace with evolutionary theology as time went by.

The Oxford Movement in a strict sense, however, petered out after 1845 when its greatest luminary, John Henry Newman (1801-1890), managed to persuade himself that the Thirty-Nine Articles (the confession of faith of the Anglican church) were compatible with Roman Catholicism. In entering the Catholic church he was joining a church whose apostolic lineage was easier to argue about than that of the Church of England.

There were two possible tactics for Continental Catholics to adopt towards the French Revolution and its continuing tradition: exorcize it or baptize it.* To exorcize it meant to fly in the face of liberal opinion and identify with a conservative ruling regime. To baptize it meant to accept liberal premises, including national religious disestablishment, substituting for the former national allegiance an international "ultramontane" union with Rome.

A word is in order about the expression "ultramontane." Its literal meaning is "beyond the mountains." Bearing in mind that Italy is girdled by mountains, thus cut off from the rest of Europe, the term "ultramontane" describes those who look for their inspiration to what lies beyond the mountains—namely, Rome, and the pope in Rome. It is quite a paradox that it should be the liberals with respect to the state who were ultramontane as regards Rome. It is, however, both easy to see logically why this should be so, and not difficult to understand why this marriage of attitudes should prove historically incompatible. The history of Lamennais and Pius IX (Pio Nono) will illustrate the options open to Catholics in the confused problem of church and state.

The issues were bitterly contested in France, the seat of the original revolution of 1789 and the hostess for two more, in 1830 and 1848. The French cleric Lamennais (1782-1854) started as a conservative. Deeper acquaintance with society and politics turned him into a liberal. As such, the ecclesiastical loyalty which he had formerly evinced toward king and pope was now vested exclusively in the papacy. He was now an ultramontane in the fullest sense. But the papacy—in the person of Gregory XVI— proved unwilling to indulge his hopes for liberal reform, however ultramontane the packaging. Forced to choose yet once more, Lamennais became a secular republican.

Lamannais's pilgrimage was reversed in the experience of Pius IX. Becoming pope in 1846, he shared many liberal aspirations till the revolutions of 1848 reached Rome. The events of this year, including demonstrations of outright contempt for his own authority, turned him into a reactionary. There was, however, it is only fair to say, no way in which Pius could escape from his predicament. Pressures were mounting for an Italian kingdom, with Rome as capital, replete with the constitutionalist forms favored

*The expression belongs to Vidler, *op. cit.*, p. 69

242

No Other Foundation

by the liberals. Increasingly, Pio Nono's response was obdurate defiance.

The *Syllabus of Errors,* published by the pope in 1864, condemned just about every liberal program imaginable. The definition of Papal Infallibility at the First Vatican Council, 1869-70, ridiculed constitutionalism by asserting monarchical authority in its most extreme form. Ironically, only two weeks after this definition, Rome fell, the Kingdom of Italy was proclaimed, and the pope's temporal power ended.

But we must not lose sight of the fact that, in a significant way, the pope had got there in time. His declaration of absolute spiritual power more than made up for the loss of his temporal position. It is, certainly, from this time that one can date the excessive modern veneration for the popes. A French cleric at Rome in 1842 reported that people did not even raise their hats to the pope in the streets. By 1870, the pope had become semidivine. A leading French bishop spoke of Pius IX as the continuation of the Incarnate Word. All this was surely an exaggerated reaction. It evidenced a longing for the sacral that was being driven out of daily life. It marked a dissatisfaction with the ultimate banality of modern secular state leadership.

Stirrings in Oxford; stirrings in Rome; stirrings in—Glasgow. Under the enormously gifted and spiritually dedicated leadership of Thomas Chalmers (1780-1847) a split took place in the Scottish Church in 1843 over the issue of state control. It originated in the desire of local congregations to have the power to reject the nominee of the patron of a living.

The patron of a living was a person or body in whom was vested the right to name the minister of a particular church. Considering that the congregation had to live with whomever happened to be named, the desire was not unreasonable. Indeed, the Assembly of the church thought so, too, and passed the Veto Act in 1834 allowing this procedure. However, when patrons appealed individual cases to the civil courts their ancient rights were upheld. Repeated pleas to Parliament in London failed to redress the grievance and, in 1843, in a massive act of conscience, 451 ministers out of a total of 1,203 left the church rather than suffer ecclesiastical matters to be determined by the state against the will of church members. As Vidler writes (p. 60):

This entailed their giving up their parish churches, their manses, and their endowments, and starting afresh with no material resources. It was a magnificent, and perhaps an unparalleled, piece of renunciation in the cause of a great principle.

Amazingly, however, from a purely human point of view, the newly constituted Free Church exploded into vigorous and visible life almost overnight. By 1845, five hundred new places of worship had been opened and a substantial sum had been raised for building manses. Between 1843 and 1853, most tellingly, the missionary budget of the fledgling church more than doubled from a substantial 4,373 pounds sterling to 9,518.

It is convenient to close this chapter with the Scottish example because it illustrates two things, negative and positive. Negatively, as Vidler points out, the isolation of the Free Church from the general flow of intellectual and social life in many cases produced aridity and detachment after a while. The church found itself, quite often, insufficiently in the world to be salt to it. It tended to react to what seemed—and generally were, let us admit—more and more outlandish intellectual and theological fashions by withdrawing further into a cocoon. It was not giving battle on all fronts.

Positively, of course, it was able in one great period of time to affirm Christ's statement that his kingdom is not of this world. Against all social, political and economic commonsense, one-third of the church chose the wilderness rather than compromise the cause of sound teaching and the principle of a responsible pastorate. In so acting, it gave the greatest possible refutation to the evolutionary theology that was beginning to dominate the seminaries and emasculate the churches.

There is a God whose law does not pass away and whose promises do not fail. To seek his kingdom and his righteousness is the all-sufficient guarantee of our physical as well as our spiritual well-being. Such statements were beginning to sound nonsensical in the mid-nineteenth century. At all times they are the belief of those who are "fools for Christ's sake."

For Further Study

Darwin, Charles. *Autobiography of Charles Darwin.* Edited by Nora Barlow. New York: W. W. Norton & Co., 1969. Somewhat melancholy document. Short.

De Maistre, Joseph. *On God and Society: Essay on the Generative Principle of Political Constitution and Other Human Institutions.* Edited by Elisha Greifer. South Bend, IN: Gateway Editions Limited, 1959 Written in the first decade of the nineteenth century. Some wisdom but obvious reactionary impulses dilute its value. Interesting for this reason. Also short.

Heller, Erich. *The Disinherited Mind: Essays in Modern German Literature and Thought.* New York: Harcourt Brace Jovanovich, 1975. A tour de force of literary and intellectual investigation. Interprets the development of the humanist conflict between science and feeling, "fact" and "faith" from Goethe to the early twentieth century. Beautiful literary style.

Schleiermacher, Friedrich. *On Religion: Speeches to Its Cultured Despisers.* Translated by John Oman with an Introduction by Rudolf Otto. Harper & Row 1958, "Friends" may do more harm than enemies.

19

A Mission Reaffirmed: Las Casas, Wilberforce, Hudson Taylor

I F IN THE LAST CHAPTER we looked at the church on the defensive, in this chapter we shall look at the church on the attack. And by attack, I mean what attack should always mean for the Christian church: truly giving, forgiving and being merciful, as our Father has given, forgiven, and been merciful to us.

We shall be talking about the church's remarkable missionary endeavors in the nineteenth century and her efforts both before and during the nineteenth century to alleviate suffering at home. While private individuals otherwise employed were often important, especially in domestic good works, the leaders and pioneers were usually involved full time—or at least soon became so if they were not at first. This being the case, it is worth making a preliminary observation about "full-time service," so-called.

We are, of course, aware that as Christians, bought with a price, our whole body and all our activities are dedicated full time to God. We are stewards not only for money, but for talents, time, affection, hospitality. Thus, full-time service refers more to specific functions than to a particular category of Christian. It is a difference in detail or deployment, not of principle.

A crucial further observation is, therefore, in order: that the most basic preparation for full-time service, in the usual sense, is the recognition that it represents no higher calling than one's present occupation. In other words, if one is not totally dedicated to God right now, there is no reason whatsoever to suppose that by putting on the mantle of a pastor, missionary, or whatever, one will be miraculously transformed into a dedicated servant.

It is unfortunate—tragic—that the proper discipline and ordaining of the local church is largely bypassed nowadays. In effect, someone is rubber-stamped after training at an appropriate institute, and duly declared fit to assume this or that full-time responsibility in the church. There is little place for a careful appraisal of a candidate's qualification to serve, judged by his humble exercise of God's gifts in a settled congregation for a suitable length of time. If the seriousness with which churches look at budget problems and so-called practical issues were applied to the far more practical matter of the training and appraising of God's servants, there would be far fewer square pegs in round holes.

One has but to return to Jesus' teaching: first show yourself faithful with the one opportunity given; then you will be entrusted with more. This is the key to Christian advance. For God is not so wasteful as to enlarge the boundaries of opportunity for agents who consistently neglect or "butcher" what has already been given them to do. It is salutary to reread the history of men and women God has especially used. Hudson Taylor, for example, had already learned the meaning of full dedication in the unromantic setting of industrial Barnsley and the back streets of London before ever setting eyes on China. He did not suddenly become *the* Hudson Taylor when he arrived in Shanghai.

What is true for the individual Christian is no less true for the corporate church. A vision of the church as a whole, a vision of one's relationship to the surrounding world, has always been a result, not a cause, of the spiritual vitality of the local congregation. There is a specific logic here: if the local assembly lacks vitality, if it is not a mutually caring, servant church, it will never pick up its larger responsibility to care for the church elsewhere and non-Christian society round about. It may, indeed, maintain a certain level of responsibility inherited from the past, which it fulfills chiefly in financial terms, but its boundaries will not be enlarged.

As usual, historical perspective is important if we are to appreciate what was going on in Christian missions at this time. The nineteenth century was the first century in the West in which it was becoming clear that the former Christian dominance of culture was passing away. This was largely hidden to contemporaries and to superficial later observers because so many details seemed to proclaim the opposite. But, inexorably, the very structure of life and thought was becoming non-Christian, and—as is plain in the less praiseworthy aspects of mission advance—Christian activity was more and more being forced into an alien mold. In the twentieth century we are living in the shadow of this fact—or, rather, amidst the results.

But the nineteenth century was also the age of the most dynamic expansion of the Christian church since the first and second centuries. Is this one of the "details" to which I refer above? Surely, this fact contradicts or qualifies the analysis just presented? Obviously, I do not think so. It is clear to me that the de-Christianization of the West is closely related to the Christianization of the rest of the world. I think the judgment and mercy of God are evident in what was going on.

As the flame began to flicker in the West, God sent forth sparks so that the fire would burn anew elsewhere. This statement prompts another objection, however. I emphasized above that missionary activity is a result of vitality in the home churches. Was there really such vitality in an age I have been describing in rather bleak terms? Without ignoring or minimizing the continuing work of God's Spirit in the Western churches, it is plain that the real secret of the nineteenth-century missionary movement lies in the profound revivals of the eighteenth century.

A missionary movement on this scale does not start up overnight; it depends upon a general preparation of the soil. It responds to a natural desire sown in the hearts of thousands and thousands of believers all over. That the first impressive cluster of Protestant missions dates from around 1800 tells us that the great domestic revival was now ready to burst its local bonds. The huge number of congregations either formed anew or revived and expanded in the eighteenth century, and which continued on into the nineteenth century, provided the basic missionary pool. And the early mission societies established around 1800 were both an existing channel for mission service and an inspiration to many others which came into being thereafter.

As I say, this is not to minimize what went on in the nineteenth century. It is only to point out the genesis of the movement. It is to point out that the pioneer impulse and the spiritual foundations were already there by 1800. We are so present-minded that we find it hard to think in terms of generations, let alone centuries.

No Other Foundation

But it is instructive to realize that Hudson Taylor sprang out of the Wesleyan revivals. Not directly, of course. Rather, his own family had been revived in the eighteenth century. Wesley, indeed, had stayed at the Taylor home. Out of a dedicated, godly lineage came Hudson Taylor, born in 1832. Out of a dedicated, revived church came the subsequent missionary advance.

I also spoke of God's judgment and mercy, however. One can perhaps see this by comparing the church in the West with the church overseas in the past seventy years. This fact comes as a surprise to us, but the most amazing, dynamic and truly apostolic workings of the Spirit in the church have taken place not in the West but in the so-called Third World and where the church is persecuted.

There is absolutely no place here for "Third Worlders" to congratulate themselves or, as is common to see nowadays, for Westerners to be uncritically adulatory of anything African, South American, or Oriental. The churches of the Third World, in the wake of revival, have the same problems to face that the Western churches once faced, including the matter of doctrinal clarity. But God's judgment upon the West, which has received so much light, is evident in the withholding of his blessings. And his mercy upon the church elsewhere is evident (where this is the case) in the sovereign bestowal of great spiritual gifts.

This overall perspective is not easy for us to grasp yet it must be understood. It has been difficult for the English to adjust to no longer being a worldwide imperial power. It is likewise hard for the Western church to wake up to the emerging balance of forces. God's strategy is not ours and there may be further reasons for the special upbuilding of the church elsewhere which are unknown to us because we cannot see the exact shape of the future.

What cannot be ignored, nevertheless, is the heroic role which God has, in fact, given to the Western church in the last 150 years in "seeding" the rest of the world. The Jerusalem church played a similar role, a long time ago, eventually being eclipsed by its offshoots. From Jerusalem, and Antioch, came the Western church.

In general terms, we have already covered some of the important facts determining the nineteenth-century missionary movement. Let us be more specific about some of the details.

Just as the Pax Romana (the Roman peace) aided the great

expansion at the start of the Christian church, so the Pax Brittanica (the British peace) aided it in the modern period. And if the Roman peace covered a small world, commensurate with the general limits of the first Christian church, the British peace covered virtually the whole world, commensurate with the new global mission.

Necessary improvements in travel and communications to facilitate the commercial and colonizing ventures of Britain and her European rivals were going to help the missionary, too. Lands once closed to the Gospel were opening up. It is surely no accident, either, that the countries with the strongest industrial and commercial base—principally, Great Britain, the United States, and Germany—were the ones which had experienced the most fruitful spiritual awakenings. These lands produced a disproportionate number of missionaries who were able to penetrate overseas wherever their ubiquitous national flags allowed. And just as Paul's Roman citizenship came in handy more than once, so the citizenship of a great Western power frequently saved missionaries from the most direct forms of persecution.

It is well known that the advent of British power in India in the eighteenth century is closely connected with the disappearance of any one commanding native ruler capable of providing order and leadership. The overall failure of the Third World to withstand the political and economic challenge of the West was, to some degree, paralleled in the cultural and religious sphere. The impact of buoyant Western economies and technologies had the effect of disintegrating native cultures and therefore creating a vacuum into which Christianity could step.

The slow reversal of this situation in the twentieth century, with Third World powers developing independent arsenals, not to mention exporting their religious ideas to a pagan West, may, incidentally, explain the timing of the missionary expansion. It is hard to imagine effective, foundational Gospel teaching in the late-twentieth century Third World (particularly the Orient), such as was possible in the conditions obtaining till the mid-twentieth century. The great non-Western leaders of the non-Western church are mainly the children and grandchildren of men evangelized in less perilous times.

Be that as it may, in the nineteenth century the superiority of Western material culture was so great that it was quite natural to

No Other Foundation

accord a superior place to Western religion. Indeed, without exaggerating the contrast, it is true that Christianity entailed certain teachings and attitudes—such as social responsibility and individual honesty—which proved an effective challenge to indigenous doctrines and ways of life. Helping to introduce native peoples yet further to the Gospel, the foundation of Christian schools, essential avenues for learning the language and expertise of the West, were and continue to be powerful agents of evangelization.

Meanwhile, the pioneer work of Christian doctors and nurses in mission hospitals made tangible that Gospel whose outworking is summarized in the parable of the Good Samaritan. It is very easy for armchair critics of Western missionary activity ignorantly and callously to brush aside this sort of contribution which still, of course, goes on apace. It has taken one or two secular anthropologists of recent years to appraise a little more favorably the obvious benefits wrought by missionaries.

Just as the skeptic tries to claim that the Reformation is explicable in economic and political terms, so also he tries to "explain" missionary expansion in the nineteenth century. As we observed of the Reformation, however, one cannot understand any movement without looking at all of its facets. Of course there are economic and political factors, both in the Reformation and the missionary movement. But neither can be "explained" in such a way. Deep and genuine spiritual commitments were amplified in effectiveness by the providential ordering of human circumstance.

The nineteenth century was not, certainly, the first time that the church had reached out to the Third World. There had been an earlier, Catholic missionary expansion in the sixteenth century, accompanying the great period of Spanish and Portuguese colonization. Even so, there is no real comparison between the sixteenth- and nineteenth-century movements, whether in terms of extent, impact or cross-denominational involvement.

I have already sketched in the relation between the eighteenth-century revivals and the explosion of missions. God had prepared his church, as he was also preparing his world, for this endeavor. It is worth noting, though, that not all churchmen saw missions in a favorable light. Listen to this speaker at the 1796 General Assembly of the Church of Scotland, arguing against missionary work overseas: "I cánnot otherwise consider the enthusiasm on this subject than as the effect of sanguine and illusive views." Another speaker thought that "to spread abroad the knowledge of the Gospel among barbarous and heathen nations seems highly preposterous, in so far as it anticipates, it even reverses, the order of nature." (cited in Vidler, *op. cit.,* p. 248) The latter speaker sounds like a Darwinian before his time, implying that the "natives" have to be brought up to a certain level of culture before they can receive the highest cultural blessing—the Gospel. Both speakers remind one of the medieval reluctance to preach to the Moslems.

In any case, the impetus to missions was not to be thwarted. Around 1800, society after society was founded: the Baptist Missionary Society (1792); the London Missionary Society (1795); the Church Missionary Society (1799); the British and Foreign Bible Society (1804); and the Methodist Missionary Society (1813).

It was not only societies; great individuals were also setting out at this time. None is more justly famed than the remarkable English cobbler, William Carey, who went to India under the umbrella of the commercial East India Company.

What was true in the Protestant world was also becoming true in the Catholic world. Seemingly, the deep shock of the French Revolution and the Napoleonic epoch provoked a powerful spiritual reaction. With the principle of clerical celibacy, the Roman communion had a body of men and women who could often be more entirely engaged in mission than married Protestants. This has to be qualified to the extent that one does lose the example of family life, which is a neglected but vital element in evangelization and in the building up of churches.

The Roman mission outreach also benefited from authoritative, centralized direction, which permitted a concerting of strategy, and deployment of resources frequently missing in the often fractured Protestant efforts. Not that one saw no effective strategy in Protestant mission. After all, the best strategist is not Rome, or London, or New York, but the Holy Spirit. And where, as in the case of Hudson Taylor, one was prepared to be a Christian fool and break the human rules, the results could be staggering. The China Inland Mission, founded by Taylor in 1865, had no denomination, no papacy, behind it; it had no carefully planned system of financing. Yet it became larger and more effective than

No Other Foundation

any other mission in China. Indeed, it was precisely this sort of spiritual freelancing that was inhibited in denominational mission strategy.

In the early years of the twentieth century, the missionary movement began to lose steam. This, again, is a statement that requires explanation, parallel to the explanation for rooting the missionary expansion in the eighteenth-century revivals.

Surely the extent to which the Gospel has been proclaimed throughout all the world is greater than ever before? The work of translation and the use of the media, radio in particular, have brought people under the influence of the Gospel proclamation who were unreachable in the past.

All of this is certainly true. Then in what sense can the missionary movement be said to have lost steam? In this sense, that just as the freshness and vigor of the Western church began to disappear as the impulse of revival died down, so the thrust of missionary effort—following a generation or so behind—began to fail. The missionary structures, of course, remained, and produced an illusion of past glories. But rigidity began to mark activities which had once been open and flexible. Some principles were betrayed, not wilfully, but because the successors of the pioneers did not bring to the application of these principles the same quality of utter and original dependence upon God.

Not that a hard and fast line may be drawn. It would, for example, be easy to note that the Chefoo mission school for the children of China Inland Mission workers did not offer a Chinese education but rather the Oxford curriculum. But the reality was more complex. Each child spoke a native dialect incomprehensible to his fellows, so Mandarin would have had to have been taught. And is it just for parents obeying an individual calling from God to gear their children ahead of time to the same calling, by failing to equip them to return to their native Western culture?

Perhaps what must be stressed, after all, is overall spiritual priorities. As long as one keeps firmly in mind that the Christian is a sojourner, the problems of sojourning can be placed in true heavenly perspective. When this truth is to any degree lost, then problems such as child education, financial support, the deployment of workers, and the like, become primary. It is as though the missionary task cannot go forward till these matters are straight. Missions and individual missionaries are hamstrung by concerns that are proper to unbelievers, not to the children of a bountiful Father.

All of this, however, is only to say that mission outreach, in common with the general outreach of the church, is subject to certain laws. These laws are that men are sinful and that no one vehicle of God's working, in the entire history of the church, has ever remained consistently useful for more than two or three generations. It is hardly surprising, therefore, that—save for a few cases of internal reviving—the most original outreach in twentieth-century missions has been identified with brand-new enterprises. But this is all very general. Let us look more particularly at the weaknesses of nineteenth-century missions.

For understandable reasons, Christianity tended to come across as a European product. A foreign, imperial aroma tended to hang around many mission stations. There was, in other words, a blurring of the distinction between the essential and the incidental. When Hudson Taylor shaved his head and grew a Chinese "pigtail" the opposition changed from ridicule to indignant criticism, to the effect that he was a disgrace to England.

Likewise, it was axiomatic that the missionaries be politically subservient and conservative, carefully cultivating relations with the appropriate embassies or consulates. When Taylor broke with all mission precedent in China and ventured into the interior, beyond the protection of British coastline establishments, he was pilloried both as a potential disturber of Chinese sensibilities (endangering, perhaps, the rhythm of the all-important British opium trade) and as an irresponsible authoritarian leader, exposing young, female Western missionaries to the hazards of China.

Actually, it is clear that just as Taylor had learned to "die" before God could use him, so the China Inland Mission, as an organization, had to "die" before it could become the instrument for evangelization that it became. We have had occasion before to observe how this sort of dying is a corporate as well as a personal matter. Most missions were not prepared to so die, and therefore often betrayed the "deaths" of their member missionaries.

This circumstance, which continues to hinder mission work, was and is often encouraged by a principle of organization that Hudson Taylor firmly jettisoned: having the all-powerful headquarters back in the West. Taylor insisted that the people best able to judge strategy were those bodily engaged on the spot. This did not mean that others, at home, were not able to offer sound advice. It meant that the balance should be tipped towards the field workers. This may seem obvious enough but it was revolutionary at the time. The degree to which Taylor's stance was untypical is the degree to which missions, as European- or American-based enterprises, appeared to ape the Western commercial enterprises with which the Third World was familiar.

The other side of the coin of the identification of Christianity with the West was the tendency to reject or look down upon all aspects of native culture as inferior. Indeed, one can see here a tie-in to the prevailing Darwinian tide discussed in the last chapter. However, the apostle Paul at Athens did not ridicule the Athenians. He selected the one open aspect of their outlook— ultimate uncertainty—and capitalized upon it. The "Unknown God," he said, is Jehovah and Jehovah has revealed himself to us through his Son. This Son has been sacrificed and resurrected for us. If, repenting of our sinful self-dependence, we accept his sacrifice, we shall also be spiritually resurrected and have new life.

In a way, it is a reflex of genuine love and humility to take the trouble to know the mind of the other man, and not alienate him unnecessarily by ignorantly treading on all his pet corns. The great Indian evangelist and church planter, Bakht Singh, was unable to accept the Gospel in India, nor yet in London, because of its false associations. It was only in Canada, in particular circumstances and through reading the New Testament to himself, that he finally believed and was able to overcome his deep, underlying anti-Western prejudice.

In mission history there have, of course, been many wonderful exceptions. William Carey, the former cobbler, became one of the two or three greatest Sanscrit scholars who have ever lived, making independent contributions to the study of Indian culture. Likewise Henry Martyn, who burned himself out at the age of thirty-two, produced a translation of the New Testament in Urdu which stands as a classic of Urdu literature. His deep knowledge of Moslem thought, coupled with his genuine appreciation for what was positive about it, gave him a point of contact with learned Moslem scholars which was second to none. Being, in addition, an uncompromising evangelist, his debates (if only we had full record of them) would make fascinating reading.

Carey and Martyn loved the people to whom they knew God had sent them. There was something appropriate, therefore, in their dying abroad. Taylor did, Carey did, Martyn did. In our own day, in south India, Amy Carmichael did.

Seemingly, however, for every Carey and Martyn there were a score of insensitive, arrogant missionaries. The result of this was not, by any means, a lack of fruit, *per se*, but a tendency for the fruit to be among the poorer sections. The more sophisticated ruling classes were unable to overcome the blow to their pride from the missionaries' brusque rejection of values they held dear. Not that there is not also, here, a fulfilment of Jesus' warning that the rich and wise, in their independence, will tend to refuse the Gospel. All the more reason, therefore, to be careful with such. The Gospel is unpalatable enough to the natural mind, without also demanding that the convert make obeisance to the trappings of Western culture—a Western culture which presented an increasingly brutal and opportunistic face to the Third World.

In the chapter title, I referred to Las Casas, and a few words about him are in order here because he was a great pioneer, well before the nineteenth century, in the compassionate understanding of indigenous cultures and peoples. Bartholomé de Las Casas was a fiery and able Dominican missionary sent out from Spain to Latin America in the middle decades of the sixteenth century. He insisted that the Indians were human beings and must be treated as full subjects of the Castilian crown. He insisted that they were fully capable both of being educated and of becoming responsible, baptized Christians, on the same footing as any European. He was under no illusions as to the barbarity and perniciousness of many indigenous customs, but he recognized that the best way to conquer is through love. He did not, in other words, go to extremes like some of the Catholic missionaries in India and China who tended to dilute the Gospel to suit their clientele.

It is very much to Las Casas's credit that the Spanish law in the colonies was remarkably liberal towards native peoples. Sadly, this law tended to be disregarded wholesale as time passed, by a jaded and corrupt colonial and ecclesiastical administration. Typical, however, of Las Casas's objectivity is this fine comment on the natives of Florida in the 1550s. He wrote that they were still "in that first rude state which all other nations were in, before there was anyone to teach them. . . . We ought to consider what we, and all the other nations of the world were like, before Jesus Christ came to visit us."

One last point to mention. It is tragicomic how missions often

No Other Foundation

exported historically conditioned and unnecessary appendages to Christian life into the foreign setting. Neo-Gothic and baroque building styles look a little absurd in the Tropics. The details of English episcopal dress which owe their inspiration to the riding attire of eighteenth century gentlemen are ridiculous enough in twentieth-century England, let alone in the Third World.

More seriously, while there would seem no escape from the denominational distinctives of the West as long as missions were initiated by particular churches, it does seem unnecessary to foist upon other peoples differences which are often rooted in accidents of Western history. Efforts, of course, have been made to overcome these problems—the Church of South India, for example. And Hudson Taylor, after early mistakes, quickly fostered a genuine interdenominationalism in the China Inland Mission. The efforts of native believers, however, have been the most impressive, whether the Little Flock of Watchman Nee in China or the hundreds of Indian assemblies associated with Bakht Singh.

One incidental result of founding denominational off-shoots abroad was that the mission churches would be subsidiary to the mother churches, the leadership being overwhelmingly Western. In the last decades, certainly, this problem has been faced up to, with the leadership of the indigenous churches being increasingly indigenous. The danger now, against which Watchman Nee warned, is the opposite: that indigenous leadership becomes a principle in itself, suitability for spiritual direction being judged more in terms of quotas and skin color than of biblical eligibility.

There is not space to elaborate upon theological declension as a cause of mission debility. It is obvious enough that with the growing acceptance in the West of a theology that denied the Fall, missions would have to suffer. If there is no Fall, a uniquely *Christian* salvation loses meaning, and the wind is taken out of the sails of missionary motivation as traditionally experienced.

Like much pastoral work in the West, missionary work assumed a "social work" profile. The end of missions becomes the creation of suitable living conditions in which indigenous peoples could begin to realize their natural potential. What is and was forgotten about this drift, is that the model in this case was far more slavishly Western than ever the full Gospel could be. Indeed, old-fashioned missionaries were criticized for not spending more time and effort introducing the Third World to the joys of industrial development. How quickly does the counterfeit gospel become shopworn.

Finally, we must briefly address the gigantic efforts made by the church in the West to deal with the deep scars created by industrialization and the tendency of men to exploit one another. To start with, one must confess that our forebears, sometimes in the name of Christ, permitted, encouraged or even participated in structural denials of the Gospel.

I say "structural" as opposed to "functional." No Christian is perfect. In our daily functioning, we sin in word and deed. But structural sin means the "baptizing" of sin—pretending it is all right. In the name of profit or convenience or social acceptability, Christians engaged in slavery and various forms of industrial practice. They justified the degradation of their neighbors by spurious appeals to Scripture or the urbane conviction that if the poor will always be with us then we must not detract from the truth of Jesus' words by alleviating their poverty.

It needs to be said that such practice and such justification were totally alien to the Gospel. They are not a fruit of the Gospel but a deviation from it. To prove it, Christians rose up all over, individually or in groups, to remedy the sins of those who took Christ's name in vain. The history of Christian social action, particularly in the late-eighteenth and the nineteenth centuries, is remarkable. In the wake of the great revivals, Christians not only sent themselves abroad; they sent themselves to their needy neighbors.

This epoch is not, of course, the first since 1500 in which the church showed itself willing to care for people's practical needs. I have earlier spoken of the social conscience of the Reformers and of Catholic bishops like Charles Borromeo of Milan. The Pietist concern with orphans and the derelicts of society testifies to a basic understanding of the Gospel. Wesley was generous to a fault—what a wonderful fault!

Yet, notwithstanding these precedents, the nineteenth-century record was still remarkable. Of course, it had to be, because the need was increasing in geometrical progression with escalating population, galloping industrialization, and the more and more efficient reduction of large masses of the lower classes to faceless factory slaves. The nineteenth century is full of great pioneers in the alleviation of suffering. The great names must not cloak the fact that there were hundreds and thousands of unknown Christians behind them. Nevertheless, the few whose names stand out deserve their prominence: Elizabeth Fry, Lord Shaftesbury, George Müller, Hannah More, William Wilberforce, and others besides.

The work of Wilberforce, along with Thomas Clarkson, in the movement to abolish the slave trade and slavery was perhaps the single most hard-fought and impressive struggle. It can never cease to amaze anyone studying the movement how patient and indefatigable were the abolitionists. Voltaire may have fought for a few years to rectify social injustice in France; the abolitionists had to maintain their crusade for decades on end.

Perhaps this crusade should remind us, in closing, that the cultivation of sin is always easier than its eradication. It should remind us that the cost of dealing with sin is very great. The living proof is our Lord and Savior who suffered a death unimaginable in its dimensions in order to redeem creation from the effects of our disobedience. The root of all fruitful mission and all effective social work is in a serious emulation of Christ—becoming like him in his death, sharing his sufferings, as Paul put it.

For Further Study

Bentley-Taylor, David. *My Love Must Wait: The Story of Henry Martyn.* Downers Grove, IL: InterVarsity Press, 1976. Despite the title, a perceptive and dispassionate study of the great ambassador to the Moslem world. Martyn's genuine interest and tremendous expertise in the culture of the world he confronted is being re-discovered in our own day as particularly important in speaking to Islam.

Coad, F. Roy. *A History of the Brethren Movement: Its Origins, Its Worldwide Development, and Its Significance For the Present Day.* 2nd ed., rev. Greenwood, SC: Attic Press, 1976. A strange suggestion but this British movement had a great impact on missions, not least in the person of the patient, indefatigable George Müller, helper of the helpless at home and abroad.

Miura, Ayako. *The Wind Is Howling.* Translated by V. Griffiths. Downers Grove, IL: InterVarsity Press, 1977. Remarkable autobiography of a Japanese novelist, "from nihilism to Christianity." Would that more such works were as honest and restrained—and well written!

Orr, J. Edwin. This author has put us in his debt by documenting in a readable, informed way the movement of God around the world in more recent times. In his *Evangelical Awakenings* series (five vols. Minneapolis: Bethany Fellowship, 1975) he covers Africa and Eastern and Southern Asia. This is *not* to say that the only awakenings are officially "Evangelical"! Consider, for example, the following record of the French Catholic missionary Charles de Foucauld:

Foucauld, Charles de. *Spiritual Autobiography of Charles de Foucauld.* Edited by Jean-François Six. Translated by J. H. Smith. New York: P. T. Kenedy, 1966. He spent himself in the barren soil of north Africa.

Woodham-Smith, Cecil B. *The Great Hunger.* New York: Harper & Row, 1963. The tragic story of the Irish potato famine which was *ideologically* beyond the reach of many Christians to lift a finger. A lesson to be learned.

20

The Dynamics of Contemporary Theology

BY TALKING ABOUT THEOLOGY, I am not trying to be academic. I wish to speak of it in a direct way, so as to enlighten, not obscure. I hope it is clear by now that what men think is important. To speak about the theology of the twentieth century is better to understand many dimensions of contemporary church life.

I am going to concentrate on the dynamics of theology, not theology *per se*. What I mean by this is that I want to get at the energizing or motive forces behind theology—this is what the word "dynamics" means. I am not, in other words, going to attempt a short course in biblical, systematic, and philosophical theology, disgorging the ideas of a host of men from Barth, Brunner, and Bultmann, to Niebuhr, Tillich, and Pannenburg.

Reasonably, in the compass of a chapter, one must look for principles, endeavoring to be as scrupulous as possible about one's generalizations. In naming some names and not others, I am not thereby indicating greater intellectual or spiritual stature, but simply greater apparent impact, or else more obvious suitability as barometers of the theological climate. One or two figures of obvious influence will also be treated separately in succeeding chapters.

If there is one thing that most commentators on twentieth-century theology would agree upon, it is the decline of reason, or a faith in reason, in theological thinking. In other words, nineteenth-century theology built upon the eighteenth-century Enlightenment, confident that it could discover the ideal natural, "enlightened" theology—*real* Christianity. By using reason, it would strip away myth and fable to get to the heart of things. By contrast, twentieth-century theology, schooled by such shattering experiences as two world wars, even apart from the obvious failure of nineteenth-century theology to reach its goal, turned from reason and embraced an irrational approach.

If, as I say, most commentators would agree upon this, I should like to qualify the judgment by saying that if, in general, it is accurate, it is specifically inaccurate if it leads anyone to suppose that contemporary theologians do not place their trust in their own reason, their own minds. One can be just as humanistically dependent on one's own reason, as opposed to Scriptural revelation, when one disavows reason, as when one embraces it. At base, natural religion, the religion of the Golden Calf, issues from man's own head—with a Satanic assist. Mainline twentieth-century theology is just as "natural" as nineteenth-century theology in this sense. That its trappings before 1900 emphasize reason over faith, and after 1900 emphasize faith over reason is less important than the common genealogy.

Having said this, it is still important to track down the "spoors" of twentieth-century man-made religion. And if these spoors emphasize nonrational processes, then they owe a very great debt to Freud.

Freud's influence is, in fact, far more pervasive than we realize, simply because we have accepted so many of the ideas and terms that he either originated or popularized and so think of them as a part of common wisdom. We betray his influence when we speak of a mother or father complex, an inferiority complex, unconscious "drives" and motivations, or the "ego" as if it were a separate part of a person.

As with Darwin, however, so with Freud: if Freud had not come along, we would have had to invent him. Not in the sense that we needed him, but in the sense that the drift of thought in the West had already anticipated Freud's work. If, that is to say, one can probe into animals and plants, and if, according to evolutionary theory, man is a continuous part of the same natural order, then he, too, can be probed. Seeing as man has cognitive and emotional processes which appear to differentiate him from other animals, why not investigate the "circuitry" of these phenomena? By so doing, one will make possible the healing of those elements in human beings which require a different type of therapy from that employed by the medical doctor.

At once, we sense the great dangers here. If we have a fairly clear idea as to what constitutes physical disorder, do we have as clear an idea about so-called mental or emotional disorder? What if, for example, to take actual cases, belief in a personal God who intervenes in our lives and whose Son was crucified, resurrected, and will return to judge the world is taken as evidence of mental disorder?

But how does Freud fit in with twentieth-century theology? Simply, by providing a natural explanation for religious beliefs including those beliefs which are clearly supernatural. Thus, belief in a Father God is clearly and quickly related by Freud to the actual relationship between the believer and his or her own father. His famous essay, *Moses and Monotheism,* may be read with interest in this connection.

Indeed, Freud's work, especially as elaborated and refined by others following after, such as Jung, strengthened the idea of a purely man-made religion. All manner of things, such as prayer, good neighborliness, and so on, could be explained as reflexes, products of family life, heredity, environment. We all have a friend who has presented us with this argument. Thank Freud! However, to be fair, as I indicated earlier, it is bigger than Freud. He was the brilliant man who wrote the play for the preexisting plot. His followers have been staging it ever since. To complete the image, many theologians have enjoyed more than just walk-on parts: they have delivered the benediction.

Although Freud's influence has been immense, within the overall context of the acceptance of the Darwinian view of man, theologians might still not have been so receptive without having digested an extremely potent body of ideas associated with the name of Kierkegaard. Many people who are familiar with the names of Darwin and Freud, have not heard of Kierkegaard. I had students once who identified the name with, alternatively, ''a race of supermen'' or ''a leading commander of German forces during World War I.''

Soren Kierkegaard (1813-55) was, in fact, a Danish theologian, or philosopher, or thinker (he is not easy to pigeonhole). Out of the anguish of a tortured and troubled life came a stream of strangely powerful, almost poetic, books which challenged the establishment religion of contemporary Denmark and hit out at the fashionable Hegelianism of the day which seemed to substitute intellectual intoxication for a living faith.

Rejecting the Hegelian legacy of a world moving steadily towards a paradise on earth, he emphasized the apocalyptic, somber side of the biblical message. Rejecting the assumption that by one's reason one can unravel the nature of faith and all religion, he stressed a virtually blind faith as the real key to religion. Only when the reason is humbly sacrificed, can one, by pure faith, a trembling faith, enter God's sanctuary. Neither ecclesiastical authority nor theological systems and propositions can act as the handmaids of faith. Truth, he said, in a famous and much-quoted sentence, is only grasped by a person struggling for his life in 70,000 fathoms of water. Until one has tasted the experience of relinquishing all rational and other supports, until one has, as it were, launched out into the deep, blindly stepping on to the water, one has never come to grips with faith.

More could be said about Kierkegaard and many have said it. What I have so briefly sketched is, nevertheless, at the heart of his influence upon our own day. Obviously, there is much that is attractive. Though he has, perhaps justly, been criticized for not fully grasping the Hegelianism which he so savagely attacked, his onslaught upon humanistic rationality is a tour-de-force and well worth the reading. But he is better as a critic than as a constructor. There is about his thought something elliptical, not quite on the printed page, which is only saved from fuller identification with the plays of Ibsen and Strindberg by stopping short of outright cynicism.

It is not always easy to exemplify in a direct way what is biblically discomforting about Kierkegaard's thought. His assertion that the history of the church is one of increasing degeneracy which began at Pentecost when the Apostles admitted 3,000 to the church in one day, is noteworthy, however. This assertion contains three indices to Kierkegaard's flaws as an interpreter of Christianity. First, he generalizes from an exaggerated and ultimately destructive attack upon the Danish church to the church at all times and in all places. Second, he is guilty of a selective and subjective use of Scripture whereby portions found useful become weapons, while other sections, such as the account of Pentecost, are so much chaff to be thrown away. Third, for a man so intent upon demonstrating the mystery of faith and the seemingly arbitrary actions of God, he has a curiously human and prosaic idea of what might or might not be possible for God's Spirit. After all, why *not* 3,000 souls in one day?

Some of the roots of Kierkegaard's unbelief are easy to pinpoint: faith was so subjective, so personal, so non-fraternal, that the idea of faith by the wagon load was monstrously offensive.

Having spoken already of Freud, we may appreciate that it is not hard to find clues to Kierkegaard's theology in his family history, relations with friends, and reaction to the smooth-flowing streams of theological debate in the Berlin he knew as a student. I am not going to search for such clues, however. It is safer and better to evaluate a body of ideas in its own terms. Ultimately, faith for Kierkegaard was so subjective, so beyond historical verification or buttressing, that it seemed to have little relation to the faith which Abraham evinced or the faith which Paul described when he made the statement that if Christ is not raised, then neither will we, so "let us eat and drink, for tomorrow we die."

If, in fact, Kierkegaard's slant on faith owed much to his own life experiences, one can see how a twentieth-century world, beginning to suffer corporately the sort of alienation, lostness and lack of confidence that he privately endured, might discover in his works its own favorite theology. In the process, Kierkegaard's ideas would be bowdlerized and sometimes misunderstood.

His own preparedness to blurr the boundaries between formal exposition and personal anecdote and attack has, however, invited an unusually nonsystematic use of his ideas. Furthermore, an apparently deliberate attempt to translate the tensions and ambiguities of his own life into a form of discourse full of surprise and paradox is bound to encourage confusion. Perhaps the confusion of his readers was something he desired, along with the confusion of his ecclesiastical opponents who could not always be certain whether they were being admonished or punished.

How precisely did Kierkegaard come to influence theology when he had been forgotten for half a century? The negative answer comes first: that the typical nineteenth-century alternative to what Kierkegaard stood for was so exhausted and discredited by 1900 that sooner or later he was bound to come into his own. But in coming into his own it is important to clarify that his influence would not drive people back towards truly biblical faith.

As self-authenticating or self-justifying, Kierkegaardian faith could, of course, be equally embraced by secular as well as religious thinkers and, indeed, modern existentialism in its secular as well as its religious wings, owes a great debt to him.

"Doing one's own thing" may sound far removed from high-flown philosophical debate, yet the idea of being consistent to oneself by acting in character is central to existentialism. Here, in point of fact, is a good example of a whole body of thought coming down to the masses in the form of a crude slogan—"Do your own thing." We are Freudians and Existentialists without even knowing it, like the man who discovered he was speaking prose.

I am still not being precise enough, however, about Kierkegaard's theological impact. It was facilitated by an immensely influential work written in 1906 by an Alsatian theologian called Albert Schweitzer (1875-1965). His *Quest for the Historical Jesus* rang the curtain on the old-style liberal theology. He argued that the nineteenth-century attempt to study Jesus and the New Testament rationally, in terms acceptable to modern scholarship, was bankrupt. All the volumes, all the research, proved one thing only: Jesus, the historical Jesus, whoever he was, *if* he was, was undiscoverable. The standards of proof required by modern scholarship denied the possibility of ever coming to a conclusion. He might have gone a step further and said the same thing about all scholarly investigation which proceeds from the humanistic trust in mind alone.

In any case, the impact of his book was such as to combine with the drift of contemporary events, above all World War I, not to mention the current popularization of Freudian thinking, to provide the ideal climate for the rediscovery and application of Kierkegaard. Was Jesus rationally undiscoverable? Kierkegaard might have echoed from the grave: "I saw that fifty years ago." And Kierkegaard's writings gave the comforting assurance that faith in Jesus does not depend upon what you can or cannot know. Indeed, serious pastors in the liberal tradition had reason to acknowledge the apparent truth of Kierkegaard's position, for liberalism had produced spiritual as well as theological barrenness. No wonder faith was at a low ebb; it had been misplaced.

The most famous pastor to capitalize upon the situation, particularly as during World War I he contemplated the ruins of Western liberal optimism, was Karl Barth (1886-1968), the Swiss theologian. In a few sentences one cannot hope to summarize the work and shifting viewpoints of the twentieth century's most able theologian. But we must say something.

He had, indeed, been impressed by Schweitzer's book, and though the Bible figures almost more prominently in his writings than in those of any other contemporary theologian, it is a Bible which is not in itself an objective repository of truth. Rather, it is a book which contains the truth, ready to be revealed to men by faith. This sounds quite orthodox, on one level. On another level, it introduces us to Kierkegaard's influence upon his thought.

For the subjective use of Scripture which this attitude also implies, could allow Barth, despite the Apostle Paul's belief to the contrary, to treat the Resurrection as a spiritual event—an essential thing to believe in—but not necessarily an historical event. This begins to sound like belief in belief.

With Kierkegaard, Barth would warn Christians not to clutch at the concrete fact, not to encumber one's faith with the flotsam of historically unverifiable events. But just as Kierkegaard's insistence on faith turned out to deny the substance of biblical faith, so Barth's characteristic insistence on God's omnipotence and majesty, compared to man's insignificance, in effect removed God from the scene. If contact between God and man is difficult and remote, if he only speaks through his word to us in a somewhat arbitrary, revelatory way that can hardly be checked against Scripture as it stands, then man—and we *are* fallible men—can be excused for ''doing his own thing.'' There is, in fact, a definite, though qualified, universalism in Barth's theology.

No orthodox Christian would deny that we only understand God's written Word by his intervention. But the fact that he has created us and given us speech is evidence of a primary intervention on the basis of which, through the self-same medium of speech, he can mediate to us the news of redemption. As a man begins to take seriously the speech of God, his level of understanding becomes more and more profound. If, indeed, he does not reject the testimonies of God but receives the Gospel, then the life-giving Word of God takes root in his very own being, God's law being written on his heart. Indwelt by the Spirit, whose sword is the Word of God, he becomes the agent for the remission or confirmation of sin to all whom he knows.

So far, we have been dealing with systematic and philosophical

No Other Foundation

theology, more than biblical. What became of the critical study of
the Bible which was central to nineteenth-century theology? Did
it shrivel up overnight? Mysteriously, it did not. What happened
was worse.

If Kierkegaardian thinking encouraged a subjective approach to
faith, it further stimulated the already subjective elements within
biblical criticism to which we referred in a previous chapter. It
provided, as it were, a "respectable" religious backing for a sub-
jectivism which was rationally disreputable.

The new preconceptions were, accordingly, more daringly
imaginative than the old ones, less inhibited in their unblushing
manipulation of Scripture to suit pet theories. There is a risk here,
if one would understand that all twentieth-century biblical scholarship is being so described, of discounting much valuable
spadework. But the methodological framework, without which
there has never been any considerable scholarly enterprise, was
seriously warped. And at some time, every scholar working
within such a framework has to locate his own research in order
to explain its significance. Frequently, therefore, the empirical
findings of a researcher may be beneficial, but the introduction
and conclusion to his work enter the realm of fantasy.

All in all, a few comparisons may be made between nineteenth-
and twentieth-century biblical scholarship. Both have been
equally ready to assume the autonomy of the human mind, unaided by God's Spirit, in examining Scripture. Both have been
ready to draw conclusions from obviously incomplete evidence.
Both have been singularly unwilling to be silent where the evidence is ambiguous. More overtly in our own century, the biblical
text, in a highly selected form, has been used to bolster current
fashions in religious thought. In this last connection, the "de-
mythologizing" approach of Rudolph Bultmann (1884-1976),
which has been the most influential in the field of biblical scholarship, has led the way. Despite what to any objective analysis
must appear its blatant shortcomings, the methodical stripping
from the Gospel narratives of allegedly mythical accretions, in
order to reveal the original story underneath, has given powerful
backing to the quest for a form of Christianity disembarrassed of
its supernaturalism.

But as, I think, C. S. Lewis pointed out, the process should be
called not *de*mythologizing, but *myth*ologizing, for all one does in
stripping away inconvenient concepts from the Gospel record is

expose to view the myth that one has already committed oneself to. The purported discovery of such a private myth in the Bible adds appropriate "religious" value to it, gives it a religious "tone."

Spiritual declension precedes intellectual declension. If we discount the commands of God's Word, we shall soon find reasons to assert that the Bible is not actually trustworthy. Reverence for God's Word, our capacity to speak of it as does the Psalmist in Psalm 119, depends upon inner submission. It is this inner submission which fortifies us against outward ridicule—it is, after all, not easy to be a man or woman of the Word in our day. It does not matter where you look, the Bible is everywhere being discounted, even while it is being read.

This is not less true than in the past; it is more true, for our culture is in open rebellion against words themselves. Frequently, where the Bible appears to be followed, it is actually made to follow—to justify a personal experience. All of us do this to some degree, but we do not have to do it systematically. It is at this point that Christian biblical scholars sometimes fall into a trap. Such a Christian scholar would dutifully warn a new convert not to take too seriously the emotions generated by difficult experiences in life. We cannot, he would correctly say, place our trust in our feelings, but in God's objective commands and promises. If it seems dark today, it will be light tomorrow. Unfortunately, owing to a prevailing academic respect for the mind, he fails to apply the same sound analysis to the hasty conclusions of the intellect. What he needs to understand is that the finite mind, no more than the finite heart, has sufficient grounds in and of itself to reach conclusions at variance with the Word of God. This is not to discount the intellect, nor yet one's feelings, but to indicate their objective limitations.

We must get rid of a silly inferiority complex about things intellectual and scholarly. Why counsel one's congregation not to doubt God when things seem to go wrong, and yet fail to offer similar counsel to ourselves—if we are teachers—when the Word of God seems hard to square with our finite and ephemeral judgment on a textual issue? Let us be consistent and let us be patient. If we are not, a form of consistency *will* emerge: we shall encourage the congregation to listen to their own feelings and seek that divorce, or indulge that inclination which is at variance with scriptural command.

"I have seen a limit to all perfection," the Psalmist says, "but

No Other Foundation

thy commandment is exceedingly broad'' (Ps. 119:96). Blessed is the man whose delight is in the law of the Lord, on which he meditates day and night. He is like a tree planted by streams of water, yielding his fruit in season.

For Further Study

Barth, Karl. *Protestant Thought: From Rousseau to Ritschl.* Translated by B. Cozens. New York: Simon & Schuster, 1969. A big, difficult book in which I am suggesting the first chapter as an example of the qualities of his perceptions with regard to the Enlightenment. Yet eventually he is himself torn by the dilemma described in Heller's *Disinherited Mind.*

Bultmann, Rudolf. *Jesus and the Word.* Translated by L. P. Smith. New York: Charles Scribner's Sons, 1958. You can read this book and find many insights alongside questionable statements. Why? Because of the method: read "View-Point and Method," pp. 3-15.

Freud, Sigmund. *Dora: An Analysis of a Case of Hysteria.* New York: Collier Books, 1963. Gives a fair idea of his approach.

Kierkegaard, Soren. *Kierkegaard's Journals.* Edited and translated by Alexander Dru. New York: Harper & Row, 1959. You need to fathom Kierkegaard to get hold of the subjective in his main writings.

21

Orthodoxy in a Pagan Setting: Illusion and Reality

I N THE EARLY CHAPTERS of I Samuel we are introduced to the history of a godly man chosen out of a godly people which had largely forsaken its calling. In the book of Daniel, we encounter a small group of godly men set down in a pagan culture. These two situations seem to characterize the church's position today. On the one hand, an orthodoxy frequently untrue to its calling; on the other hand, orthodox individuals living out their lives in an alien context. In the first case, God reaches down to his people, providing a faithful leader, Samuel. In the second case, God provides a testimony to pagan society in the persons of those who completely trust him.

These alternatives and the challenges they embody are not always perceived. Hence the words "illusion and reality" in the chapter heading which evoke the problem of failing to see the wood for the trees. This failure, this lack of spiritual discernment, is observable in the three great areas of personal life, corporate church life, and testimony to the world at large.

In exploring these areas it is worth stressing that, in analyzing twentieth-century church life, it is very difficult to be objective. With the best will in the world, it is easy to become fixated upon problems which are minor, missing altogether matters of far greater import. We can, in other words, see more at a glance than might be true of past history, but without sufficient perspective to measure relative significance. One can only seek to adhere the more closely to the universal benchmark which is God's Word written.

No Other Foundation

"A double-minded man," James tells us in his Epistle, "is unstable in all his ways and will receive nothing from the Lord." He makes this remark after telling us to have faith in God and to seek our wisdom from him. This is in line with what the Lord himself said about trusting him. The gentiles, he noted, are always planning for tomorrow. But you, he said, must not have this mentality. You must realize that God is in charge, and if you depend upon him he will always be in charge of you. It is as if the gentile, the unbeliever, supposing he lives in a world of chance, cannot, for that very reason, leave anything up to chance. He must determine his own destiny. The believer, knowing that God determines his destiny can, for that very reason, be content to leave things up to God, without fear or anxiety.

It is precisely this which distinguishes the believer from the unbeliever in practice. It is not the only thing, of course, for there is also a basic stance of love and mercy which goes along with such practice. But the point is that one *can* be foolish enough to love to one's own apparent hurt; to give without counting the cost; not letting one's left hand know what the right hand is doing—precisely and only because we know ourselves to be in the hands of an Almighty Father. Thus, everything stems from a simple, clear realization of our dependence upon God and the results of it.

Because this is so central, it is hardly surprising that our difficulties focus here. Much of the time we make what Christ calls the rule an exception. Thereby, we help guarantee that we receive from God, if not nothing (as James says), then at least very little.

Christ seems to emphasize an openness towards tomorrow, towards such issues as material need, and our responsibility to those who demand things of us. But we often close the door to such openness, not by outright denial so much as by regulating quite fully our program for tomorrow, determining what we can or cannot do purely with reference to our own opinion as to our time, strength, or capacity.

Likewise, we hedge ourselves about with so many guarantees of our future material security that there is precious little room left for God to show us how *he* can provide for our needs. Further, there is little incentive for the needy to look to us for succour when our social lives are so geared as carefully to exclude interlopers.

Is it God's blessing or our own planning that we can relax over the paper night after night by the fire or in front of the television? Is it God's blessing or our own planning that we enjoy material security, with ample balances in the bank—our tomorrows sunny, our holidays assured, our retirements guaranteed? A still small voice may not tell us: "This night thy soul is required of thee." But it may warn us: "Their blood be upon thy head." None of these things in itself is bad—that must be underlined. If, however, they reveal a disordering of priorities, they are cancerous, fit to be plucked out and burned.

This is not a sermon, though, but an essay about history. Yet, "history is philosophy teaching by example," and I enter into this sort of spiritual detail to make vivid one of the great dilemmas of the contemporary, orthodox church: that it is infrequently salt, infrequently so dependent upon God as to realize the benefits.

And this is true because a church is made up of individuals. And it is individuals who are living like this, giving substance to the gibe that the Christian church is the bourgeoisie at prayer. As a matter of fact, it does not matter whether one substitutes "proletariat" here. The point is, such an identification with the transient values of the age that the outsider can legitimately suppose that Christian convictions are a parasitic growth, a wart on the flesh of an otherwise unblemished worldliness.

Too often, then, it has been the case in our age that the individual believer has embraced illusion instead of reality. He has read the law of Christ in church, preached it to others, but become a shipwreck himself. Eli performed the ceremonies but his sons Hophni and Phineas, like Israel, played the harlot. Will God judge us less culpable when our advantages are that much greater?

Predictably, what is true of the individual is magnified in the case of the corporate church. One of the insistent claims of the sociologist is that churches are first and foremost socio-economic groupings and only secondarily religious ones. If, indeed, any one congregation is predominantly this or that socially and economically, then the sociologist has a right to his analysis. And it is not enough to say to him: "But poor people are also Christians. Look at such-and-such a congregation across town," for the sociologist will retort with an indulgent smile that all this only proves his

No Other Foundation

point—that, indeed, there are many social, ethnic and economic groups and they divide neatly along social, ethnic and economic lines. Like all people, he will continue, they have something we might call a "religious impulse" but this is clearly less important than the other impulses, for the good reason that the lines of demarcation follow these impulses so closely.

I am far from saying that the matter is as simple to argue as this. The average sociologist is incurably naive, opinionated, and thick-skinned. He tends to be more sensitive to data that can be quantified than to subtle nuances which resist such clumsy manipulation. Furthermore, he is not used to giving the benefit of the doubt. The decimal point is his absolute.

Having said that, has it not always been true in Christian history that one sign of real spiritual vitality in a congregation has been the human diversity of the flock? In other words, the key point of contact is Christ; anything else is incidental and, by being incidental, advertises to the outside world that Christ is truly the heart of the church. It need hardly be added, as qualification, that the human diversity of a congregation is no sign, by itself, of Christ's centrality. It is a fair index but not an infallible one. A biblical glorying in the Cross of Christ, as Paul understood it, is primary.

We must speak, however, in more diect terms of the church in its pagan setting, and one of the best ways to do so is to recall what marked the church in the first few generations after Christ. A firsthand experience of Christ and his leading came first, followed by sound doctrine and discipline, both accompanied by a dynamic outreach to the world.

What most clearly evidenced the firsthand experience of the early church was its emphasis upon the essentials and its lack of emphasis upon the incidentals. Thus, to illustrate from our previous discussion, it was the concern for the whole Gospel, to serve God who is no respecter of persons and who desires that no man should perish, which brought the incidental result of a church which leapt the boundaries of race, creed, and social origin.

If it had aimed at this incidental result—as, indeed, some churches do in our day—you may be quite sure that the results would have been ephemeral. Only in Christ Jesus are all made one. The mark of firsthand experience is that just as no two believers will be alike (because they are distinct persons), so no two congregations will be alike.

It is worrying to see advertising for this or that church model—from California, Texas, Florida, wherever—or this or that pattern of action, which strays much beyond the simple biblical principles. For what it tends to encourage, despite caution, is a dependence upon subcriteria, substandards. By subcriteria and substandards I do not mean things which are inferior but things which are derivative, things which are simply the localized application of the main principles.

To seek to enact in one place what occurred in another is excellent if it leads to the same repentance and dependence which may have characterized the original experience. But if it is, in effect, a short-circuiting process, whereby one plugs in the model, much as one places a cartridge in a cassette recorder, then it is self-defeating. It probably reveals misplaced guilt about the absence of obvious "spiritual success." The fact is, no two congregational "wiring diagrams" are the same; only the power is constant.

All of the foregoing is particularly relevant to a discussion of the church in the world for one solid reason: that what is very clearly portrayed in the effort to apply the success formula of one congregation to others is a leading facet of the common mentality of our pagan age. This is the package-deal mentality, the streamlined approach to all problems.

If you have read about advertising techniques, you will be aware that the greatest effort of the advertiser is to condition the mind of the consumer. Once that is done, almost anything can go. In other words, you condition the consumer to identify totally incidental or superficial aspects of a product with essential quality, such that he will actually shop for the superficial, believing that thereby he is getting the real thing. The use of sex in advertising is just one example here.

Applied to the church, this boils down to seeking spiritual renewal not by the hard biblical route but by some incidental, superficial method which, one is promised, will deliver the goods. I do not wish to be overcritical but I cannot help seeing a lot of familiar salesmanship in the claims one reads for this or that plan of church renewal. Like all good sales pitches, one speaks in terms of ultimate benefits while actually selling a brand name.

No Other Foundation

This is to say, that one is disarmed by the soft-sell assertion that, of course, we all desire renewal, etc. Then we are told that congregation X achieved renewal in this way. Therefore—here comes the hard sell—are you not being spiritually irresponsible if you do not at least give this a try?

In such ways we not only clutter our house with useless products, but we clutter our church with useless schemes. We dissipate our spiritual energies, we tragically frustrate what may be genuine spiritual appetite by accepting a twentieth-century mess of pottage. Thereby, we take the edge off our desire for the sincere milk of the Word. Thereby, we forget what is the armor of the Christian warrior. Finally, by partaking insincerely of that meal which commemorates our Lord's sacrifice for us, and which tells us that we are all indeed made one in him and are partakers together with him in his sufferings—by making a practical mockery of this deep communion, the congregation grows sick and dies.

If the twentieth-century church has often adopted the standards and techniques of the surrounding world and often, as a result, forfeited the chance to change that world, it has also had a hard battle over that second characteristic of the early church, sound doctrine and discipline.

Calvin, you may recall, insisted on these two principles before he would assume the leadership of the Genevan church in 1541. The truth should be known and the truth should be lived: that is what doctrine and discipline mean. They are to be understood, of course, in the context of a central aspect of doctrine: love. For love is at the heart of the Gospel and at the heart of the Truth. As Paul further reminds us, discipline itself must be exercized in love.

The dangers that the orthodox church in our day have encountered as regards doctrine have led to one extreme or another: either there has been laxness in doctrinal statement and teaching, allowing Christians, sometimes by default, to wander into strange waters; or there has been an over-rigid, over-particular, doctrinalism which has frequently muzzled the church's witness by erecting artificial barriers to fellowship and driving away possible seekers.

In both cases there has usually been a decline in true church discipline. This latter phenomenon is both a result of the doctrinal stance and a reflection of worldly mentalities. Laxness or lack of clarity over doctrine inevitably leads to a weakened sense of discipline. For, if certain mental attitudes are tolerated as long as one gives the formal assent to Christ's saving work, then certain physical and social acts are tolerated too, for the same reason. In effect, one becomes a double Antinomian, making a working distinction between belief and confession, practice and profession.

Overstrictness in doctrinal matters can, on the other hand, lead to harsh discipline which in turn frequently generates deep hypocrisy. The degree to which there may be in both these cases a reflection of worldly mentalities is the degree to which the world preaches a sort of vacuous tolerance as a new first commandment, while also inculcating a sort of universal hypocrisy whereby the crime is in the discovery, not in the act. One might reflect here upon the various misdemeanors of public officials as revealed to the public, and the actions which go unrecorded.

However one tampers with doctrine, there is a price to be paid. Overrigidity produces church members who are either less than human or else hypocritical. Insufficient teaching leaves one wide open to the influences of the age. One cannot be silent in the congregation about all the practical and theoretical matters which affect daily life and not expect that the church will soon begin to reflect worldly opinion and conduct.

A footnote to these considerations is the appalling adoption of "efficient" secular methods of raising money. The *normal* "Christian" fund-raising letter, spewed out at regular intervals by a computerized addressing system, is hardly distinguishable from those stultifying notes about subscription renewal to your favorite magazines. Just change the letterhead and edit the pious phrases. I say this is appalling: but it merits more than a resigned shrugging of the shoulders and "It's cheaper this way" or "People just won't give otherwise." It is, in very truth, a grievous insult to the Body of Christ in the light of Paul's teaching in 2 Corinthians 8-9. Is not giving a privilege and a blessing? Is it not an echo of God's "inexpressible gift"? And is not a gift—a *gift?* Yet we are poked and cajoled. Such "gifts" are not worth having—at least in that way. And we who give? If our motive is to obtain a book offered as an inducement, then, verily, we have our reward.

The third and last characteristic of the early church was a dynamic outreach to the world. Here, too, the problem of illusion and reality looms up. To some degree we have already discussed crucial aspects of this in talking about the life of the individual and

No Other Foundation

the congregation. Let us focus here upon two special aspects: intellectual outreach and conventional evangelism.

Orthodox believers have overreacted to a sense of intellectual inferiority, to a sense of being outside the mainstream of modern thought, including theological thought. Thus, if the modern world has taken to identifying competence with academic degrees rather than with apparent merit, Christian institutions have slavishly climbed onto the bandwagon. Christian publications, like other minority publications, overcompensate by painfully listing all the letters that may be legitimately tacked on after an author's name.

More seriously than this, the Christian has often believed the world's own propaganda, that knowledge and reason are the keys to life, by displaying unjustifiable jubilation over this or that new finding which substantiates the biblical record. Let us, however, make no mistake here. First, the drift of serious scholarly endeavor in the last generation has made it much easier to argue the orthodox Christian case, whether as regards Scripture or as regards more general issues. One may contemplate much of the lifework of W. F. Albright, the greatest Near Eastern archeologist of this century. One may note the revival of the conviction that there was, indeed, an historical Jesus who is discoverable and that Schweitzer was hasty in reading the last rites. One may take courage from the long-overdue attempt on the part of a few scholars to place biblical history in its natural cultural setting, thus avoiding many of the crass errors of the critics.

Second, it is certainly right and proper to argue one's case in the forum. But there is a double danger here. One may naively suppose that one will be heeded for demonstrating one's case. In fact, while the world claims to be governed by hard data, it is actually governed by inner convictions. Further, one may be captivated by the world's own intellectual stance, which is to assert the primacy of the mind. The mind is, thus, the master of the text of Scripture, instead of being its bride and handmaid. Thereby, Scripture is discussed and judged always in human terms, never in its own terms. And scholar is compared with scholar, not Scripture with Scripture. The Word of God is made void by the traditions of Renaissance scholarship.

When one operates in this way, the positive scholarly results subtly discount Scripture, as if Scripture has value because a scholar tells us so. It is reminiscent of the pontifications of some child psychologists about aspects of infant behavior which have been perfectly obvious to mothers ever since the world began. Yet one is supposed to credit the researcher with a "discovery" when, until yesterday, he was resolutely refusing credence to the mother's humble testimony. Christian scholarship has one ultimate purpose: rescuing a dying world.

Some of the remarks made earlier about patterns of church renewal are applicable to the subject of evangelism. An astute columnist in an English newspaper, some years ago, wrote a propos of an evangelistic crusade that the very degree to which the organization involved was careful to work hand in glove with established churches, not upsetting anybody's boat, was the degree to which, judged by past revivals, a revival would probably not result.

This pragmatic observation in no way detracts from the necessity for evangelization, however. It simply underlines that our concern is to follow God's commandments; the Holy Spirit has control of the harvest. "The wind blows where it lists." And "My thoughts are not your thoughts"—so often God uses what is strange, bizarre, or merely commonplace, to accomplish spectacular ends.

The role of illusion and reality in evangelism is clear from contemporary observation. The illusion lies in accepting the worldly emphasis on numbers as the criterion of spiritual effectiveness, with organizational efficiency as the pathway to success. Yet the evangelism of the early church was ridiculously small fry—but ridiculously effective! This brings us to a concluding remark.

We have a view of efficiency which we hold dear in the modern world, and it can and does influence the church. It is a view of efficiency modelled essentially on the machine. It is not, therefore, particularly human. Furthermore, machines have been known to break down. But life, especially the life of the church, is about people. The highest value here is not efficiency; it is love. And while love may be served by efficiency (by turning up on time to help a person in need, for example) it can never be subservient to efficiency.

In other words, a late start to a church meeting caused by an opportunity for the pastor to minister to an immediate need, should be occasion not for grumbling but for rejoicing. The clockwork schedule of the average church service, while understandable and commendable in certain respects, can become a trap. Any possible freedom of spiritual expression within the hallowed church hour may thereby be denied, and many impulses to praise die on the lips of the congregation.

Likewise, on a private level, though the Lord is a God of order and it behooves us to live in an orderly fashion, the basic conditions of that order may involve priorities which negate purely human conceptions of what is appropriate. Order, in the usual human sense, is far below hospitality, for example, in the list of virtues. Thus, relative domestic disorder—the possible sacrificing of yet another piece of wedding china—is a small price to pay for giving "a cup of cold water" to one's neighbor. A late meal on the table, or dust on the picture frames, is a mere bagatelle—indeed, absurd to even think about—if we are laying ourselves out for others.

We have to make a decision as to whether we are to cultivate godly efficiency or secular efficiency. Godly efficiency does not average out problems and accept a margin of loss. It aims for 100 percent and nothing less. "If thine eye offend thee, pluck it out." Is this just a figure of speech? Tell that to someone whose torture for Christ has involved the gouging out of an eye. To have compromised would have saved the eye. "Be ye therefore perfect as your heavenly Father is perfect."

For Further Study

Lloyd-Jones, D. Martyn. *Preaching and Preachers*. Grand Rapids, MI: Zondervan Publishing House, 1972. Deals with a fatal weakness: inadequate teaching and little preaching.

Maier, Gerhard. *The End of the Historical-Critical Method*. Translated by E. W. Leverenz and R. F. Norden. St. Louis: Concordia Publishing House, 1977. Very acute; every theological student needs to digest it. Warning: the translation (especially the early parts) is wooden—or worse.

Packer, J. I. *Evangelism and the Sovereignty of God*. Downers Grove: InterVarsity Press, 1961. Clear principles expounded without judgmental attitude.

Smith, David R. *Fasting: A Neglected Discipline*. Fort Washington, PA: Christian Literature Crusade, 1969. A short but balanced treatment of something which is usually too obvious for us to see.

22

The Reversed Scenario: Anti-Christ and Anti-Church in Late-Twentieth Century Perspective

T HE KNOWLEDGE OF GOD is too wonderful for us; too high, that we could attain it (Ps. 139:6). This is an important fact to have in mind and heart as we come, finally, to questions of the immediate present and future. For these things are revealed not to the wise, but to babes and sucklings. Obedience to the Father is the secret to understanding the word of the Father. We must not shrink from obeying what we know to be true; it is the only way to receive further knowledge of the truth. And to bear witness to the truth is, first, to offer life, and only secondly to mediate judgment. The truth itself is a judgment, without our having to make it so. He who *is* the Truth is alone qualified to render final judgment.

Jesus warned that we must take stock before entering his service, just as one calculates the costs before building a tower. One aspect of taking stock is to have the spiritual courage to look candidly at our own day, our own culture, our own church.

When we pray for a person to believe in Christ, when we urge the Gospel, we are demanding a great deal. We are asking someone to choose between the visible and the invisible, between what seems concrete and what seems insubstantial. It is a hard decision and, in fact, one can only admit to the hand of God in it—otherwise, who would make it?

In any case, as ambassadors for Christ, we cannot afford to be

No Other Foundation

guilty of demanding of others what we do not demand of ourselves on a daily basis. There is but one guarantee for us in a continuing commitment to unseen reality: that nothing whatever can separate us from the love of God in Christ Jesus our Lord. Jesus, indeed, shrank from the cup of his suffering but bowed to his Father's will. We are to tread the same path: being realistic enough to see that the cost is great, and obedient enough to go ahead anyway.

When Daniel was shown signs of things to come, he was utterly overwhelmed: "I, Daniel, was overcome and lay sick for some days. . . . I was appalled by the vision" (8:27); "I turned my face to the ground and was dumb . . . no strength remains in me and no breath is left in me" (10:15, 17). We shall find ourselves sharing Daniel's experience of grief and awe if we are sensitive to God's Word. But may we also copy Daniel's response: sacrificial prayer to God, confessing his own sins and those of his people, becoming one with them as Christ, supremely, became one with us.

Outward form means so much to us that it is not easy to appreciate that God really does look on the heart. There is not a shred of evidence to suggest that because apostasy is couched in religious terms or uttered with an ecclesiastical inflection it is thereby less offensive or less real. Rather, there is overwhelming evidence that it is precisely this sort of apostasy that is most repugnant to God. As Jesus said, the fate of Capernaum in the Judgment will be far hotter than that of Tyre and Sidon. Our feelings are far more deeply aroused at deception practiced by the judge than at deception practiced by the criminal—and we are right so to feel.

For this reason, I find it difficult to comprehend why people invent all sorts of extenuating circumstances to excuse the expression of outright heresy by church officers, as if they had more claim upon our tolerance in this regard than the rest of the congregation. The reverse is true. That they also administer sacraments and preach and mingle a judicious amount of truth with their falsehoods is regarded as a redeeming feature when it is, in fact a scandal. It is a scandal that the counterfeit coinage of human values should be passed off for the currency of God.

A good example of human values in the church is social justice. But, one asks, is not the Bible emphatic about the need for social justice? It is; but the way it is, is crucial. The Gospel insists, as John puts it, on the man who claims to love God, taking care of the needs of his neighbor. What is the difference? In Gospel justice, all purpose and value comes from God; in social justice, all purpose and value stems from society itself.

A literary critic and historian has pointed out that the very word "society" as a concept only developed in the West from the sixteenth century. As I have just indicated, "society" implies a value system which only has meaning in a social context. Thus, just as in the sixteenth century one saw the acceleration of the idea that the visible state is supreme and omnicompetent, so it was accompanied by the germinal idea that morals and values are defined only in the visible social setting.

The phrase "social justice," like all similar phrases ("social history," for example), is therefore more loaded than it first appears. Most who use these phrases are not aware of these antecedents, but their personal convictions correspond to the hidden meaning of the words. Placed within the stream of modern theological thought, God's justice is seen to have meaning only in a social context, from which alone it can gain meaning. Naturally, therefore, if God's justice as revealed in the Bible seems to contradict the supposed best interests of society—over matters like abortion, divorce, sexual permissiveness, and the like—then so much the worse for God.

Although the logic of social justice is not always pressed to its conclusion, one can find the basic articulation of the argument in such twentieth-century theologians as Reinhold Niebuhr and, behind him, Ernst Troeltsch, and behind all of them, Karl Marx and Hegel. The fatal spiritual misapprehension of these thinkers comes from spiritual ignorance. They take Jesus' statement about the law being fulfilled in love of one's neighbor and conclude that to love one's neighbor—presumably in a tangible way—is to fulfill the law. What they fail to perceive is that Christ is talking about a quality of love which is God's and which, accordingly, directs attention first and foremost to Christ and not to the human agent.

It is a fair rule of thumb that only that love of neighbor which can also draw people to Christ is truly a reflection of that love for God which is its source. One easily forgets that the story of the Good Samaritan was given in answer not to the question "What shall I do to inherit eternal life?" but to the question "Who is my

No Other Foundation

neighbor?'' The neighborliness Jesus was explaining, itself sprang from an antecedent commitment of the whole being to God, as Jesus' previous conversation with his questioner demonstrates (Luke 10:25). It is love of God that breeds love of men, never vice versa. But these things are not understood, save by the person who has been given the mind of Christ. They are, as Paul points out (1 Cor. 2:6-14), spiritually discerned.

This is not to say that one does not welcome the beneficial actions of a nonbelieving neighbor toward oneself or others. These actions are an echo of the fact that God desires harmony between his creatures and that traces of our original creation in God's image remain, buttressed by the general influence of God's Spirit living in those who are redeemed. They are not, however, saving graces in themselves nor are they, save incidentally, such as to draw attention to God. Rather, they usurp God's place. Whatever the appearances, in reality there is no point of contact between Christianity and Marxism.

This said, we open up for ourselves a yawning chasm of hypocrisy if we are not absolutely, wholeheartedly and practically seeking the good of our neighbor. It is here that Jesus' definition of neighbor applies. A neighbor is one who scorns our theology, pillories our values as antihuman, and gossips behind our back. He may reject well-meant efforts to be pleasant, possibly attributing our generosity to guilt feelings. He is a person who most thoroughly deserves the condemnation of God and, for that reason, will only grasp the severity of God's love and the compassion of his justice when it is actually revealed through us.

Universalism is closely tied to social justice. If the flaw in social justice is that it is justice in purely social terms, it is not surprising to find universalism in the same stables. For if society is the supreme value, the idea of any unit of society being damned is unthinkable. Hence, modern justice is reluctant to punish criminals; it prefers to think in terms of therapy. After all, there must be something wrong with a unit of society attacking society; analysis and treatment is called for.

Likewise, modern theology is reluctant to accept the basic implication of Christian salvation which is that man is fallen. More than this, one may notice a hidden implication in universalism: heaven cannot be union with God outside human history but must rather be a dimension of human history projected into the future.

Heaven, the abode of God, also has a purely social meaning. It represents man's yearning for something better, social justice being the means to realize such amelioration.

Along with universalism goes the modern insistence that all religions are, at base, the same. The question is usually put like this: Surely there are many ways to God and to insist on just one is unreasonable? This question is already loaded, however, and misleading. The real issue, which is skirted, is not one of ways but of destinations. Are there not, then, many ways? Yes, indeed, there are. And each one leads to its own destination.

One can easily caricature the effort to bring all religions together under a common denominator and then fail to see that division, per se, within the Christian church, is a poor advertisement for the harmony of the body of Christ. It is necessary to point out the glaring deficiencies in the theology of church union associated with the World Council of Churches. But, as with the issue of social justice, a yawning chasm opens up before us if we are not deeply grieved by the divisions in Christ's body which hinder his coming and if we fail to make positive personal and corporate efforts to heal such divisions.

As I see it, the sin in such divisions is not so much in theological and ecclesiological differences, per se. This side of Christ's return, we must acknowledge the likelihood of differences. After all, one does not have to read too much between the lines of the Book of Acts to see differences of emphasis as between, say, the believers in Jerusalem and those in Antioch. Furthermore, granted the fact of different emphases which have spawned different denominations, an incidental spinoff benefit is that so many hedges are set up to prevent as rapid a decline into overall apostacy as might be likely otherwise.

No, the sin is rather in allowing minor differences to prevent the practice of major harmony. This was not allowed to happen in the Acts, and that it is characteristic of so much believing Christianity in our own day is a deep offence to Christ, our one Head. If we suppose for a moment that those elders of the church in Ephesus represented several physically distinct household congregations, then we might ponder the fact that, equally, the pastors and elders of all parts of the Body of Christ in any fair-sized community are, in God's sight, as the "elders of the church in ——ville." Would that these elders would more fully act as such, bearing one another's burdens, rejoicing and weeping at the successive joys and trials of the various congregations.

So far, two issues which have a lot to do with action have been emphasized. Let us deal now with an issue that has to do with thought, bearing in mind that, ultimately, thought and action cannot be separated. This is the so-called Death of God theology. This theology, popularized by (Anglican) Bishop John Robinson's *Honest to God* in 1963 and by a rash of works since, is a sort of theological demythologization.

Just as the textual demythologizers purported to be getting at the core message beneath the "myths" in the New Testament, so their theological counterparts claimed to be getting at the essential ideas or realities beneath the crust of old-fashioned, hackneyed doctrines. They claimed, indeed, to be finding what was truly universal and enduring in the bloated "epic" of traditional, orthodox Christianity. And just as the textual experts had a ready-made idea of what the core-text would be like when they found it—which certainly lent wings to their search—so the theological experts very clearly perceived that the universal theology they sought would complement the idea of a universal human religion, honoring man as he might be and in a purely terrestrial setting.

Thus, the notions of a heaven "up there" or a hell "down under" were discarded as picture language for universal human perceptions of justice. To embrace the concepts of heaven and hell as literal destinations was, therefore, ridiculous; it was to confuse the illustration with the reality. Likewise, "God" had to stand for a sense of value focus among men. "God" was the idea of a universal good. To think in terms of a God in whose image we are made would, therefore, be a naive and crude interpretation of a piece of religious prose-poetry, the actual aim of which was to dignify humanity by relating it to a mythical Creator-God.

One might turn the criticism of these demythologizers upside down by noting that if they claim that traditional biblical religion is anthropomorphic (the divine in human terms), their own belief is deomorphic (the human in divine terms). For if God is not the controller of man's destiny, then man must be. And this, in the end, is what much of late-twentieth century theology is all about. There are exceptions or partial exceptions, but the generalization is fair.

ol professor, a Baptist, Harvey Cox. It includes this

Conservatives, as usual, are partly right in the arguments
against the ordination of women. Unlike enlightened,
liberals, they know full well this is not just an equal oppor-
emale priests would, despite themselves, modify the mean-
s. But what the Conservatives fear, I welcome: a Christian
iched by the presence at the altar of the Great Mother, the
n, the Whore of Babylon, and the Virgin Queen. So the
are right in their panic but wrong in their conclusion. If the
gs together, at least for a moment, not only Spirit and
y East and West, but also the conscious and unconscious,
d the conceptual, then the ordination of women is not only
, as the Prayer Book says, "meet and right."
g now the ecumenical movement has focussed on unifying
What a boring prospect! . . . What I long for is an "ecu-
ty which will reconcile not so much the churches as the
ments of the human family, which will bring together not
minations but the "separated brothers" and sisters who
ithin each one of us. This means that we can no longer
ee-quarters of the race who are not Christians, nor the 51%
en. And the moment of reckoning is here.

d quotation is a couple of passages from a book by a
an Catholic feminist, Mary Daly: *Beyond God the*
ard a Philosophy of Women's Liberation (Boston:
ss, 1973):

at another form of reversal has been the idea of redemptive
niquely in the form of a male savior. . . . A patriarchal
son is exactly *not* in a position to save us from the horrors
al world. Does this mean, then, that the women's move-
to, seeks, or in some way constitutes a rival to "the
In its depth, because it contains a dynamic that drives
tolatry, the women's movement does point to, seek, and
primordial, always present, and future AntiChrist. . . .
at the mechanism of reversal has been at the root of the
"AntiChrist" must be something "evil." What if this is not
? What if the idea has arisen out of the male's unconscious
men will rise up and assert the power robbed from us? . . .
this perspective, the AntiChrist and the *Second Coming of*
ynonymous. [p. 96]
ond, then, between the significance of the women's revolu-
Christ and its import as Antichurch. Seen in the positive
n which I have presented it, as a spiritual uprising that can
nd sexist myths, the AntiChrist has a natural correlative in
the Antichurch, which is a communal uprising against the

Sooner or later, those who make gods out of themselves meet one another on the common ground of their mutual divinity. This is one way of viewing the rapprochement between Eastern and Western thought in our day. In an important sense, this rapprochement is only a footnote to a universal tendency in the thought and action of man in rebellion against God. This tendency can be plotted in terms of idea and in terms of deed.

Ideologically, spiritual declension traces a long descent from the rejection of the personal, infinite God, who loves but is not a part of his creation, to the acceptance of an impersonal, abstract principle, which is pantheistic in the sense of being all that there is, past, present and future. All nonbiblical religion can be plotted along this descent.

By an odd paradox, the ideology that produces real community among men is not the one that says that we are all part of god (pantheism) but the one that says that we are not God at all, but are made by God (biblical belief). The explanation for this is simple: if there is an objective, personal God, the well-being of each of his individual creatures depends upon Him, not upon oneself. Thus, the path of well-being for each person contains the potential for harmony through being directed to the same personal objective of obedience to God.

By contrast, if each one of us is "god" through being part of all that there is (which is, by definition, "God"), then the full realization of our individual "godness" will depend essentially upon ourselves. Pantheism, which is the religious form of pure humanism, is self-absorption raised to a doctrine. The various forms of meditation, whereby one is promised a fuller realization of one's unity with all that exists, all alike cut one off from anything and anybody else. This brings us quite naturally to the deeds which complement this tendency.

If spiritual declension traces a path from the biblical God to outright pantheism, this same declension in practice traces a path from unselfish dependence on God to utter self-centeredness. It comes as a surprise to most people, who identify pantheism and the mysticism which accompanies it with the nonmaterial, to discover the crass materialism at the heart of most oriental religion.

Materialism is not machines and Gross National Product but a mentality. It is the mentality which derives from the quest to realize to the full one's "godness." It is basically antisocial and

No Other Foundation

basically concerned to taste to the full all kindred aspects of universal divinity in order to appreciate one's identity with all that is. Hence the idea of cycles of existence in which, successively, one experiences poverty, riches, sexual abstinence, sexual promiscuity, family life, solitary life, and so on.

There is, however, another angle to this. If the poor are people enduring a stage in their total life cycle, their condition need not be—indeed, must not be—alleviated. In other words, there is here a built-in rationale for ignoring the poor and unfortunate while enjoying one's own plenitude. Where some sort of social conscience has been evident in Hinduism and Buddhism, it has been an inconsistent, sectarian offshoot which has paid tribute, willy-nilly, to the fact that man really is made in the image of a loving, personal God.

The reason for dwelling on these matters is that what has usually been discussed in the context of the Orient must now be discussed in a Western setting. The growing refusal of people in the West to be their brothers' keepers, to intervene when their neighbor is robbed, beaten, or killed, reflects two things: a loss of dependence upon a God who commands and rewards sacrificial neighborliness, and an accelerating instinct towards self-protection which is the natural breeding ground for religious ideas which rationalize it.

In the midst of the trend towards human self-divinization, one thing is forgotten. It was Nietzsche, whose prophecies now supersede Kierkegaard's, who saw that if God is dead, man is dead, too. He had come to this realization before 1900. We are now hearing a swelling chorus of voices which chant that man is dead, and good riddance to him.

Man, in this context, is not the spiritual being whom God made and of whom the Son of Man is the agent to restore the humanness which was God's creation gift. No, man is a being crippled with hobbling obsessions and socially useless values like freedom and personal dignity. This man must be finally discarded in order that mankind—the conglomerate—can survive. Yet, the high priests of society recognize the social value of religious language and liturgy. Like Machiavelli and Marx and Jung, they know the impact upon people of traditional symbols and words. Therefore, religion is by no means done with—which brings us to a final consideration: the religion of the future.

We are familiar with the s
versal religion and an Anti-
rejection of the Gospel of Jes
conscious of, though we wou
of the times, is specific hints

"Large oaks from little ac
seem, even if regrettable and
But if we are trained to see
instance of apostacy yet
malady, we shall be better p

Yet another image is usefu
visualize the growth and dest
a multistage rocket. As with
ground and proceed into orb
Each one must play its pa
Nevertheless, none of the b
rocket, assumes meaning sa
eventual function of that cap
the capsule represents the
anti-Christian religion which
orbits before Christ's return
means whereby the supports

First and foremost, comes
then more openly. Then, e
upon this denial: the structur
upon the Word of God are
God's Word having become
brace a system of values at
being. Given over to a reprob
the Reprobate.

For reasons which are too
clearly the vital biblical idea
loving submission is rejected,
proved an important focus an
religion opposed to the Gos
what I mean, I shall quote at l
thinkers who presently (or
denominations and who woul
what they think is basic Ch
Times religion editorial (Oct.

Divinity Sch
statement:

Frightened
they advance
symbol-blind
tunity issue. F
ing of the Mas
sacrament en
Scarlet Woma
Conservatives
Eucharist bri
Flesh, not on
the intuitive a
just, it is also

For too lon
the churches.
menical'' uni
scattered seg
divided deno
reside deep
ignore the thr
who are not

The secor
radical Rom
Father: Tov
Beacon Pres

I propose t
incarnation u
divinity or his
of a patriarch
ment points
Christ''? . . .
beyond Chris
constitute th

I suggest t
idea that the
the case at al
dread that w

Seen from
Women are
There is a
tion as Anti
perspective i
bring us bey
the coming o

social extensions of the male Incarnation myth, as this has been objectified in the structures of political power. [p. 140]

These are sickening words, delivered with all the arrogance of an evil confident of its own powers. Does not one feel a little what Daniel must more deeply have felt as God drew aside the curtain of the future for him?

We seem to be faced, in other words, for the first time in history, by a powerful and well-prepared anti-Christian movement which claims to be more truly Christian, more truly spiritual, than anything based on the Bible.

In a different setting, we are beginning to see a repetition of an ominous process which took place in the first century of the Christian church: the Jew who had recognized Jesus as the Messiah, and who therefore rightfully belonged in the synagogues, was thrust out. Henceforth, Judaism precluded Christ Jesus. Likewise now, the Christian, true in word and deed to his Master, is being steadily pushed into the outside aisles of many major denominations. Increasingly, the Gospel is identified with old-fashioned minorities in the larger denominations or miniscule groupings elsewhere. Meanwhile, just as true Judaism supposedly resided in the Christ-rejecting synagogue, so true Christianity is supposed to be represented in the Christ-rejecting churches.

If we are to be precise about the lineaments of this monstrous reversal, we might express it in a series of substitutions. The authoritative text of God's Word is replaced by a demythologized Bible, plus other religious books. The creedal interpretation of the Bible is replaced by an arbitrary extrapolation bolstering the concept of a purely human, social fulfillment. The truly catholic, Christian Church to live and proclaim the Gospel is replaced by the Anti-Church which lives and enforces the values of human liberation, freed from all constricting biblical absolutes. Finally, for Christ, the so-called male incarnation myth, is substituted the Anti-Christ, who liberates from all false distinctions, granting a new unity to all mankind.

How is one to conclude? The Bible is clear that true love, true family, true community and true freedom only come when we find our identity in Christ. It is already beginning but it is going to be acceleratingly true, that these values will disappear. In this context, our love will be desperately needed. The sharing of real

No Other Foundation

family life will be a sought-after premium. The existence of true community in the Church will be a startling, almost unbelievable, miracle to the outsider coming in.

There is, however, no room for romanticism here. These fruits do not grow without obedience, without "abiding in Christ." My friends, said Jesus, are those who do what I command (John 15:14). The call, then, is to so abide. And to so abide is to listen afresh, with a very literal heart and mind, to the instructions of our Master, as also to his encouragements. Further, we must maintain the essential marriage of love and sound doctrine: the love which gives the doctrine meaning, and the doctrine which explains the love. What is love if God is not love? And what is doctrine if there is no love when we explain that salvation presupposes damnation?

The first chapter of this book noted how man chose to make a name for himself, built a city and a tower, and then saw his scheme destroyed by God. We look forward, of course, to a city with true foundations—that is our great hope.

In the meantime, we must recall what was also discussed in that first chapter: how God chose out Abram and gave him a name. Our calling is to live worthy of the very great Name by which we are named—even Jesus Christ. At his name, forcibly, all men will one day bow. We have the privilege of bowing in voluntary submission now. And—"No longer do I call you servants, for the servant does not know what his master is doing; but I have called you friends, for all that I have heard from my Father I have made known to you" (John 15:15).

For Further Study

Anderson, J. N. D. *Christianity and Comparative Religion*. Downers Grove: InterVarsity Press, 1971. The author's gifts of analysis and fair presentation are here employed to good account.

Macaulay, Ranald and Barrs, Jerram. *Being Human: The Nature of Spiritual Experience*. Downers Grove: InterVarsity Press, 1979. A much-needed antidote to many wrong-headed tendencies; not only in terms of telling critiques but also in terms of positive biblical exposition. Never have we more needed to be reminded that salvation is the recovery of "humanness" in Christ.

Schaeffer, Francis A. *The Church before the Watching World*. Downers Grove: InterVarsity Press, 1971. In some ways this summarizes the author's basic message, in simple words and few pages.

Solzhenitsyn, A. *The Gulag Archipelago,* 3 vols., trans. T. P. Whitney New York: Harper & Row, 1974-76. Although this is very long it is also calculated, for that reason, to impress itself on our minds. I believe that no congregation should be without someone(s) who have read every word and are able to distill the essence to the rest: "If you are not ready now, you won't be ready then."

Vitz, Paul C. *Psychology as Religion. The Cult of Self-Worship.* Grand Rapids, MI: Wm. B. Eerdmans Pub. Co., 1977. It is enough to say that the book lives up to the title.

The Spiritual Counterfeits Project (Berkeley, California) has an excellent issue of its *SCP Journal* devoted to "holistic medicine." This field is a good example of the rapid ordering and unifying of anti-Christian forces within the world today.

Bibliographical Note

MY INDEBTEDNESS in preparing this book to a great many other books which I have read over the last twenty years, often in a desultory fashion, is too great either to ignore or to document. However, where an original idea is taken knowingly from another author I have made acknowledgement in the text.

Otherwise, in three places in the story where my own tread was sufficiently uncertain as to require the use of a guide, I have made selective use of directions offered by those more familiar with the terrain. For aspects of the early church, for portions of the Middle Ages, and for the nineteenth century, I have been steadied by, respectively, Michael Green's *Evangelism and the Early Church,* Grand Rapids, MI: Wm. B. Eerdman's Publishing Co., 1970; Jeffrey Burton Russell's *A History of Medieval Christianity,* Arlington Heights, IL: AHM, 1968; and Alec R. Vidler's *The Church in an Age of Revolution: 1789 to the Present Day,* Harmondsworth, Eng.: Penguin Books, 1972.

This is not to say that I wholeheartedly concur in all of the judgments of these authors—nor, I am sure, would they in mine. Russell, in particular, stuffs his well-written account of the medieval church into a bunk-bed dichotomy between reason and faith, as his subtitle *Prophecy and Order* forewarns.

Index

To save space and help the reader, various subjects and persons have been grouped together in the Index. Thus, for example, Karl Barth and Paul Tillich will be found under the entry *Theologians, theological thought and scholarship;* Augustine of Hippo is listed under *Church Fathers and leaders (up to A.D. 450);* and Charles Dickens appears among *Authors and thinkers cited and/or discussed.* A quick perusal of the Index will acquaint the reader with the particulars of its arrangement.

110, 139, 219
Great Schism, 116-7
Greek culture and the church, 24, 54f.,
75, 109-10

Heretics and heretical movements,
33-42, 43, 52, 57-8, 62, 63, 77, 86,
100, 103-5; Adoptionism, 40; An-
tinomianism, 277; Arius and
Arianism, 40-1, 71-2; Cathari (Albigensians), 86, 103-4, 105, 110;
Children of God, 104; Christian Science, 32; Deism, 193, 223; Docetism,
40; Donatism, 39, 48; Gnosticism,
38-40, 55; Jehovah's Witnesses, 32,
39; Judaizers, 35, 37-8; Manichaeanism, 39, 103-4; Marcion, 39,
61; Monophysites, 40; Montanism,
38; Mormons, 32, 39; Nestorianism,
40; Neo-orthodoxy, 233, 267;
Nicolaitans, 39; Pelagianism, 38;
Sabellianism, 40; Servetus, 166;
Socinianism, 219; Unification
Church, 39; Unitarianism, and Universalism, 187, 219, 223, 267, 284-5,
290-1; Valentinus, 38-9
Hinduism, 288
History, Christian concept of, 75, 79,
120, 122, 133, 226-7, 267
Holland, 134, 169-70, 176-7, 179-80.
See also: Netherlands
Holy Spirit, 26, 27, 38, 40, 86, 129, 159,
160, 207, 211, 251, 279
Huguenots in France, 168-9, 182
Humanism, humanists, 14, 75, 100,
118, 144, 162, 164, 180, 218, 235. See
also: Enlightenment; Renaissance
Humanistic religion, 11, 39, 219-20,
223, 287f.
Hungary (and Huns), 70, 134, 148, 149,
168, 178, 182

Index of Prohibited Books, 131, 146
India, 210, 249; Christianity in, 211,
249, 254, 256; religious ideas from,
36, 249
Individualism, 123-4, 144, 151
Indulgences, 133
Industrialization, Industrial Revolu-
tion, 108, 176, 192, 249, 255, 256, 257
Inquisition, 166, 169; Roman, 146
Investitures Contest, 86-90, 101
Ireland, Irish, 79, 183

Islam, Moslems, 47, 51, 71, 90, 97, 251,
254
Israel, 12, 16, 31, 48-9, 93, 154, 159
Italy, 76, 134, 238; church in, 72, 144,
148, 149, 241-2; Renaissance in, 122f.

Jerusalem, 26, 31, 47, 48, 50, 75, 96-7,
248, 285; Council at, 49, 62; Temple
at, 31
Jews, ch. 1 passim, 23f., 46, 58, 60, 61,
79, 160, 162, 192, 217; and Christianity, 25, 27-8, 31-2, 35, 37-8, 47,
93, 97, 99, 100, 201, 291
Judgment of God, 31-2, 43, 79, 120,
141, 159, 207, 247, 248, 281, 282
Justification by faith, 136-8, 143, 147,
149, 193, 199
Just Price, The, 99

King James Version of the Bible, 138

Law, and personal freedom, 123, ch. 13
passim; in Bible, 14f., 53, 57, 58,
159, 191; and justice, 137, 158f.; in
medieval church, 99
Lay piety, lay reform, 86, 95, 123-5,
131f., 142, 144-5, 149, 192-3
Liberalism, 238. See also: Church
movements
London (England), 98, 192, 197, 246
Lord's Prayer, The, 16, 53, 106
Lord's Supper, Eucharist, 45, 53,
150-1, 167, 172, 290; changes in,
83-4, 147. See also: Mass, The
Love, as central to doctrine, 276, 279,
283-4, 292
Luther, Martin, 21, 73, 75, 130, 133,
135-40, 145, 199; influence of, 139f.,
146-9, 199; and Lutheranism, 134,
142, 168, 177, 181; Ninety-Five
Theses and Address to the Nobility,
138
Lyons, persecution at, 46, 47, 113

Madison Avenue methods in church,
27, 101, 275f.
Mary, Virgin, 81-2, 124; and Mariology, 105f.
Mass, The, 53, 83-4, 126, 146, 147, 149,
151, 184; laity and, 95
Massachusetts, Puritans in, 172-3, 175,
209
Meditation, 120, 185, 287

302

No Other Foundation

Mediterranean world, 24, 46, 47, 70, 71, 81, 135
Mercy, 16, 73, 120, 245, 247, 248, 272
Missions and Missions leaders, 79, 90, 94, 243, ch. 19; Baptist Missionary Society, 251; British and Foreign Bible Society, 251; Carey, William, 251, 254-5; Carmichael, Amy, 255; Church Missionary Society, 251; Las Casas, Bartolomé de, 140, 255; London Missionary Society, 251; Martyn, Henry, 254-5; Methodist Missionary Society, 251; Pietism and, 186, 197; Reformation and, 151; Revivals and, 147-8, 250; Roman Catholicism and, 151, 250-1, 255; Taylor, Hudson, and the China Inland Mission, 140, 246, 248, 251-6
Monasticism and its leaders, 77-9, 82, 85-6, 91, 98, 101, 106-9, 118, 219-20; Barnabites, 142; Benedict of Nursia and Benedictinism, 78-9, 85, 101, 106; Bernard of Clairvaux, 50, 97, 106-9, 112-3; Boniface, 79; Brethren of the Common Life, 126, 132; Capuchins, 142; Cistercians, 106-8; Cluniac, 85-6; Dominic and the Dominicans, 108, 255; Francis of Assisi and the Franciscans, 108-9, 113-4; Jesuits, 146, 182; Norbert and the Premonstratensians, 108; Oratory of Divine Love, 142; "Spirituals" (Fraticelli), 109, 114; Theatines, 142
Moravians, 186, 196-7, 199
Music, and singing in church, 53-4, 73, 107
Mysticism, 38, 112, 119f., 236, 287-8

Nature, concepts of, 110, 123, 193, 206, 218, 232
Natural religion, 193, 223, 229f., 261-2
Netherlands, 104, 126, 134, 168, 169-70, 176, 178f.
New English Bible cited, 28
New York State, "burned-over" district of, 215
North African church, 39, 47, 74

Oberlin College, 214
Oxford, 197, 199, 242; "Holy Club" at, 193, 199

Paganism, 77, 81-2, 115, 154, 227, 230, 271
Pantheism, 109, 287
Papacy, 75f., 82, 97, 125, 126, 130, 162, 226, 241-2; "Babylonian Captivity" of, 116-7; corruption of, 118, 133-4; and the Great Schism, 116-7; growth of power of, 75f., 87f.; individual popes: Leo the Great, 51, 76, 88; Gregory the Great, 76-7, 78, 82, 87, 94; Gelasius I, 87; Leo X, 87; Gregory VII, 87, 88-90, 96; Innocent III, 116; Boniface VIII, 116; Clement V, 116; Paul III, 145-6; Gregory XVI, 241; Pius IX (Pio Nono), 241-2; reform movements and, 85, 86-90, 133-4, 142f., 168
Paris, 119, 163, 168; Pantheon at, 225
Parochialism, 12-3, 15, 18
Pax Romana and Pax Brittanica, 248-9
Philanthropists: Abolitionists, 214, 258; Clarkson, Thomas, 258; Francke, Hermann, 186; Fry, Elizabeth, 258; More, Hannah, 258; Shaftesbury, Lord, 258; Smith, Hannah Whitall, 186; Wilberforce, William, 258
Philology, 130-1
Pilgrimages, 96-7
Political developments, 70-1, 98-9, 117-8, 125, 133-5, 157f., 235f.; and concept of community, 148, 152, 226; and constitutionalism, 117, 146, 150, 167, 168-9, 222; growth and fear of centralization, 133, 146, 168-9, 176-80, 226; and monarchy, 117, 146, 149, 242; public ethics and, ch. 13 *passim*, 226, 283
Political leaders:
Alfred the Great, 85; Attila the Hun, 71; Brandenburg, Elector of, 177; Catherine de' Medici, 168; Charlemagne (and Empire of), 72, 85, 134; Charles II (England), 171; Charles V (Emperor), 134-5, 138, 142, 144; Clovis, 71-2; Cortez, 134; Cromwell, Oliver, 178, 183; Elizabeth I, 168, 170-1; Gustavus Adolphus (Sweden), 178; Hapsburg dynasty, 176, 178; Henry IV (Emperor), 86-7, 89; Henry IV (Navarre, France), 168; Henry VIII (England), 145, 170; Herod Antipas, 23; Herod the Great,